ZIMBABWE TOWNSHIP *music*

Joyce Jenje-Makwenda

First Edition 2005

© Joyce Jenje Makwenda

Storytime Promotions
Box M163
Mabelreign
HARARE
Zimbabwe

Cell: 011 70 30 79 or 091 340 703
website: www.zimtownshipmusic.co.zw
Email: storytime@zol.co.zw

All rights reserved. No part of this publication may be reproduced or utilised in any form or by any means, electronic or mechanical, including photocopying, recording or by any information storage and retrieval system, without permission in writing from the publishers.

ISBN: 9780797427914

Editor – Gibson M. Mandishona
Graphic Design – Takesure Handiseni
Index - Patrick Nyamhunga
Origination – Zimbabwe Expressions
Printing - ORT Printing Services

Z MBABWE TOWNSHIP
music

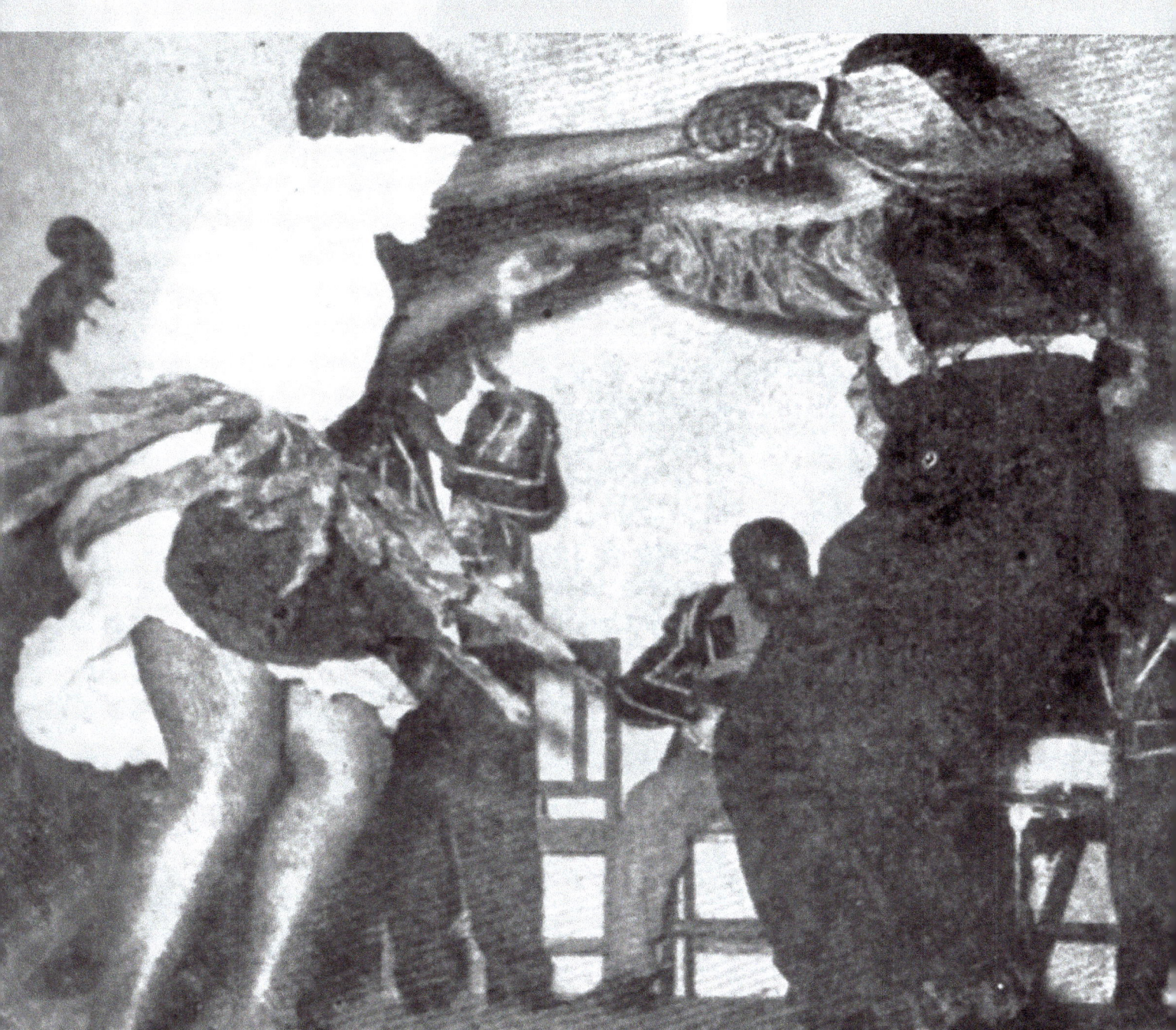

I AM GREATFUL TO........

This book was made possible with a fund from THE FORD FOUNDATION; thank you for the generous fund which went a long way towards script writing, editing, research and final publishing. Special mention goes to Dr. James Murombedzi, for understanding this project and for his encouragement.

Thanks NORAD for funding the first draft of this book, in particular Thore Hem.

My special gratitude to the Zimbabwe College of Music for facilitating the project.

The National Archives of Zimbabwe played an all-embracing role as an invaluable store house of historical material.

DEDICATION:

To my late parents, David (Murehwa) Jenje and Canaan (MaDube) Jenje, for passing on to me a time-honoured heritage, which I shall in turn bequeath to tomorrow's youth.

Various artists who contributed to the evolution and unfolding of Zimbabwe Township Music Early urban dewellers, who created and nurtured a vibrant and never-dying musical tradition.

Cool Crooners (Makokoba) Bulawayo 2000

Foreword by Dr. Herbert M. Murerwa

As one of those who grew up in Mbare, or old Harare, our cherished pastime as boys was to participate in musical activities. Innovative boys would meet at the Mai Musodzi Boys' Club, where they were exposed to a variety of musical instruments. So it was; that talented township musicians picked up their preferred instrument; be it guitar, drums, piano or saxophone. And certainly, Mai Musodzi was thus the launching pad of the Zimbabwe jazzartists of yester-year:Kenneth Mataka, Evelyn and Simon Juba, Remmington Mazabane, Josaya Hadebe, Moses Mpahlo-Mafusire, Sonny Sondo, Dorothy Masuka, Simanga Tutani, Faith Dauti, Chris Chabuka, Andrew Chakanyuka, Jonah Marumahoko; the list goes on and on.

In Bulawayo, particularly Makokoba Township, there was a complementary upsurge of township jazz, stimulated by a Boys' Club akin to Mai Musidzi, which was to be the stables of Paul Lunga and the like. Individual instrumentalists were then simultaneously paralleled by musical staging groups, which offered the desired entertainment and social escapade, to an otherwise dull township environment. These were the Bantu Actors, De Black Evening Follies, City Quads, Merry Makers, Golden Rhythm Crooners, Cool Four, Epworth Theatrical Strutters; to mention a few.

I am delighted to note that, a woman who grew up in modest Mbare surroundings, Joyce Jenje - Makwenda, took upon an innovative and onerous task of chronicling the times and trends of Zimbabwe Township Music, resulting in an accessible and user-friendly ethnomusicology compilation. She needs to be highly commended for having spent long, arduous and solitary hours of dedicated research, which are the building blocks of her book; a culmination of several years of fact – archiving.

Zimbabwe Township Music goes back seventy years ago or more, when early rural migrants converged into the emerging urban centers; and in quest of social entertainment, moulded a musical niche, which was a fusion of indigenous traditional lyrics and borrowed rhythms. Even today, after several transformations, township jazz boasts of a perennial continuity; of young aspiring artists, who persist to spur forward a dynamic jazz initiative. The narrative is in no way exhaustive, as to include the various musical forms or individual artists currently on the contemporary scene; Gospel, Pop, Hip-Hop, Sungura, Urban Grooves, Afro-Mbira, R & B; and what have you. Rather, the book charts major milestones, which unfolded to give birth to the archetypical Township Music.

Indeed, Joyce's book is a challenge for today's youth; to expand and further develop our understanding of Zimbabwe's musical legacy. It is an excellent source-book and essential reading for enthusiasts of Zimbabwe Township Music.

Dr. Herbert. M. Murerwa; June 2004.
Minister of Higher and Tertiary Education

Women who Set the Ball of Jazz Rolling

Lina Mattaka

Evelyn Juba

Prudence Katomeni

Virginia Sillah

Faith Dauti

Dorothy Masuka

zimbabwe township music

Preface by Barbara Makhalisa Nkala

REMINISCENCING ON ZIMBABWE TOWNSHIP MUSIC

In Zimbabwe, music has always been an integral part of daily life, complementing home-based tasks, such as stamping mealies, grinding corn, field harvesting or threshing millet. As such, music abounded in the countryside, as well as in towns. Bulawayo, where I grew up, was awash with musical entertainment for both the young and old folks.

I mastered tunes of the time from my father who sang in his baritone voice, particularly in the mornings before going to work. I recall such soulful pieces as; "Lindi Mwana Wakanakisisa", "Lizofika Nin' Ilanga Lenkululeko", and *"Ndafuna funa"*. The same tunes were also aired regularly over the community loudspeakers. I never saw the legendary singers actually performing. I am now over- thrilled with joy, that Joyce has captured the yester-year songs on both video and print-form.

Dorothy Masuka hit the charts in the fifties when she popularized "Iyo Phatha Phatha". Later on, Dotty, belted other popular songs : "Imali Yam' Iphel' Eshabhini", and "Hamba Nontsokolo", which alongside some songs of Miriam Makeba, became the talk of shops and township homes. At boarding schools, competing groups sang versions of the tunes, for evening entertainment.

In the early sixties Spokes Mashiyane and Lemmy Special visited Zimbabwe from South Africa, at a time when parents were hesitant to allow children to attend the shows, even during daytime. I managed to sneak into one such show, and I was thoroughly enthralled by the smooth blending of pennywhistles, guitar and drums. There was "Tsaba-tsaba" and Kwela jive, amidst whistles and shouts for encore.

Soon pennywhistle music became widely popular, and so was the rapid manufacture of these aluminium and plastic instruments, which in turn sold cheaply. It became commonplace for young people to entertain their peers with pennywhistles , crude banjos and make-shift drums.

"Omasiganda", of the likes of Sabelo Mathe and Josiah Hadebe, sang "Uzangenzani Malayisha?", "Sabona Fish" and "Gwabigwabi Ngilentomb' Yam'", to mention a few. Hadebe was an adept composer whose songs reflected a fascination and caricature of city life , including romantic escapades of the 50's/60's ; such as buying buns or sweets for the loved one. The "Omasiganda" played guitar music for "Tsaba-tsaba" jivers and "Amarabi" dancers. John White, plied the Bulawayo-Gweru train, entertaining passengers for token money. He sang a mixture of Shona, Ndebele and English, and would introduce himself characteristically: "Yimi uJohn White, igabazi elidala." (It's me, John White, the veteran performer).

When the KwaNongoma College of Music was established in Bulawayo during the late 1960s, I intended to be trained as a music teacher, much to the distaste of my parents, who visualized "Omasiganda" as cheap entertainers . I continued with schooling, but with the love for music, which ran in the family. At school we sang Zulu and Xhosa lyrics, Negro spirituals and hymns of the Brethren in Christ Church. We also used to watch the Zion Christian Church men sing , gyrate and dance. At Iminyela Beerhall men sang "Imbube" and danced "Ingquzu".

During the Jairos Jiri fetes (60's- 70's), there emerged electronic bands, guitars and drums with a Western influence of Afro-Jazz and Rock'n Roll. Bulawayo then became a brisk hub of music and dances.

Joyce Jenje- Makwenda has produced a well-researched Zimbabwe Township Music video, now complemented in book-form. Books are a priceless asset as they constitute a sustainable archive of our culture. As one of the pioneer writers, I am certain our progeny will be enriched by such wealth borrowed from the past.

Barbara C Nkala; July 2004.

Tinashe Mukarati

August Musarurwa

Simangaliso Tutani

Township Music has come full circle!

Paul Brickhill

Roger Hukuimwe

Paul Lunga

EDITOR'S NOTE

Zimbabwe Township Music evolved on a parallel trend as the 19th century slave work songs, hymns and spirituals; with melodic elements borrowed from African traditional lyrics. Having known Joyce as an adept researcher/archivist and jazz music lover, it's no surprise that she has authored the Zimbabwe Township Music story-book. Township Music developed simultaneously in the urban environments of Harare and Bulawayo, where early settlers took to music like a bird takes to song at dawn. The event symbolised running away from the urbanization spectre which demanded a myriad of social adaptations. Thus, the township dweller had to survive in this strange, alien and newly-found cold city. The historical trend was characterised by choir music, giving way to Omasiganda, vocal groups and mixed popular bands.

Over the years, Zimbabwe Township Music artists have experimented, improvised and sung their way with ecstatic tunes that proved irresistible and unforgettable. The music nurtured a new identity which outwitted urban boredom, ushered in family entertainment, and finally bridged the middle passage between the generations of jazz/blues lovers.

Alike politicians during the colonial period, Zimbabwean musicians braved their way forward, despite being subjected to overt and covert racism, which was then a grim reality, but which nevertheless created an innovative and sleek idiom-jazz expression. Joyce's deliverable is not an exhaustive offering on the broad subject of Zimbabwean music, as obviously several talented artists could not be included in a narrative that aims to chart only major trends.

Although Township Music is often played in exclusive hotels, it is in no way a genre preserved for the elite. Both young and old alike derive joy and pleasure from listening to it. It is music to revel in, to work in, and to sing along to; as opposed to music designed solely for listening to.

Zimbabwe Township Music will prevail and outlast, as living memory; as a vivid chronicle of men and women who honed their talent and repertoire, often mimicking the penny whistle or be it Skokiaan versions.

Gibson M. Mandishona, August 2004.

impact of the guitar on township music

Josaya Hadebe

Shamiso Chitsinde

Jacob Mhungu

John White

Louis Mhlanga

CONTENTS

INTRODUCTION.	14
The Beginning 1930s-1960s	14
The Mid Sixties	29
Then the Seventies	33
The Jazz Revival	43
VENUES	48
TOWNSHIP MUSIC PROMOTERS	59
INFLUENCES ON TOWNSHIP MUSIC	67
Kwela	71
Influnces of Zimbabwe Township Music Abroad	75
The visit of Louis Armstrong	77
THE RECORDING HISTORY	80
POPULAR GROUPS/MUSICIANS AND THEIR MUSIC	86
THE BANTU ACTORS/MATTAKA FAMILY	87
Kenneth Mattaka	87
The Bantu Actors	88
Lina Mattaka	89
Bertha Mattaka-Msora	90
Edisson Mattaka	90
THE MERRY MAKERS	91
Agnes Zengeni	93
Emma Moyo	93
MOSES MPAHLO-MAFUSIRE/	93
THE DE BLACK EVENING FOLLIES	93
OMASIGANDA	97
Josaya Hadebe	97
Jacob Mhungu	98
John White	98
AUGUST MUSARURWA	100
EPWORTH THEATRICAL STRUTTERS	103
DOROTHY MASUKA	106
THE CITY QUADS	108
PAT TRAVERS	111
THE MILTON BROTHERS AND FAITH DAUTI	113
THE GAY GAETIES	115
ALICK NKATA	117
JEREMIAH KAINGA	118
RUTH MPISAUNGA	119
ALBERT NDINDA	120
CITY SLICKERS	121
SAFIRIO "MUKADOTA" MADZIKATIRE	123
SUSAN CHENJERAYI	124
THE MARSHALL BROTHERS	127
SIMANGALISO TUTANI	128
ANDREW CHAKANYUKA	131
CHRIS CHABUKA	132
ELIAH BANDA	133
GEORGE SISIMAYI	134
WOMEN SET THE BALL OF JAZZ ROLLING	135
Lina Mattaka	136
Mabel Bingwa	137

Victoria Chingate	137
Sylvia Sondo	138
Flora Dick	138
Tabeth Kapuya	138
Florence Modikwane	139
Kristine Dube	139
Joyce Ndoro	139
Faith Dauti	140
Evelyn Juba	140
Grace Jones	140
Dorothy Masuka	141
Rennie Jones Nyamundanda	141
Margaret Pazarangu	141
Miriam Yafele	141
TOWNSHIP MUSIC/JAZZ: A GREAT REVIVAL	142
Cool Crooners	147
Harare Mambos	149
Virginia Sillah Jangano	150
Fanyana Dube	151
Paul Lunga	152
Friday Mbirimi/Mbare Trio	153
Basil Kumpeu	155
Biddy Patridge/Mhepo	156
Moses Kabubi/Summer Breeze	157
Jethro Shasha	158
Hilton Mambo	160
Fungai Malianga	161
Ava Rodgers	163
Bob Nyabinde	165
Jabavu Drive:	166
Phillip Svosve	167
Roger Hukuimwe	167
Timmy Makaya	168
Ernest Sando	168
Louis Mhlanga	170
Jazz Inivitation	172
Prudence Katomeni	172
Dumi Ngulube	173
Duduzile Manhenga	174
Maita Women's Ensemble	175
Africa Revenge	176
TODAY'S PROMOTERS	178
Irene Gwaze	182
Jackie Cahi	182
Penny Yon	182
Sam Mataure	183
Gibson Mandishona	184
SOCIALITES	186
PICTURE OF THE 50'S AUDINCE	186
PICTURE OF TODAYS AUDINCE	186
INDEX	187
Bibliography-Sources referred to and further reading	187
Glossary	187
Musicias/Personalities	188
Groups/Bands	191
Tunes/Songs	193
Places/Names	194
Venues	195
Events/Publications	195
Picture Credits	196
ACKNOWLDGEMENTS	198
Authors Biography	199
Epilogue	200

zimbabwe township music

INTRODUCTION

Mbare (The cradle of Township Music) 1958

During the 1930's black Zimbabweans left their communal homes in search of jobs in towns, and in the process a dynamic urban 'Township Culture' emerged. The townships attracted people from Zambia (Northern Rhodesia), Malawi (Nyasaland), Mozambique (Portuguese East Africa) and South Africa.

Townships became a melting pot for a variety of cultures. Traditional music took many forms, as depicted by the Shona, "Shangara", "Jerusarema," "Muchongoyo" and "Mbira". The Ndebele varieties included, "Isitshikitsha", "Iqhuzu" and "Imbube", all of which were accompanied by different types of dancing. Malawian or Zambian music was performed, in the form of "Gule" or "Nyau".

included, "Isitshikitsha", "Iqhuzu" and "Imbube", all of which were accompanied by different types of dancing. Malawian or Zambian music was performed, in the form of "Gule" or "Nyau".

Initially people of different ethnic groups would gather to sing and dance in streets, where they would often be dispersed by 5.00pm. Mbare Market became the forum for musicians and instrumentalists (guitarists, saxophonists and pennywhistlers); here different tribes would gather to provide a variety of entertainment especially on Sundays.

Later, as burial societies developed, people gathered during weekends at the house of one of their members to pay subscriptions and to console through singing. The burial societies were formed on tribal and ethnic lines.

Subsequently, these society groups began to play at beerhalls where they would get money for their performances.

A typical form of singing performed by the burial societies was "Makwaya Music". The term "Makwaya" is generic from 'choir', as people sang in groups in a similar fashion to church choir music. However, the influence of Shona and Ndebele story - telling tradition dominated the "Makwaya Music" theme.

Some of the earliest "Makwaya" would begin with a narrator telling a story, and the accompanying group would back in chorus. After supper people gathered around the fire, where an elderly person would tell fiction stories, mostly aimed at ridiculing someone (sometimes in praise). The song "Baba va Ngirande"(The father of "Ngirande"), is a typical example of combined story - telling and "Makwaya" music. It began with the story teller introducing himself, then narrating a story followed by music which pokes fun at a greedy man who eats alone, taking no heed of his wife or children.

"Baba va Ngirande" was recorded in Masvingo (Fort Victoria) by Hugh Tracey in 1933.

Baba va Ngirande

SHONA	ENGLISH
Ndini Dhawura manzi	
Wameso makuru	I am Dhauramanzi
Ndino kuzivisai	the man with big eyes
norungano rwomunhu	I want to tell you a story
waikara gore rezhara	about a person who was a glutton
Aive nemukadzi asi	This was during the drought
wakanga asingade	he did not want to see
kuti mukadzi adye	his wife eating sadza
sadza kana mukadzi	If his wife cooked "sadza"
akabika sadza zvonzi	he would say don't give
usapa vana ipa in	it to the children give it
baba vaNgirande	to me the father of Ngirande

The early songs depicted the traditional situation of mixing story-telling with song; a trend that has persisted until today, whereby musicians use narration in song to emphasise a point.

In some cases during the story telling, the audience would respond in chorus (dzefunde), which is a positive acknowledgement. After a short break they repeat the chorus as the leader singer continues with story-telling. The choirs (makwaya) often narrated tales to reflect what was happening those days, for instance at the gold mines.

Gold and other minerals were mined on a large scale using modern machinery, with the miners wearing protective metal hats and other such paraphernalia which, was a novel development providing a form of music fascination for many people. Mineral resources in Zimbabwe partly led to the colonisation of the country. The digging and accompanying noise had some influence on people; thus early "Makwaya" sang about gold miners, and events associated with mining activities.

Dinah

NDEBELE	ENGLISH
Dinah Dinah Dinah *(Narrator)* *Kudhala abelungu* *bengaka nyatheli elizweni lethu* *labe nsundu sasingena* *lwazi ngelitshe lemali* *sebefikile bahamba* *kulowonke umhlaba* *bahlolisisa befumana inotho* *baze bafika eqaqeni olwa* *luse dhuze lamanzi* *lapho okwakuhlala* *intombazana igama* *layo lingu Dinah*	Dinah Dinah Dinah (Narrator) Long before the white people came to this land Local people people did not have indepth knowlede of gold trading When the white man arrived he explored throughout the country looking for wealth, until he reached the peack of a mountain close to a village where a certain girl lived

The early township musicians of the 1930's used to perform in the open, and bystanders would throw money tokens to them. They did not have musical instruments, but depended on vocals and foot stamping to produce the desired sounds. Musicians of the 30's - 60's brought joy to the townships as they provided entertainment which people craved for.

In the early days most people did not have radios, which were popularly known as 'saucepan' (wireless); furthermore gramophones were expensive. Gramophones also required needles, as well as frequent repairs and maintenance. The cost of such items inhibited people's access to desired entertainment.

There was also bioscope (cinema), which showed Western films, especially with American fashions. Western culture was thus creeping in through the electronic media. This was then termed "civilisation", and everyone apparently desired to be associated with the trend.

During the late 1930's loud - speakers were installed in townships by the municipal councils. This was ostensibly in order to enable news broadcasts to reach the majority blacks who did not own radio sets. But alongside the radio news bulletins and a sprinkling of musical programmes, the authorities also utilised the facility to keep people in check by broadcasting official harangues in the form of police messages and other warnings. Nevertheless, the musical broadcasts were a welcome respite to entertainment-starved urban communities. Later on, local musicians began to imitate Western music particularly Jazz, as this was closer to African rhythms. Country Western, Calypso and other types of music had limited influence, as jazz was more dominant.

The introduction of musical films in the early 40's also introduced people to Western dancing styles, apart from American jazz which

zimbabwe township music

was becoming popular. The loudspeakers, radios, and bioscopes encouraged the formation of properly organised local bands. The electronic media also encouraged professional performance among musical

grammophone

groups, whereby patrons paid fees to watch the shows. The popular halls then were Mai Musodzi in Harare and Stanely Hall in Bulawayo.

At first music tunes were copyrights, but soon traditional music was interwoven with jazz to produce what is popularly termed: "Township Music". There are marked

jazz with traditional music alongside popular music from neighbouring countries. Gradually the music product became "show business", with

Evelyn Juba

Kenneth Mattaka leading the first organised musical group: The Bantu Actors (1932).

At about the same time in Bulawayo, Evelyn and Simon Juba, with Remmington Mazabane as conductor, formed a vocal group, the Merry Makers. Like many other bands of the 30's, the group started without a guitar, and only introduced it afterwards. At the time local singers were greatly influenced by church music, negro spirituals and swing-tempo styles.

similarities between American jazz and African traditional music, of which the former is a by-product of the latter. The drum and the "call- and- response" styles are typical, where the choir backs the lead singer. Musicians fused

People living in the townships were by law, neither permitted to drink clear beer nor brew it. They were also not allowed to be in the city centre after 7pm. However, during the 1940's

zimbabwe township music

(Josaya Hadebe's visit to the Bantu Sports Club (Johannesburg) ended in a riot as the crowds followed him through the tunnel obstructing the soccer spectators from all sides of the field)- Zonk Magazine April 1951.

Jacob Mhungu

Jacob Mhungu was a popular "Masiganda" who followed the footsteps of the earlier masters. He became widely known in the 50's, although he had started his music in the 40's. There was also Gweru-based John White who used both the "Ukuvamba" mode of playing the guitar, as well as the Hawaian bottle method style.

John White played his guitar on trains, entertaining passengers in the 4th class or "Mbombela", which was then an affordable

people began organising "Tea-Parties" where beer was served from a tea-pot instead. They would also organise "Birthday-Parties" or "Mabhavadheyi", as a way of circumventing the prohibitions of the police. Often, at such parties they would hire a one-man band musician "Masiganda"; a term derived from the Afrikaans word "musikaant", meaning musician.

Some celebrated "Omasiganda" musicians were Josaya Hadebe, George Sibanda and Sabelo Mathe. Beside playing at tea-parties, they also performed in the streets as African Troubadours. "Omasiganda's" music was similar to Western country music, having been influenced by such musicians as cowboy Jimmy Rogers, who was a folk hero in the 40's. Josaya Hadebe used to dress like a cowboy after watching Western movies which were popular at the time.

The "Omasiganda" guitar style was called "Ukuvamba," and played on a few guitar chords. "Ukuvamba", derives from "vamping", which was a popular guitar method in Southern Africa.

Hadebe, Sibanda and Mathe were among the first to record with Gallo in 1948, but as they ceded all their royalties to Gallo, they died poor.

Alick Nkata

and sociable way to travel.

Other notable "Omasiganda" were Daniel Mukondorwi, and Marko Takaingofa, who often performed jointly with John White. Ali Bentule from Mozambique was also acclaimed for his tremulous singing style.

Some one-man guitar players preferred not to be associated with "Omasiganda", since the latter were more of street musicians. Jeremiah Kainga was one such musician. He composed "Imi Munosara nani Ndaenda", which was recorded by the Mahotella Queens in the 1960's. It was later recorded by Temba Ndlovu, a Zimbabwean musician based in Germany in the 1980's. The song has retained its popularity, but

August Musarurwa

of Negro Spirituals and traditional music, which often supported political protests, but encouraged people to participate in football, boxing and sporting activities. One of their popular compostions in the 50's, and which is still functional in educational programmes is: "Kudzidza Kwakanaka" (Educational is rewarding).

Kudzidza Kwakanaka

SHONA	ENGLISH
Kudzidza Kwakanaka Kunoita rudzi rubudirire, Dzidzai mose vatema, kuti chidza chisvike kwatiri.	Education is rewarding it makes a nation prosper Be educated black people so that we may be enlightened.
Nyika yazo pinduka nesu ngatipindukewo.	The world is changing and we should also change.

it sadly never benefitted its composer, due to problematic issues relating to royalities and copyright.

Alick Nkhata, a guitarist and one-man band musician, did a lot to preserve early township music. He worked for the Central African Broadcasting Corporation (CABC) in Lusaka, before he transferred to Harare (Salisbury), then the capital of the Federation of Rhodesia and Nyasaland and worked for the Federal Broadcasting Corporation. Whilst there, he used his position to record memorable contemporary music.

August Musarurwa was a musician of the 40's, known for his tune "Skokiaan", which was about the illicit alcohol brew. It was first recorded in 1951 by the Cold Storage Band, later named the Sweet Rhythm Band. An instant hit, the composition was subsequently recorded by several musicians, including Louis Armstrong, Nico Carsten, Robert Delgado, Sandy Nelson, James Last, Joe Carr, Paul Ankar, Paul Lunga, Hugh Masekela and Herb Albert.

The Epworth Theatrical Strutters was a family musical group based at Epworth. It consisted of Andrew, Peter and Nesbitt Kanyowa, including their nephews. They sang a mixture

Herewith, people were made aware of the rewards of education; which equips us with knowledge and expertise for a better life and a better future.

The De Black Evening Follies broke away from the Bantu Actors and formed their own group in 1943, led by Moses Mpahlo Mafusire. They were the first to introduce beauty contests in their variety shows. The 1940's were characterised by large bands due to the influence of such groups as the American Count Basie and Duke Ellington Orchestras. At one time the De Black Evening Follies numbered twenty five in the group.

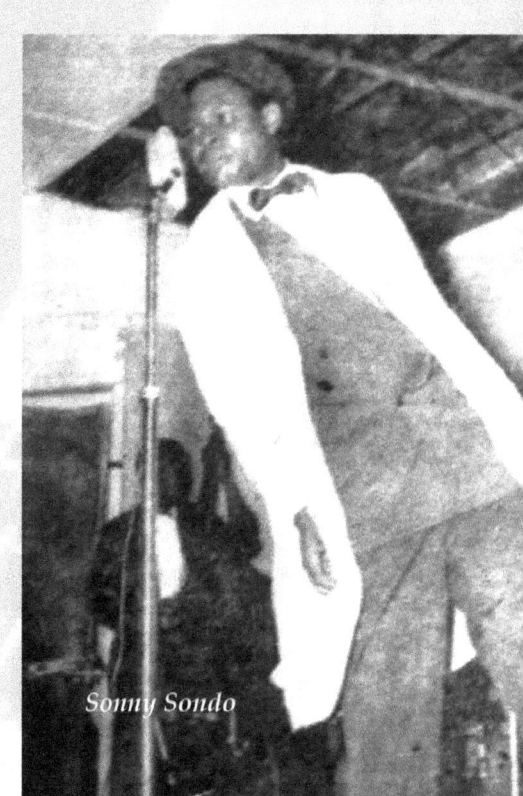
Sonny Sondo

The De Black Evening Follies

Township", which was produced by Polydor in Germany. The album was banned the same year because of political overtones on one of the tracks: "Lizofika nini Ilanga" (When will the Day { of Freedom} Come?).

They also recruited female musicians of the likes of Mabel Bingwa, Faith Dauti, Sylvia (Benya) Sondo, Christine Dube and Joyce Ndoro, who in turn became quite popular in the 1950's. Follies' songs were mostly influenced by American jazz and other music forms with traditional and Indian flavours.

Sonny Sondo, a popular showman of the De Black Evening Follies, broke away from the group in 1953 to form the City Quads. Popularly known as the "The Boys", the City Quads took the country by storm. They were the first group to record a long-playing album in 1961, entitled: "Music in the African

LIZOFIKA NINI ILANGA

NDEBELE	ENGLISH
Lizofika nini ilanga lenkululeko come	When will the day of freedom come
Lizofika nini ilanga lenjabulo come	when will the day of happiness come
Abantu abensundu bayahlupheka	Black people are suffering
Kudhala Kudhala Kudhala	It's been long, it's been long.

The 1950's witnessed a shift from the big band sounds of the 1940's to the formation of musical trios and quartets. Besides the City Quads, there were also the Cool Four, who made their debut with Dorothy Masuka during the Rhodes Centenary Exhibition (1953).

Members of the police band, which often played on state occasions, also formed splinter groups in 1957, such as the City Slickers and the Twelve Bar Blues.
These bands were relatively well equipped, as they could use police band instruments. They subsequently became popular in the townships.

The 50's were symbolic of the peak of Zimbabwe popular music, as they were also the decade of the short - lived Federation (1953-63). It was a

City Quads

Pat Travers

Eileen Haddon

period of disillusionment during which several outspoken personalities were jailed or detained without trial.

There were, however, some white liberals who voiced dissenting views, such as Eileen Haddon, editor of the Central African Examiner, a newspaper which was popular among the black majority. They envisaged the concept of the Federation as an opportunity for genuine partnership. The Inter-racial Association undermined the colour bar by organising multi-racial concerts with bands such as the City Quads, De Black Evening Follies and the coloured group Arcardia Rhythm Lads. The Lads were led by Pat Travers, musician-activist who viewed the show business as both a way of bringing people together, and as weapon to fight the colour bar. When requested to perform in hotels reserved for whites, Travers invited and brought in black colleague artists. Because of his popularity among the white community, hoteliers compromised by allowing him to perform alongside his black counterparts.

Traditionally women sang at funerals, in churches and in community choirs. Those who performed on stage accompanied by western instruments such as guitars, were often labelled as cheap "public girls". Despite such negative social prejudices, and discrimination based on race, class and gender, black women musicians championed their own liberation. The first female singers to make a name for themselves were Lina Mattaka, Evelyn Juba and Victoria Chingate. Interestingly these women had support from their husbands, with whom they shared the stage, as was exemplified by the Mattaka's and the Juba's. The couples soon became role models in society, where marriage and morality were highly respected.

Victoria Chingate

Similarly, Chingate's husband, an MP in the Federal Parliament, was a member of the social Gamma Sigma Club, which organised Christmas parties and family picnics. Chingate was a music promoter, who gave his wife moral support. He would also invite politicians, educationists, and the township elite to watch his wife perform at concerts.

In 1954 **Victoria Chingate** formed the Gay Gaeties, a female musical group of nursing sisters based at Harare Hospital. The public did not expect

zimbabwe township music

Dorothy Masuka 1959

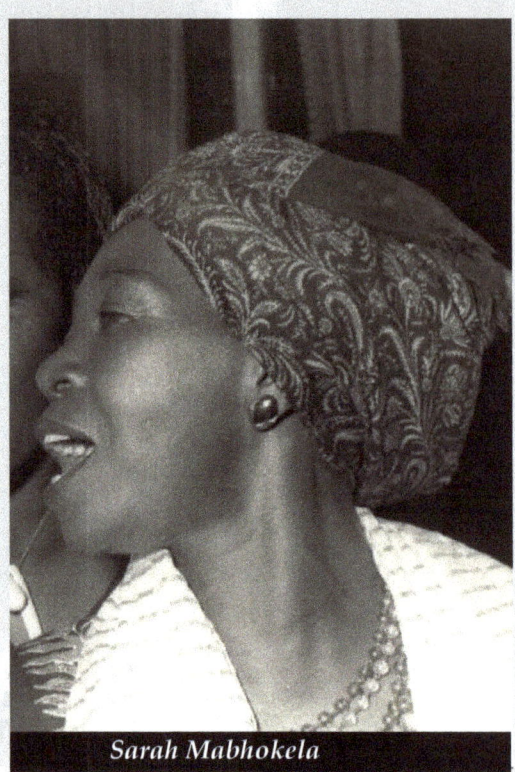
Sarah Mabhokela

Dorothy Masuka graced the 50's musical scene and became the talk of the town. A singular woman who achieved popularity in her own right was Sara Mabhokela (Mhlanga), who sang "Imi Munosara Nani Ndaenda", a Jeremiah Kainga composition which he had originally recorded with Ruth Mpisaunga. The Mahotella Queens later sang their own version of the same tune which apparently became even more popular.

"educated" women to participate in a career normally associated with women who were considered as social misfits. However, the black nurses could no longer withstand the prejudice and discrimination which inhibited them from participating in Christmas festivities. Thus, music became a welcome social outlet for them.

As the group continued to shine and perform, white nurses became attracted to the music and eventually joined the social gatherings. The group would perform a play about a mother, who for some reason did not want to have her child operated on. The play became popular; attracting the attention of hospital authorities, and making the gathering a non-racial event. The Gay Gaeties sadly disbanded, after Victoria Chingate left for overseas to further her nursing studies.

Tabeth Kapuya, once a member of the Gay Gaeties, decided to go solo and did reasonably well for sometime. Faith Dauti, the "Shot Gun Boogie," joined a family musical group, The Milton Brothers. She was to become one of the most prolific township jazz musicians of the 50's. During the same period, Martha Banda led a successful singing career alongside the City Quads. Some of the women who graced the jazz scene, although for a short while, were Miriam Yafele who teamed up with the Mubvumbi Brothers in which her husband was leader, and Margaret Pazarangu who was discovered by the De Black Evening Follies, before joining the African Melodians.

Most women who sang during the 30's-60's performed jazz or traditional music, or a mixture of both. Such music did not require a lot of dancing, though musicians such as

Lina Mattaka 1991

zimbabwe township music

Sylvia Sondo, Joyce Ndoro, Mabel Bingwa and Faith Dauti often sang "Cha-cha-cha" (Rhumba) music with some graceful dancing.

Sylvia Sondo was leader of a musical group, The Yellow Blues, which groomed the famed 60's-70's musician, Susan Chenjerai.

Despite prevailing prejudices on women, female musical success was rapid during the period 1930-1960. This was partly because there was little entertainment at the time, for which women filled the gap, and partly because female performers were a new development and novel phenomenon.

Few women musicians ever play instruments, in line with contemporary culture and tradition. The general attitude was that musical instruments are meant for men. It is felt women will not have enough time to learn or play musical instruments due to household chores and domestic duties.

Lina Mattaka in the 50's was exceptional, as she could play the organ and piano, which she still does to this day. She feels strongly that women ought to be serious enough to play musical instruments. In the olden days, women singers had to be backed by such male groups, as the police band or the likes of Simangaliso Tutani and his colleagues, who were products of the Boys' Clubs.

Boys' Clubs, which were organised by the City Council Department of Social Welfare,

The Boys' Club

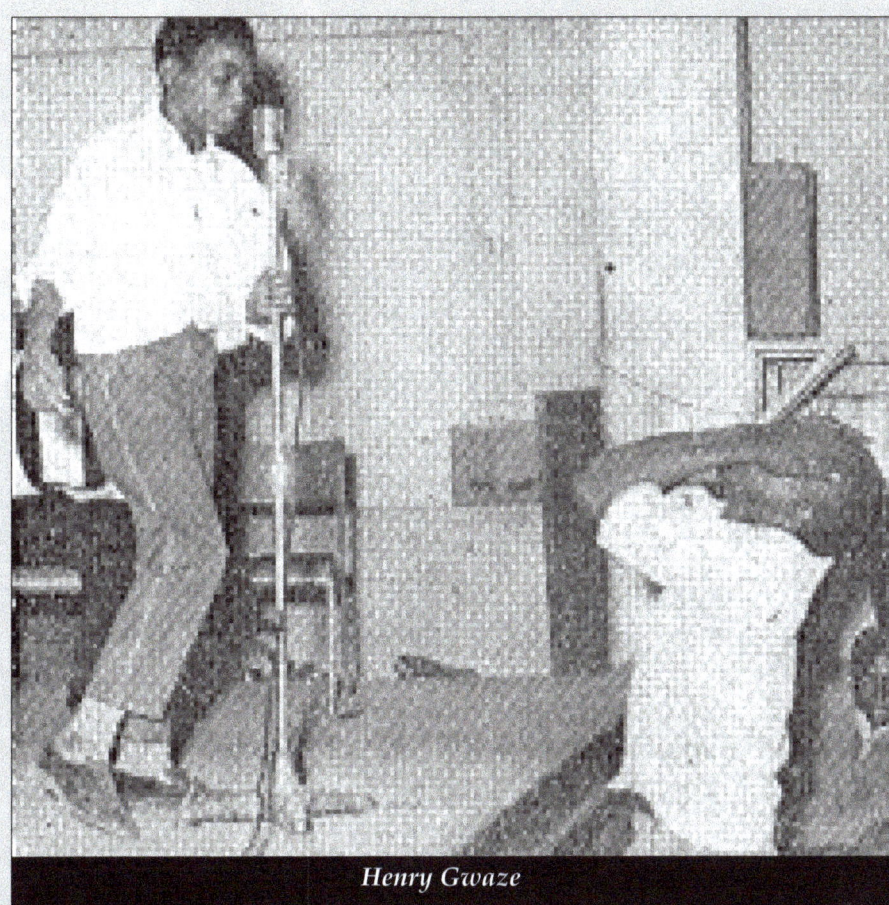

Henry Gwaze

Teenagers had to yell with excitement last saturday when little Harry Gwaze rocked and rolled at the De Black Evening Follies show in mai Musodzi Hall. At the mike is Harry immediately, in front of him is one of his admirers who had to leave his seat and place his hands on his own head!. A real admirer.

BOY'S CLUB ENTERTAINS CHILD PATIENTS

Salisbury, Monday (1956) **The Central African Daily News**

The air at the General Hospital was filled with music and song yesterday afternoon as two choirs composed of boys from Salisbury African Boy's Club sang songs in the latest jazz tempo to patients and members of the hospital staff.

The boys had particularly gone to the hospital to entertain the child patients of Ward 7 as their custom every year when Christmas is approaching.

...continued on next page

Under the leadership of Mr. T.C.G. Chigoma of the Welfare Office, and Mr. J.B. Matsvetu the boys had collected some money with which they bought sweets to give to the little patients. The firms of Messrs Sun Valley and Victoria Bakery generously donated some fruit and cake respectively to be given the sick children.

The musical programme proper started off at a lively pace when the choir of the bigger boys gave a very good account of itself by singing some of the songs on the current Rhodesia hit parade. The smaller boys who followed up also won the hearts of the audience. And so it went on until the programme was cut short when a heavy downpour of rain sent entertainers and audience racing for shelter.

Commenting on the generousity of the boys after the show Mr. T.C.G. Chigoma said, "………..these little boys do something for their friends here at the hospital every year."

Simangaliso Tutani

The City Crackers with Mabel Pindurai

zimbabwe township music 26

played a crucial role in moulding upcoming musicians in the townships. The boys learnt how to play different types of instruments; guitars, saxophones and drums. There were also other forms of vocational training in Mbare, which included welding instruction and carpentry. The De Black Evening Follies promoted young musicians through their annual Christmas Talent contest. They included females in their programmes, which led to the discovery of talented women; Christine Dube, Mabel Bingwa and Margaret Pazarangu, among others. The Follies also formed an educational trust for the less fortunate children, and young people whose aptitudes were discovered at the talent shows. The fund was administered by Sonny Sondo, when he was still with the De Black Evening Follies.

In Bulawayo there were also Boys'/Cultural Clubs similar to those in Harare. Here young people would be taught or would be engangeed in various activities, such as music, sporting, camping, hiking and mountain climbing. Oliver Gwaze who now owns the Red Fox Hotel, which has assisted several jazz artists, is grateful to have been involved with the Boys Clubs, particularly where sport and vocational activities were concerned as they prepared him for life today. "Like now I do not hesitate going canoeing." he remarked.

Musicians, such as those of the Broadway Quartet who were popular in the 60's, and Paul Lunga, a jazz survivor, all started with the Boys' Clubs.

Musical groups in the townships held variety shows which incorporated comedians and sketches in between the songs. The arrangement made the shows more lively and broke the monotomy of music, as the shows ran from 7pm-11.30pm. Quite often, the same musicians doubled as comedians. Moses Mpahlo Mafusire and Jonathan (Joe) Chabata, performed humorous episodes as part of the musical show. Sonny Sondo also performed similarly. A famous commedian of the 50's was **Albert Ndinda**, nicknamed **"Magaisa"**, who used to devour three loaves of bread on stage in five minutes.

As Ndinda became popular, he travelled throughout "Central Africa," performing to crowds and to a variety of audiences. He later became a politician and trade unionist. As the country's political situation grew more tense, "Magaisa" fled to Europe.

Drama acting played an important role in early township entertainment. Musicians Sam Matambo, Steve Mtunyani and Sonny Sondo of the City Quads; as well as Pat Travers of the Acardia Rhythm Lads, and Victoria Chingate from the Gay Gaeties, all belonged to a group; The Runyararo Drama Group. The producer of the drama shows was Monica Marsden, who endeavoured to make township life a little more interesting. She also fought the colour bar through entertainment, by organising and staging drama shows in the City Centre. The white

Albert Ndida (The Bread Eater)

community soon realised that blacks could also act well in drama. The Drama Group later won a coveted prize at a contest which was organised by Barbara Tredgold, at the Anglican Cathedral.

The then Ministry of Information would produce commedy films which they took around the country (mobile cinema). One of the popular commedians of the 50's-60's was Tickey (Andrew Kanymeba) Drama thus provided an indirect channel

Runyararo Drama Group 1954

for educating the community; on health, social and political issues.

Township jazz performed in the halls, commonly known as "concerts," was mainly for the elite audience in the township, as this type of entertaiment was associated with Western or "modern culture". There were other forms of entertainment such as "Mahobo" parties, which drew their membership from the black working class. Such parties were held in the bush where "Skokiaan" beer was brewed, and often amid unwarranted romantic affairs.

The decent township folk shunned the "Mahobo" parties and wished them banned. However, the parties slowly transformed themselves into township "Shebeens", where people drank "Skokiaan" beer and alcoholic spirits, such as whisky or brandy. "Shebeens" thus became as popular as night clubs. At the time, black people were not allowed to be in the City Centre after 7.00pm; thus if there was no concert in the township halls, people would converge at "Mahobo" parties. There was also a spectacular dance by women at these parties, which became a big attraction to men. Township residents increasingly visited the parties for social entertainment, where grammophone music was the order of the day.

In the mid-sixties the city council raised fees for hiring entertainment halls, making them unaffordable to ordinary musicians; and consequently making the "Mahobo" parties more attractive. Coupled with the political upheavals the mid sixties thus marked the gradual decline of township music, which had become a symbol of identity of the urban African.

Following the Unilateral Declaration of Independence and under the declared state of emergency, it was illegal for people to be seen in large groups. Any such grouping, even a social party, came under heavy scrutiny as the authorities endeavoured to thwart political dissent. The concerts were the meeting point of black educationists, businessmen, politicians and ordinary people. Township people supported the music which became partly a unifying force among the urban dwellers. During the 1930's -1960's the music scene was a reflection of the various activities within the urban townships; it came to an end in the mid 1960's, mainly due to the unbearable political situation. Some musicians left the country, including commedian (Magaisa) Albert Ndinda and Daniel Madzimbamuto, organiser of music festivals, who had been detained without trial. Simangaliso Tutani, a young township musician, left for Zambia with The Broadway Quartet, which remained there until Zimbabwe attained its independence in 1980. In the same vein Sonny Sondo went to work in Zambia at Rokhana Mines, where he eventually died. Jacob Mhungu was also in Zambia pursuing both jazz music and the liberation struggle. And so followed Dorothy Masuka and Eileen Haddon of the Intercultural Association, who both found haven in Zambia. Thus several artists who were involved in township music, either as musicians or as promoters, went into exile. Those who remained in the country found their musical activities heavily curtailed by political constraint.

Dorothy Masuka

THE SIXTIES MOOD

MID SIXTIES

The OK Success Band

L to R: Virginia Silla, Christine Nyandoro, Gladys Motsi, Joseph Kashala,
Back: Daniel Katatu, Joseph Nsabila, Andrew Ngoyi, Godfrey Sikubuyo.

As township jazz temporarily phased out, other forms of music gradually crept in, such as West African Highlife and *"Cha-Cha-Cha"* from the Democratic Republic of Congo (DRC). Some music bands from the DRC who performed in Zimbabwe at the time, are still active in the country. These include, the Limpopo Jazz Band, OK Success, whose original members have since become permanent residents of Zimbabwe. South African groups who toured the country, introduced the popular "Mbaqanga", also known as "Simanje-Manje" in those days. The Mahotella Queens and Izintombi Zesi ManjeManje ofetn toured the country.

Rock 'n Roll music appealed to the young as it was given lots of media airplay. The foreign-based music was further promoted by recording companies then baseinSouth Africa (Gallo) and France.

The Mahotela Queens

The music, which included Rhumba and "Simanje-manje", alongside Western forms typified by Rolling Stones and Beatles, flourished due to regular airtime on radio.

A popular local musician was Elijah Banda of the Great Sounds, which recorded "Anopenga Anewaya". "Cha-Cha-Cha" was used as the basis for fusion. Eliah Banda and his group were among the few to record music during the time, as there was only one recording company. Another popular song was "Ndati Bhutsu Yangu Yapera Hiri" (The soles of my shoes are worn out), composed by Nelson Jera of the Zebrons. It was a typical Rock 'n Roll song with lyrics in Shona, originally recorded in the late sixties. The song was again recorded by Rob Kruger in 1993, and it still appeals to contemporary audiences.

George Sisimayi in the late 60s recorded a "Cha-Cha-Cha" song which he had translated into Shona; "Ndapera Necha-cha-cha Amai" (Mother I am overwhelmed by "Cha-Cha-Cha"). When he went to the recording studio his intention was to record a "Kwela" song, but he was advised that "what is selling these days is 'Cha-Cha-Cha' ". However the flip side of the record was a "Kwela" which he had originally earmarked to record.

"Kwela" music reached its peak in the 60's, having evolved in the 50s. The Gallo company was recording "Kwela" songs mostly in Bulawayo. The archives have master tapes with just the title, "Bulawayo". The song writers are being sought as there is need to re-issue the songs. The "Kwela" craze also gripped Harare, where Rufus Nkonde recorded with the Rhodesia Broadcasting Corporation during the late sixties and seventies. The new music originated from South Africa, with influence from Spokes Mashiyane and Kid Marongrong, (Albert Rurulimi), now with Gallo Archives in South Africa. At one time "Kwela" records sales were spectacular in South Africa, according to Rob Allingham, the Gallo Archivist.

Some Zimbabwean groups began copying the "Simanjemanje" songs. The Mutanga Queens based at Mutanga Nightclub, in Highfields, rose to fame and so were Izintombi zikaMtwakazi, (Bulawayo Simanje Manje group). The Jairos Jiri Band played the same music, and had the late Eva Melusi, as one of their soloists.

During the 60's and 70's, certain Zimbabwean musicians did not focus on "Simanjemanje" or "Cha-Cha-Cha" music, which were dominant at the time. Such were Susan Chenjerai and **Safirio Madzikatire**, who sang duet comedy tunes with a social message. They recorded a song, "Ndatemwa Negogo" (I have been hit by a pointed shoe), which tells a story of a man who was discovered with a girlfriend by his wife. The girlfriend after discovering that the man was married, hit him on the head with one of her pointed shoes before running away. Susan, in the the song acted as a wife and girfriend. Another duet was, "Dai Tiri kwa Hunyani" (I wish I were at Hunyani Lake). Hunyani, now Lake Chivero, abounds in scenic

George Sisimayi

Susan Chenjerai (right) and friend

Safirio Madzikatire

zimbabwe township music 31

views. It is a picnic spot, and is also a major source of water supply for Harare.

The song was later recorded in the 1990s by the late Safirio Madzikatire and late Elizabeth Taderera (Katarina). The tune was one of the most popular recordings of the decade.

Jordan Chataika composed songs which he played on acoustic guitar. His music was mostly Shona church songs.

Jordan Chataika

At times he teamed up with Safirio Madzikatire, Susan Chenjerai and his sister, Edna. On other occasions he performed as a solo musician. These represented the few artists who focused on indigenous Zimbabwean music with minimal external influence. However, a lot of bands in the 60s were mere music copyists. Foreign music was apparently popular when entertaining patrons, either in bars, night clubs, or at private functions. The mid 60's and early 70's witnessed the "Teen-Time" era, which was a significant departure from the music concerts of the 50's. In the earlier concerts, patrons paid an admission fee and sat down to listen to the music.

"Teen-time" shows were influenced partly by a band of whites called the Cyclones, which played at the Stodart Hall, and partly by Elvis Presley and Cliff Richard type music, which was popular on radio. The latter artist eventually toured Zimbabwe (Rhodesia) on "His Summer Holiday" Show.

Jack Maravanyika, who was a youth in the mid 60s, remembers the Cyclones show, when he and his friends sat down on benches as they used to do when accompanying their parents to concerts at Mai Musodzi. The band ordered the removal of benches, so that the audience would dance, thus heralding the "Teen Time" era, recalled Jack. The popular dances were "Twist" and "Agogo", which the local bands and patrons imitated zealously.

Teen-Time music did not go down so well with the older people, as it required some hectic dancing. They preferred to listen to South African bands playing "Simanje-manje" or "Kwela" or "Cha-Cha-Cha" music from The Democratic Republic of Congo

Jack Maravanyika

(DRC), or Zambia.

A section of the young generation was not just interested in the "Teen-Time", but also belonged to a folk music club in Harare's city centre. Folk music festivals often took place at the University of Zimbabwe - Beit Hall. The folk clubs were more popular amongst the whites, with only a few blacks interested, of which Jack Maravanyika was one. The late 60s witnessed the advent of music promoters such as Nikki Onayadis, organiser of the "Neshamwari Festival". Winners at the Festival got scholarships to advance their musical careers at the then Rhodesia College of Music. Some participants of the festivals were Tendai Makwavarara, Bertha Mattaka-Msora and Jack Maravanyika.

Nikki, in addition, organized the "Eistedford competitions", which were usually held at the Harry Margolis Hall. They included choirs (Makwaya), soloists and duets.

L to R: Harry Gwaze-Guitar, Sam Banana-2+2, Joseph Msonda-(Eye of Liberty) (not identified) Jethro Shasha-Sound Effects, Bright Mbirimi (Fan), Cuthbert-(Gypsy Caravan)

SEVENTIES

Oliver Mtukudzi

Susan Mapfumo

In the mid 70's Zimbawe's music was transforming yet again, adapting itself to new trends fused with traditional lyrics which, as in the 50's, often coveyed revolutionary themes. Zexie Manatsa and the Green Arrows came up with their hit song: "Chipo Chiroorwa Tipemberere" (Chipo get married so we can celebrate). As the tune was a mixture of traditional music and "Simanje-manje", it became instantly popular. The Green Arrows performed at the New Way Hotel and restaurants at Juru Growth Point in Goromonzi District, Mashonaland East.

Green Arrows music had its origins in Bulawayo. The group toured the whole country until it finally settled in Harare, (Salisbury). Zexie Manatsa had numerous songs which often mocked other tribes, such as those of Malawian origin. "Chechule Anavala Bottom", is one such song.

Oliver Mtukudzi became a popular musician in the 70s; he revived traditional hits such as "Rovangoma Mutavara {Sango Rinopa Waneta}", a song which implicitly supported the liberation struggle. The salient meaning is: "Go on fighting, you will make it." Another of his popular hits was "Ziwere-Ziwere". He later recorded a number of long playing records, some with a mixture of traditional and "Mbaqanga" music.

Gallo (South Africa) recorded the music of Oliver Mtukudzi and Zexie Manatsa. It often seconded its producers to Zimbabwe such as Hamilton Nzimande and West Nkosi, who recorded local music in the 70's. The company also recorded Susan Mapfumo, one of the few women musicians of the 70s. Susan's music depicted the plight of contemporary women, such as in the tunes: "Ndakanga Ndakaroorwa kwa Murehwa" (I was once married in Murehwa), "Baba vaBhoyi Maita Seiko Munouya Nehalf

zimbabwe township music

The Singing nuns : Sister Getrude Matsika and Sister Tendai Maminimini

Yepeyi" (What has happened to you the father of my children, to bring half of your pay home*)*, *"Kwenya Mezi dzako Wega Makeyi"* (Sort out your own problems man!) and "Muchenjeri" (The clever one), which is a political satire. Susan Mapfumo was also a band leader, who owned a set of musical instruments which had been donated to her by West Nkosi of Gallo. She sang mixtures of "Rhumba, Mbaqanga" and traditional music.

Other popular women musicians included Jane Chenjerai, Susan's daughter, who recorded; "Usandimirire Pagedhi Unondirovesa Nababa"; (Don't wait for me at the gate or my father will beat me up); a traditional song which she adapted for backing by western- type musical instruments.

Two Roman Catholic nuns sang and played the guitar, which was rather unusual. They eventually recorded songs some of which were church - related and others focusing on married life, which appealed to the general public. The public would ask: what made the nuns sing marriage - related tunes? The two nuns wereTendai Maminimini and Getrude Matsika, now Mrs. Mushayabasa. Magna is still a nun, and based in Harare.

Virginia Sillah a well-known female vocalist recorded the song, "Ndafunafuna", which is a traditional "chiChewa" tune. The City Quads did their version in the 50's and recorded it in the 70's, topping the charts. Contemporary musicians Prudence Katomeni and Jazz Invitation have popularised the tune on radio and since recorded it.

The Tutenkhamen Band recorded "Torai Mapadza Muchirima" (Take your hoes and plough), a version of an old traditional "mbira" song, which they played on guitars. The song appealed to both the young and old because of its "mbira" beat, accompanied by modern guitars. Joseph Musabaika came up with the concept of mixing guitars with "mbira", when the Tutenkhamen Band was playing at Mushandira Pamwe in Marondera before moving to the branch in Highfields. When Tutenkhamen made a name with "Torai Mapadza Muchirima", Mushandira Pamwe Hotel bought instruments for the band. The band then did not continue with "mbira" songs, as the proprietor, encouraged them to play versions of popular hits of the day. They named themselves New Tutenkhamen.

The group produced a hit single in the 70's called "Jo'burg Bound", composed by the late Elisha Josamu who was also the lead vocalist.

zimbabwe township music

One of the few locally produced LPs during the 70s.

They later went on to produce a long playing album entitled "I Wish You Were Mine".

The Tutenkhamen thus pioneered the adaptation of mbira music to guitars, before the likes of **Thomas Mapfumo and Oliver Mtukudzi.** The latter two musicians have earned themselves world-wide acclaim for backing traditional "mbira" songs with modern instruments. One of Mapfumo's early recordings was "Bhutsu Mutandarika". As some of his music became political he was thrown into prison by the Smith Government. Mapfumo's lead guitarist was Jonah Sithole, who masterminded a popular tune in the 70s; "Chembere Dzomiramira Sabhuku Wapenga Penga", (apparently about witch –hunts but subtly alluding to political strife).

The Jairos Jiri band became famous in the 70's, as it held music festivals at the Stanley Square in Bulawayo's Mzilikazi township. The festivals became a favourite of the youth, as the bands performed different types of music; which included "Simanje-manje, Rock and Soul".

Gypsy Caravan

However, a lot of the tunes were mostly copyrights.

Several bands mushroomed at the time: Gypsy Caravan, Double Shuffle, Season, Baked Beans, Dhama, Halelujah Chicken Run, Pied Pipers, Blind Eye, Mverechena Band, Memphis Band (White Band), Limpopo Jazz Band, 4 Aces Wild Flower, Eye –Q Band, Breeze, Soul and Blues Union, Wells Fargo, Eye of Liberty, Dr. Footswitch, Stars of Liberty, Shaka, and Movement.

They sang English lyrics, mostly Soul and

zimbabwe township music

Rock with traditional flavours. They would also sing in Shona or Ndebele, sometimes in Nyanja with a fusion of Rock or Soul/Pop. The Gypsy Caravan recorded "Maybe Tomorrow", which had salient political messages, a common trait in songs of the 70's. Families were being harassed by police, with more and more young people opting to join the freedom struggle. The youth who remained behind, sang mostly freedom tunes such as; "May be Tomorrow I will be Gone".

Gideon Neganje

The Eye of Liberty and the Wells Fargo were Rock groups based in Bulawayo, with Dr. Footswitch based in Harare. These groups often sang Rock tunes in vernacular.

Eye of Liberty became popular with a song "Calling Your Name" and Wells Fargo hit the charts with "Watch Out Big Storm Is Coming", the two tunes being quasi- political. Dr. Footswitch came up with a love song "Shumayira The Woman Of My Life", which became synonymous with the name of the band.

Dhama, Soul & Blues and Movement were groups of mixed races which played to mixed audiences. Laura Bezuidenhout, a white woman who played with a mixed group, shocked the public by even visiting the African townships and making herself at home.

Four Ace Wild Flower, was a popular band of the 70's, owned by Solomon (Solo) Chiweshe, who was fortunate to have instruments of his own. The band was known for their hit: See It Fade.

The Limpompo Jazz Band and The OK Success originated from the DRC in the 60's and teamed up with Susan Mapfumo during the 70's. The Harare Mambos was formed in the the late 50's and survived the turbulent 70's, becoming a household name.

The Pied Pipers sang; "I Am A Country Boy", which was composed by Gideon Neganje, a gifted and intelligent song writer. Shaka and Stars of Liberty were formed by Zimbabweans in the UK, comprising Louis Mhlanga, Fungai Malianga, and Fred Zindi. Fred did a version of "Imi Munosara Nani Ndaenda" in the 70's, which was a Jeremiah Kainga composition. He also adapted "Kutapira Kunoita Manhanga", a popular tune of the 50's. Fred mad his mark in the 70's when jazz was not the in-thing, this group played at the famous Hundred Oxford Street Club, where jazz enthusiasts converged, to listen to flavours of South African

Fred Zindi

Crispen Matema

Jack Sadza

"Kwela" and "Marabi". Alongside they would also play contemporary soul and pop. When Fred Zindi returned home after independence, he carried on with the reggae tradition, and put up a group of youngsters, "Frontline Kids" which featured prominently in the 80's.

Zindi has since written three books: Roots Rocking in Zimbabwe (1985), Music ye Zimbabwe (1997) and The Pop-Music Work Book (Zimbabwe Versus The World) 2004. Currently he is Chairman of the Academic Committee at the Zimbabwe College of Music, and also lectures at the University of Zimbabwe. Fungai and Louis have carried on with the Township Jazz tradition.

The choral music entertainment was brought about by Bezel Chidyamatamba, who also organised choir competitions.

In the 70's one - man band guitarists became prominent, of which Ngwaru Mapundu and Jackson Chinembiri are typical. They were called "Ana Gwenyambira", unlike the one-man band of the 50s "Omasiganda". The latter derived from the word "musikaant" which means music in Zulu/Ndebele and pronounced "Masiganda". The "Gwenyambira" were one-man band musicians from Harare (Salisbury), who spoke Shona, resulting in them being called "Ana Gwenyambira". "Gwenya" means strummer; "mbira" is a traditional thumb piano, played at festivals and religious ceremonies. The word "mbira" used to signify the guitar.

During the UDI period, musicians had difficulties in acquiring musical instruments

L to R: Nicholas "satch" Chidhuza, Jeff Ilunga, Jethro Shasha, Solo Chiweshe, Laura Bezuidenhout, Webster Waungana (seated): David Marumahoko and Kaisano Tembo.

Movement

Webster Shamu

due to international sanctions imposed upon the country. They often bought second-hand equipment mostly from South Africa. The scarcity of good instruments constrained the quality of local music, which became a poor match to the live shows of South African bands which toured the country.

To complement Gallo producers such as Hamilton Mzimande and West Nkosi, some Zimbabwean producers emerged: Crispen Matema, Nikki Piccard and **Webster Shamu**. Webster was one of the organizers of a festival held at the Nyamanhindi Farm near Mutare, which was dubbed "Woodstock Festival", as it ran for three days, involving more than ten musical groups. Another organizer of the festival was the late Jack Sadza, who became Oliver Mtukudzi's Manager in the 80s.

Crispen Matema did some recordings in the 70s with the Teal Recording Label. Shamu recorded musical groups at the then Rhodesia Broadcasting Corporation. A tune to remember was: "Calling Your Name" by the Eye of Liberty, which featured on popular charts. Immediately after recording the hit, Webster joined the liberation struggle.

The popular musical venues of the 70s were the Stodart Hall in Mbare Township, near

Mushandirapamwe Hotel in Highfields

Harare city centre, and Gwanzura Stadium in Highfields, which was well known for "Pungwes" (all-night shows). Gwanzura Stadium is close to the **Mushandira Pamwe Hotel**, another popular night spot of the 70s music. The owner of Mushandira Pamwe Hotel Charles Tavengwa, contracted popular musicians to play at the night club. Mutanga Night Club also in Highfields, became a crowd puller. Kambuzuma Hall excelled in "Pungwes", especially during public holidays. In the city centre popular music spots included the Federal Hotel, Bonanza, Queens and Elizabeth Hotel The latter did not allow black patrons at certain times; but coloureds and whites were welcome anytime. Simba Night Spot, later called Jobs Night Spot, was not affected by discriminatory practices, as it was located remotely from the city centre. Other social joints of interest were the Jamaica Inn, near Harare, Mverechena in Domboshava and kwaBhora in Goromonzi District.

In Bulawayo entertainment focal points included the Stanley Square in Mzilikazi Township, the Macdonald, Pelandaba Hall, White City Stadium, Marisha and Valley Hotel, which was owned by Jerry Vera, a well-known businessman at the time.

Mutare often attraced patrons from as far afield as Harare, mostly because of the Tsimba Hotel, which groomed Susan Mapfumo, a star musician of the 70s.

zimbabwe township music

Wells Fargo: Standing L to R: Handsome Mabhiza, Jerry Tikili (seated), Never Mkuze, Ebba Chitambo and George Phiri

Jane Chenjerai

Jonah Mutumwa

The "Soul and Blues Union Band" They are L to R: Boykie Fido, Hendry, Basil, Robert, Timothy and "Bunny".

Zexie Manatsa

Virginia Sillah

Dr Footswitch: from L to R: "Jako", Stanely, Nicholas, "Taps" and Manu.

zimbabwe township music

THE JAZZ REVIVAL

Jethro Shasha (front) and Simangaliso Tutani (behind)

zimbabwe township music

THE JAZZ REVIVAL

Simangaliso Tutani

When Zimbabwe gained independence in 1980, Township music/Jazz was revived, although there was some dominance of reggae and funk music. Township music creeped in slowly back into the hearts of people. As of today, it still has a vast following, being revived by old generation musicians and their young ardent followers.

Musicians at the forefront of reviving Township Music included: Simangaliso Tutani, Dorothy Masuka, Jacob Mhungu, Jethro Shasha, Andrew Chakanyuka, Paul Lunga, Erick Juba, Bezel Kumpeu, Louis Mhlanga, Cookie Tutani, Chris Chabuka, Ben Gumbo (Pula-Pulani), Henry Todlana, Elisha Josamu, Checks Tavengwa, Jonah Marumahoko; the list is long. The contemporary Township Music reviving groups include: Summer Breeze, Cool Crooners, Jabavu Drive, Jazz Impacto, Harare Drive, Lucky Street Blues, Mbare Trio, Two Plus Two, Jazz Invitation, Africa Revenge, Tanga Wekwa Sando, and Colour Blu.

Simangaliso Tutani once organized the Body and Soul group consisting of Cookie Tutani, Chris Chabuka and Jonah Marimahoko. Apart from Cookie, the rest were old boys who used to play in the 50's, with the Pine Tops, a coloured band then based in Acardia and The Broadway Quartet. Body and Soul played at the George and Oasis Hotels, which were focal points for jazz patrons.

Simangaliso Tutani organized the first all-inclusive Jazz Festival in Harare, after a break of some 30 years. This was in 1993, and thereafter followed a spate of jazz festivals, with venues also in Bulawayo and Mutare. Jazz festivals have since been a regular feature in the major towns of Zimbabwe.

Simangaliso taught History of Jazz at the Zimbabwe College of Music. Dorothy Masuka is now resident in South Africa, and still performs jazz with old friends, Miriam Makeba, Letta Mbulu and Dolly

Dorothy Masuka

Rathebe. Jacob Mhungu once exiled in Zambia with Dorothy Masuka and Simangaliso Tutani, was a session jazz musician. In 1995 he appeared in a television

Biddy Patridge

Louis Mhlanga

Jethro Shasha was a top drummer of the 70's, having played with The Movement, and the Tutenkhamen. In the 80s he toured with Caiphus Simenya and Letta Mbulu on BUWA, a highly successful jazz act. During the same period Shasha arranged a brilliant composition; "Alouis naJane", which is a mixture of Rhumba and jazz. In South Africa Music Ye Africa performed with such greats, as Ray Phiri and Hugh Masekela. It also featured at the Sun City Afro Jazz Orchestra Band show in 1995. James Indi, a member of the group, is a brilliant guitarist, who in the 80s, composed and recorded the song; "Ndoenda". documentary *"Omasiganda"* (Township Troubadors), produced for the ZBC/TV by Joyce Jenje-Makwenda.

Louis Mhlanga, a highly successful Zimbabwean jazz guitarist, is currently based in South Africa. His early interest in jazz derived from the family, particularly aunt Sara Mabhokela, a one time township jazz singer.

In South Africa, Louis played with a group, Music ye Africa (Axemen), which included Jethro Shasha and James Indi. He is one of the finest musicians in Southern Africa, with a career dating back to the 70s. He once lived briefly in London, where he also jammed with Fred Zindi. In the 80s Louis played with The Southern Freeway, with late brother drummer Willie, and Steve Dyer, a multi-talented jazz artist.

Andrew Chakanyuka, of the 60's Broadway Quartet, composed brilliant guitar solos, and was one of the jazz survivors. He subsequently left for Zambia, where he re-united, with the Broadway Quartet, before heading for Uganda and Ethiopia.

Paul Lunga

Later he left for Switzerland, where he performed with an assortment of bands. Upon his return back home at independence, Andrew fraternised with several local jazz groups. He was also a part-time guitar tutor at the Zimbabwe College of Music. Andrew is now late.

A gifted all - rounder, was the late Elisha Josamu, whose musical career goes back to the 70's. He once played with Harare Mambos as well with the Tutenkanen band, which included the late drummer Johnny Papas. Elisha later played with the Two- Plus - Two Band, together with another survivor bassist, Checks Tavengwa.

The Harare Mambos, led by Greenford Jangano from the 60's, is a jazz outfit which was based in Harare and later at the Victoria Falls.

Paul Lunga founded the Jazz Impacto, a popular jazz group based in Bulawayo. It boasts of the finest Township Jazz musicians, the likes of Jacob Ncube who once played in several bands of the 60's, including Kenneth Mattaka's Talent Band. The late Bezel Kumpeu was a jazz survivor of the 80's-90's, with a musical career dating from the 70's.

Eric Juba based in Bulawayo, is reviving Township Jazz, being also the son of Evelyn and Simon Juba, the early Township Music champions. In the 70's Eric played with the Wells Fargo, which was a favourite of the youth because of its rock sounds. He currently

The Harare Mambos

Bezel Kumpeu

zimbabwe township music

sings with the Cool Crooners.

The Crooners are a quartet of men in their 70's; two of whom used to belong to the Cool Four, one from the Golden Crooners, and the fourth being Eric Juba. Their music is so demanding due to their vocal vibrancy and dancing skills, which arguably dispute their age. They are Ben {Pula-Pulani} Gumbo now late, Sinwametsi Sithole, Lucky Thodlana and Eric.

Moving Jazz Cafe': Philbert Marowa- Keyboard, Penny Yon-Bass, Samatha-Drums, Jonah-Guitar, Katrina-Sax/Flute, Biddy Patridge-Sax/KeyBoards

The Cool Crooners: BLUE SKY

VENUES

Stanely Sqaure (Makokoba) Bulawayo

zimbabwe township music

VENUES

Mai Misodzi Hall in Mbare

Artist who championed Township Music in the 30's often performed in the open, as there were no concert halls at the time. The musicians would also use church halls as venues of entertainment. The Methodist Church in Magaba was one of the earliest musical venues in Mbare township.

Eventually Harare groups began to stage shows at the Kaufman's centre, close to the Mbare Marketplace. It was named Magaba, and it became a venue where pioneering musicians of the 30's, such as Mattaka, used to entertain and perform. Although the centre was still used in the 50's, it grew less popular, as Mai Musodzi became more attractive due to its central location.

Mai Musodzi's original name was the Recreation Hall, as it was originally a venue earmarked for black entertainment. Besides hosting concerts of the 50's, it was a training centre for homecraft skills and other vocations such as the Red Cross. The name Mai Musodzi derives from a pioneer social welfare worker who was called by the same name.

Behind the Mai Musodzi Hall was a sub-township called the Old Bricks, which was the cradle of several musicians due to its proximity to the music scenes. One can name Jeremiah Kainga, who composed the song "Munosara Nani Kana Ndaenda", and a coloured Pat Travers, who endeavoured to use music to fight colour bar. Travers lived in a street called Dispenzura Line, (near a dispensary), behind Mai Musodzi. He used to accompany his mother to the Mai Musodzi concerts, where he met groups such as the De Black Evening Follies. Later he was forced to live in Arcardia,

zimbabwe township music

a suburb reserved for coloureds. However, he continued to bring his Arcardia Rhythm Lads, to Mai Musodzi where they often held combined shows with the City Quads.

Several musicians and socialites of olden days will remember the Mai Musodzi as their favourite entertainment joint. Christmas parties were held there; it was a prestige hall for all performing artists. Bands from Bulawayo such as the Cool Four, also staged at the venue. When this group performed at the Mai Musodzi, the entrance fees would be raised due to their popularity.

Harare, now Mbare, was Salisbury's only African township, at the time. As the population expanded Mai Musodzi became too small as a centre of recreation. The migration of people into the city resulted in more houses being built in Harare. As a result, the township grew and expanded from the Old Bricks to the New Lines, and to New Location and National, each stage having an increased number of living rooms. The housing schemes shared communal toilets, with the exception of the National Lines where each house had four rooms with own toilet and shower. To accommodate the growing population a bigger hall; the **Stodart Hall**,

Stodart Hall in Mbare

with additional recreational facilities, such as a swimming pool; was built in 1958. As such, it became equally popular but was rather more expensive to hire than Mai Musodzi Hall. Thus, some early township musicians continued to feature at the Mai Musodzi, which was more affordable. At the close of the township jazz era the contemporary musical groups were now closely identified with the newer Stodart Hall.

Macdonald Hall in Bulawayo

When it was commissioned, the older township musicians opened the stage curtains. These were: De Black Evening Follies, City Quads, Epworth Theatrical Strutters and the City Slickers (police band). Other bands which were to grace the stage were the Gay Gaeties, Milton Brothers, Capital City Dixies and Modern African Stars. The Stodart Hall was also the venue of the All Africa Festival, a Talent Show organised by Daniel Madzimbamuto, where musical groups performed to a stiff competition.

Monica Marsden with Runyararo Group

In the mid 60's the Stodart Hall became even more popular as a haven for Teen Time bands, and so as the **Macdonald Hall** in Bulawayo.

A unique supporting centre for entertainment and township music was the Runyararo Hall, in Mbare's National section, Barbara (Tredgold) who was in charge of the Church, was also a keen patron of township entertainment. She also provided space for young groups like African Kid Brothers, which was a band of youngsters consisting of George Mambo, Shelton Mazowe (leader), Kenny Tabva, and Raphael Murambiwa. Female musicians included Faith Dauti and Mabel Bingwa. Sister Barbara often organised trips for the young performing artists, with one such outing during Rhodes and Founders Holiday in Zvishavane in the 50's. It still lingers as a memorable event to those who participated in it.

Groups such as the City Quads helped raise money to build a creche in the neighbourhood, named after Sister Barbara. It is one of the best run creches, where nursery school teachers are also trained. On the same day the De Black Evening Follies were able to stage concerts at Mai Musodzi and Runyararo Halls simultaneously, as they had several musicians. A car which was on stand-by, shuttled musicians to and from Runyararo Hall to Mai Musodzi and vice-versa. Follies called such a show "a double header."

George Mambo and his group

zimbabwe township music

Runyararo Hall was famous for its Drama Club led by producer Monica Marsden. Several musicians belonged to this group; including Victoria Chingate and her Gay Gaeties, Sonny Sondo, Sam Matambo, Steven Mtunyani and Pat Travers. Monica also produced a number of plays such as "Cry The Beloved Country". The Drama club became a sensation because of its able actors and the good quality of the productions. Victoria Chingate remembered how well they were received by the audience, which was mostly whites at the time. Demand for the drama group was overwhelming in the city centre.

The group was later invited to perform at the Reps Theatre, where Pat Travers and Steve Mtunyane also performed in the play: " Under the Sun". The plot was a political satire set around the construction of the Kariba Dam. Pat Travers represented Ndabaningi Sithole, who conscientised the blacks not to build the Dam, as their labour was being exploited. A member of the audience complained to Ken Marshall, producer of the play, about actor Pat Travers, who seemed to have been politically motivated whilst acting.

Adrian Stanely also promoted black actors at the Reps Theatre. In "Cry The Beloved Country", he featured Sam Matambo, Ruth Mpisaunga and Albert Chaza.

In Highfields, a second township built after Mbare, the Cyril Jennings Hall was built to accommodate the increased need for entertainment. It instantly became a focal point for early musicians as well as politicians. Highfield township was administered slightly differently from Mbare, as it had a house ownership scheme for residents.

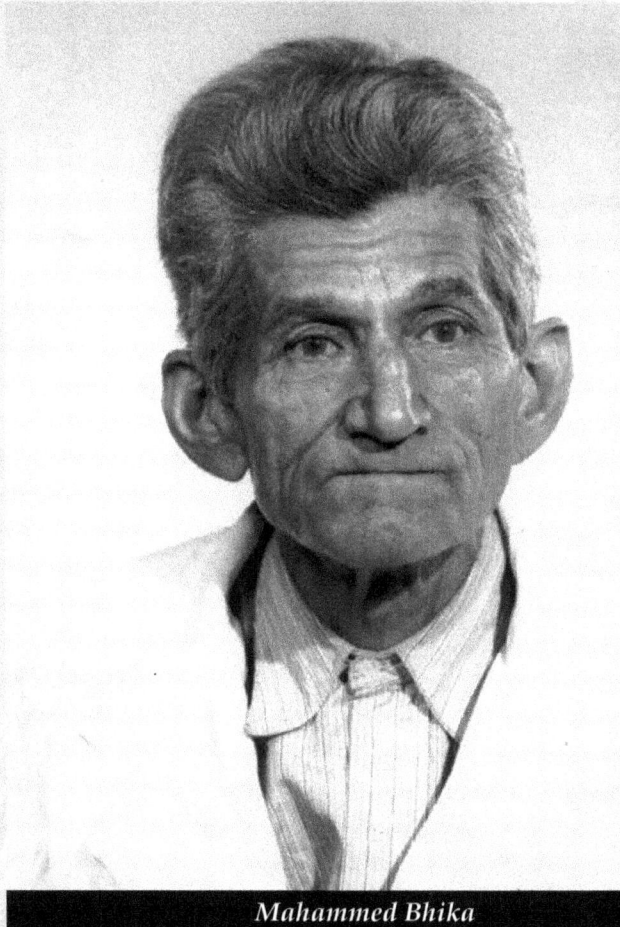
Mahammed Bhika

Although blacks were not allowed to be in the city entertainment centres, there were certain localities reserved for them. The Federal Hotel, at the time owned by Bob Bardolia of Indian descent; was one of the few multiracial places in the city centre. University students, politicians, and patrons from all walks of life converged to the Federal Hotel to listen to Township Music. The Hotel was built during the days of the Federation of Rhodesia and Nyasaland, hence its name. It was later called the Kudzanayi Hotel, and has since changed names.

Mohammed Bhika saw the need for a multi-racial venue, and built the Bhika Brothers Restaurant, also known as Karimapondo Restaurant. There, township groups played freely to people of different races. The name "Karimapondo" is from "Akarima Mapound"; which meant Mohammed Bhika ploughed "pounds", as he had a farm also. The "Karimapondo" Restaurant was later shut down due to consistent harassment of patrons by the state police.

DOUBLE STOREY HOTEL OPENED BY M.P

**Salisbury, Saturday
(17 November 1956)**
The African Daily News

A number of distinguished Africans witnessed the official opening ceremony of a first class double-storey African restaurant owned by Bhika Brothers, popularly known as "Karimamupondo", by Mr. J. Z. Savanhu, Federal M.P. for Mashonaland yesterday.

In an introductory speech, Mr. E. Bhika, the oldest son said, "I am very pleased to be here today for the opening of our African restaurant and I want to give my African friends the assurance that I will personally do everything I can to see that a high standard of service is built and maintained in this restaurant." He told all present that it was his intention to build the restaurant into a comfortable dining place for Africans in the Colony because he did not know of any place in the Colony were respectable Africans were able to dine decently and comfortably. "We intend to provide a large variety of dishes for the Africans as is provided for Europeans in this country," he said. He said that he was sure that all the requirements of a high-class restaurant would be introduced at that restaurant in due course and that everything would be done to ensure that the premises remain respectable and a pleasing place to dine for Africans. Mr. E. Bhika introduced Mr. Savanhu and thanked him for his kindness to officially open their restaurant.

"I am highly pleased and thankful to father Bhika and his sons for their greatest venture in making this first class restaurant for both low and high classes of Africans," said Mr. J. Z. Savanhu M.P. when he opened the restaurant oficially yesterday. He said that he had been told that it was built for 40,000- pounds and that a firm of Europeans wanted to buy it for 75,000- pounds but Mr. Karimapondo refused on the grounds that he had made it for use by his African friends who had helped him to progress. It was the duty of both the proprietors and the Africans to see that the highest standard of cleanliness and dignity is maintained in the restaurant. I declare this hotel duly open," concluded Mr. Savanhu.

Amongst those present were Rev, Kanyowa, Captain and Mrs. Tapfumaneyi, Mrs. Mzingeli, Messrs J.M. Chinamano, J.G.S. Chingattie and J.R.D. Chikerema, and four sons of Mr. M. Bhika. The restaurant is in Chater Road, near the Castle Brewery.

Mr. J. M. Chinamano B.A. said that the restaurant was a real pride to all Africans who will patronise it. Mr. J. R. D. Chikerema called it the Blue Lagon of Central Africa as it was like the Blue Lagoon of Johannesburg. He congratualted the Bhika Brothers for their insight of marching with the times and also the African advancement.

The Rev. Kanyowa in proposing a vote of thanks said that it was God who had guided "Karimapondo" to establish that wonderful restaurant for the Africans.

All present were entertained with tea and delicacies. During a personal interview Mr. Bhika said that they were planning to put two more storeys one as a bar for beers should the Liqour Act be amended and the other will have private rooms for African lodging.

* *In the picture, Mr Bhika, popularly known as "Karimamapondo" rushes to Mr. S. Sondo (seated) with a pound note as an "enchore" for the song 'Hasta Luego' sung during the Salisbury Cultural Club function in his hotel last Saturday. Simangaliso, vocalist seen singing, made a debut into music on that day, flanked by Sondo. The Crazy Kids, with Faith Dauti, appeared on same stage, with famed City Quads.*

> **Dartmouth Hall** was yet another popular spot those days, although it was more frequented by the coloureds. In the same league was The Palace Hotel, which also hosted township music, but was often dominated by whites. Le Coq D'or was popular in the sixties, when racism was still rife; and so was Acardia Community Hall, located in the Acardia coloured suburb.

zimbabwe township music

In Bulawayo a top entertainment centre was the **Stanley Hall**, which was built in 1935. Here, the Merry Makers made their debut. The Hall is situated in the Makokoba section of Mzilikazi Township, which has a history counterpart to that of Mbare. The Stanley was where filmshows (bioscopes) were featured for youngsters; where musicians; the Cool from Harare (Salisbury) and other towns. For family socialites, it was like the Mai Musodzi rebuilt in Bulawayo.

Bulawayo was then growing in size, becoming the second largest city in the country. The flow of people from the communal areas, as well as migrant labour, resulted in a rapid population growth. A second and much bigger entertainment center; the which had memories of the 50's. Musical groups often held their annual competitions at the Stanely Hall, something special to look forward to for Bulawayo bands and music patrons.

The Indian community patronised the Vashee Hall, situated in Bulawayo's city centre, which also attracted township musicians. A memorable event held at

Stanely Hall (Makokoba) Bulawayo

Four, Golden Rhythm Crooners, Josaya Hadebe, George Sibanda, Sabelo Mathe, Jacob Mhungu and August Musarurwa; performed their variety shows. It also hosted groups Macdonald Hall, was subsequently built. Although the new hall was more spacious and more modern than The Stanley, older musicians preferred the latter, Vashee Hall, was a combined show of the Bulawayo and Harare musical giants to fundraise for the building of the Jairos Jiri Centre. Sam Matambo, a member of the City Quads which participated

The Merry Makers

Golden Rhythm Crooners

Dorothy Masuka

John White

Josaya Hadebe

August Musarurwa

zimbabwe township music

in the show remembers how well-attended the charity event was. The City Quads put up at the Jairos Jiri home, as Mr. Jiri himself was a highly hospitable man.

At the white-dominated City Hall, township music groups were allowed to play only on special invitation. The municipal council was supportive of township entertainment; and at times it organized group shows in the City Hall.

The beer halls became popular venues, especially for the Omasiganda. Quite frequently big bands also played at the beerhalls; such as at Manuele Beer Garden and the Ikhwezi Beer Hall in Pelandaba Township. When Louis Armstrong visited Bulawayo, he played at the Ikhwezi Beerhall. Apart from hosting popular musical groups, burial societies often performed in beerhalls for fund-raising.

Early musicians frequently performed in open space, which was the case of showbiz pioneer, Kenneth Mattaka. He performed in the open during the 30's, as people gathered around to donate token money. Performing in open spaces was not out of choice for early musicians who had no proper halls. Furthermore, musicians such as the "Omasignda", found it a pleasure to sing in the open or in streets.

The "Omasiganda" performed in streets, whereby patrons would follow them in a procession. As they played music at one place, crowds would swell around and listen to them, in addition to giving them money tokens.

Jacob Mhungu, a one-time "Umasiganda", remarked that his guitar once became rather heavy to carry around as it was stuffed with money from street shows.

John White was a popular albino "Umasiganda", who frequently sang in moving trains, particularly in the Fourth Class (Mbombela). Train passengers were often entertained the whole night, as there was also no place for sleeping. Travelling time thus passed by so quickly. For offering a desired entertainment service, John did not pay for the train rides. Eventually he became popular countrywide, particularly in Gweru, his home-base.

The guitar had become a popular musical instrument, finding its way deeper into the rural areas, where the rural folk organised "Konzati" (concerts). These shows took place after the harvest. Patrons would bring a one-man band player, or "umasiganda", after putting up a makeshift hall from used sackcloth. The audience would pay "two shillings and six pence," to attend the concert.

In Mutare the Moffat and Beit Halls were the popular venues for local artists, as well as for visiting musicians. The De Black Evening Follies performed in Mutare at the official opening of the Beit Hall. On their way back to Harare, Sonny Sondo the lead singer, composed the song: "Makomo EkwaMutare" (The Hills of Mutare).

Of all the musical venues of the time, the Mai Musodzi and the Stanley Hall remained overwhelmingly popular.

Mai Musodzi

Mai Musodzi is the popular hall in Mbare, which was the focus of township entertainment in the 1950's. It groomed young musicians of the time and was the hub of established groups. The hall was built in 1935, when it was called Recreation Hall. The name was later changed to Mai Musodzi, after a social worker Musodzi Ayema, a woman who contributed a lot to Mbare's early development. Mai Musodzi is a "hall of fame" that brought hope and joy to township dwellers. Musodzi assisted the needy and illiterate in a variety of ways, be it physical education or home nursing. Some of her graduates later went on to work in hospitals. She founded women's clubs, and worked as a unifying force among foreigners and locals. She was married to a Zambian, even though she hailed from the Hwata family (clan), origin of Mbuya Nehanda (Charwe), who was sister to her father. Despite the fact that her relatives perished during the Mashona Uprising in Mazowe, Mai Musodzi was optimistic about life's brighter opportunities. She moulded a positive personality, always yearning to make a meaningful contribution to society. She pioneered Red Cross and Home Craft Clubs for township women; all this unfolding at Mai Musodzi Hall. She looked after soldiers during the Second World War, supplying them with food at the location now known as Rufaro Stadium. She was eventually "honoured" as MBE-Member of the British Empire.

Born **Musodzi Chibhaga** in 1885 in Mazowe, she survived the Mashonaland Rebellion. Later she moved to Chishawasha with her sister, where they stayed with an aunt, who was married to Chief Chinamhora. The sister later died and left her two

Mai Musodzi (standing) giving instructions to Red Cross Workers

children in the care of Musodzi, who was baptised as Elizabeth in 1907, and confirmed as Maria within the Roman Catholic Church.

Musodzi got married to Frank Kashimbo Ayema, the son of Zambian Paramount Chief Lewanika. Ayema had accompanied Colonel Hartley to Zimbabwe, to deliberate on the construction of a railway line between Zambia and Zimbabwe. He later made Zimbabwe his home country and worked for the British South African Police as a sergeant. Mai Musodzi and her husband lived in Chizhanje (Chishawasha), although they had been given accommodation in Mbare in 1928. They lived in both homes until the mid 1930's, when they finally settled in Mbare. The couple had five children, with Lucy as first –born, who was mother of Chris Chabuka, renowned township jazz pianist. One of the sons, Francis Joseph, used to play piano for the City Quads, and was responsible for bringing into the country the first Luna Park.

Francis Joseph Street has been named after him in Mbare's National section.

Mai Musodzi was a hard worker, according to grandson Leonard Chabuka. The family never went hungry, as she harvested a variety of crops from pieces of land in Mbare. Leornard also recalls her as a gender - sensitive personality, who treated all her children equally regardless of their sex. As such she worked tirelessly for her family, and community at large. Mai Musodzi died on 21st June 1952, and will be remembered for her foresight and relentless devotion to social and vocational development. The invisible inscription on Mai Musodzi Hall is that of nurturing and grooming township musicians.

zimbabwe township music

TOWNSHIP MUSIC PROMOTERS:

African Daily News

A GRAND SHOW
This Week By
☆ THE ☆
GREAT CITY QUADS
with the
CRAZY KIDS & the SHANGANI DANCERS

IN THE RECREATION HALL
SATURDAY, 28th. JUNE.
DON'T MISS THIS BIG SHOW. 2/6d. All Round

C-O-N-C-E-R-T
By The Famous
DE BLACK EVENING
FOLLIES
of Salisbury
— In the —
MABVUKU BEER
HALL
Accompanied by Dorothy
Masuka
The Famous Rhodesian
STAGE STAR
on
SUNDAY,
11th January, 1959
Admission: 2/6 All-round
DON'T MISS

zimbabwe township music 58

TOWNSHIP MUSIC PROMOTERS:

Township musicians did not have sophisticated means of advertising as we have today, yet they managed to promote their shows in a way that was highly commendable.

Only the newspapers earmarked for black readership, gave coverage to township music groups, which was not the case with "The Rhodesia Herald". The early township musicians advertised their shows in the then African Daily News and The Bantu Mirror, which focused on black people's activities. Similar pertinent magazines included The African Weekly, African Parade, Zonk and Drum. Lawrence Vambe was then Editor-in-Chief of the The African Daily News and the African Parade. He lived in Mbare, where he closely followed the rapid unfolding of entertainment scenarios.

The African Daily News and The Parade were owned by Betram and Cedric Paver, who were white liberals at the time. The Daily News was later banned in 1963, after running some wide ranging publicity and coverage for township people. Most media/papers which covered black people's concerns were eventually banned at the onset of the Unilateral Declaration of Independence (UDI).

To some extent the papers widely advertised township musical groups and lifestyles of the musicians, which went a long way in promoting and boosting the morale of musicians. A regular newspaper column of The Africa Daily News, featured music bands from Malawi, Zambia, South Africa and Zimbabwe, focusing on the latter's artists.

The articles featured both established and not-so-popular groups: Bantu Actors, Merry Makers, Gay Gaeties, De Black Evening Follies, Three Brothers, African Melodians, The African Boogie Four (Bulawayo), The Philhamonic Stars (Bulawayo) and Mashonaland Melodians.

Laurence Vambe

Mr Cedric Paver

The Melodians were led by Wilson Munangatire, and also included bread eater Albert Ndinda and Flora Dick. In 1955 the group introduced two ambitious schemes for the benefit of the public; donation of trophies for school choir competitions, and teacher training bursaries for African students.

The Woogie Boogie Songsters, founded in 1950 and led by ABC Rusike, were based in Bulawayo, also featured in the press. The group comprised of William Makore, Peter Kurete, Fyn Mqadi, Stephen Gadluma, Pasika Sibanda and Tomix Kombe. Also featured were The Kalanga Boys from Botswana. A special column focus was, Women Who Set The Ball Of Jazz Rolling.

An early nationalist, **Daniel Madzimbamuto**, played a crucial role in promoting township music festivals. He led the Cultural Syndicate which organized annual festivals and talent shows, which in turn gave the needed publicity for township musicians. Dorothy Masuka, a by-product of the festivals, gave a press conference to a packed audience of dignitaries, business executives and diplomats at the All Africa Music Festival.

At one such gathering, the festivals also publicised township musicians internationally. Black musicians pitched a high standard of performance, exemplified by Dorothy Masuka, City Quads, and De Black Evening Follies. The hectic era came to an end in 1959, when Daniel Madzimbamuto and other politicians were detained at the Gonakudzingwa Prison. Soon, the once vibrant township life became suddenly solemn and dull. The Parade at the time, vividly lamented on the lull and dearth of musical activities in the townships.

A memorable township music promoter was the late Eileen Haddon, who often entertained musicians at her house. She also provided space for dancing and rehearsals to the aspiring artists. Eileen was a founder-member of the Interacial Association, which sought to unite people of different races. Although a journalist by profession, she fought the colour-bar through organising intercultural events, where blacks and whites met freely. She also organised a concert at the Harare Showgrounds, where whites saw black musicians performing for the first time. Eileen would also visit the " Whites Only" hotels as a protest, accompanied by Blacks, Indians and Coloureds. Quite often, they would be thrown out of such premises.

The then Ministry of Information hired technicians to take films around the

The Kalanga Boys

Daniel Madzimbamuto

zimbabwe township music

country, of music groups whose history dated as far back as 1948. The popular groups then were the De Black Evening Follies, The Epworth Theatrical Strutters, and Alick Nkhata. The movies were earmarked for mobile cinema

Ephraim Chamba

shows in the townships and rural areas, where entertainment was virtually non-existent.

The Central African Broadcasting Corporation was then based in Lusaka, after which it became The Federal Broadcasting Corporation (Salisbury). Subsequently, it was renamed the Rhodesia Broadcasting Corporation after the dissolution of the Federation. The broadcasting personnel either went around recording music, or musicians would be invited to the studio for recordings, which were done on reel - to - reel master tapes. The presenters/producers at the time organised studio music shows, of which "Variety Half Hour" was typical. Benjamin Chipere hosted the music shows, whereby band leaders would deliberate on their music and historical background. The programmes were highly popular as they depicted life-styles of the township folks.

A notable presenter of the 50's was Ephraim Chamba, who also produced a musical play: "Rufaro Mumba" (Happiness in the Home); featuring the Mattaka Family. The show was led by Kenneth Mattaka, who sang alongside his wife Lina, daughter Bertha and son Eddison. "Rufaro Mumba", which was a fusion of drama, song and comedy, was aired for 13 weeks in 1959. Eddison was adept at playing guitar and piano, having learnt the latter at the age of five. Mattaka and wife Lina championed showbiz

Dominic Mandizha (left) Jordan Chataika (right)

in Central Africa in the 30's. Their daughter Bertha Mattaka - Msora began singing at the age of five

Other presenters/producers of the 50's and 60's fame were Isaiah Mpofu, Dominic Mandizha, Joseph Chaza and Ben Musoni.

Ben later worked for the Ministry of Information, recording musical films which he also presented. Whilst at the Rhodesia Broadcasting Corporation he covered recordings of both urban and rural based musicians. Sam Matambo, who doubled as producer/presenter, also sang with the City Quads. The quartet recorded a long playing album: "Music in the African Township," which was later banned because of the song "Lizofika nini Ilanga lenkululeko." (When Will The Day {of Freedom} Come?). Each time, Matambo played the song, he was tasked by the Federal Broadcasting Corporation to explain what the tune/song was all about.

Another broadcaster who brought musicians to the studio for recordings was the musician/producer Alick Nkhata, who also recorded with Hugh Tracy in the early 50's.

Fereday and Sons sponsored a trophy for the best musical group at annual competitions. The Mattaka Family won the trophy in three consecutive years, and later gave it back to the sponsors.

The business community often promoted township

music, as in the case of Mohammed Bhika's son Ismail, who would go into the townships and bring musicians to the Karimapondo Restaurant.

The Gamma Sigma Club led by Victoria and Schotting Chingate, promoted musicians by facilitating shows and Christmas parties. Victoria established a popular female musical group; The Gay Gaeties, consisting of Harare Hospital nurses. At one time the Gamma Sigma was led by Dr Edward Pswarayi, one of the few qualified medical doctors at the time.

Albert Ndinda was also a notable comedian-cum music promoter of the 50's.

A contemporary township musical promoter was Sheila Cameron, who organized Kwela musicians for a show in the early 90's, in Bulawayo. The Kwela pennywhistlers are now phased out, all having died poor.

In 1989 Henry Thodlana, jointly with the Ministry of Education and Culture, organised a Jazz Festival in Bulawayo. Most of the bands which where popular in the 50's were invited: Cool Four, Golden Rhythm Crooners, Jerry De Vorse Band, Paul Lunga; to mention a few. The festival was quite a success, with some patrons travelling from as far afield as Harare.

The late Simangaliso Tutani in 1990, revived Township Jazz Festivals of the 50's. It was a resounding success, and since then, annual Jazz Festivals have been held in Harare, Bulawayo and Mutare. A young township jazz drummer, **Sam Mataure**, took

Sam Mataure

over the organisation of jazz festivals after the death of Tutani. The trend has given rise to a spate of jazz festivals of one sort or another. Current promoters of local jazz music include Irene Gwaze of the Red Fox Hotel, Jazz 105, The Hollies Spot and Paul Brickhill of Mannenburg and Book Café and Gibson Mandishona, once patron of the Zimbabwe National Jazz Festival.

The corporate business community in Zimbabwe, has of late, been awakened to sponsor jazz festivals, particularly banks, such as Trust, Interfin and African Banking Corporation.

THE AFRICAN PARADE NOVEMBER 1959

TOO BAD, NO MUSIC FESTIVAL THIS YEAR

BAR the shouting, it's sticking out like a sore foot that there will be no All-African Music Festival this year and that's a great pity because I was beginning to look upon this performance as an encouragement to our regularly deaf singing stars, troupes and bands. The first attempt last year in the Stodart Hall wasn't anything like the premiere of "The Bridge on the River Kwai" or "There's no Business Like Show Business". But it was something — by our standards (and believe me, there's much to be desired) — which could easily have developed into a real dynamic show.

It's too bad that Dan Madzimbamuto, the Cultural Syndicate's Director is in detention somewhere in Selukwe or else he would have started things going already. It's another pity you can't petition the Director of Prisons into releasing Dan for a couple of months so that he can organise rehearsals for the Cultural Syndicate's All-African Music.

Herb Munangatire, the Organising Secretary and rest of the members of the executive committee of the Syndicate are apparently inactive. I couldn't get them to give me the lowdown on their future plans. As a matter of fact, no one has so far had the courage of saying something about the Music Festival. I don't know if they think it might be inadvertently associated with the SR National Congress, which is now outlawed.

THE POSIBILITIES

The Cultural Syndicate, I think, shoul be revived, Some of your music fans may be wondering why I am particularly worried about its untimely death. Well, there is the reason. Rhodesia-and the Federation for that matter Dan Madzimbamuto Big Gun behind the First All African Music Festival. Lieutenants don't seem anxious to continue from where he left off.

In South Africa you have got shows being produced so rapidly that there's no telling what is going to happen next. "'King Kong", "Shebeen" and the "Shanty Town Revue"—all of , them symbols of the local . talent—are great shows. Haven't seen them myself. But from what I read from critics in newspaper columns (unless they're pulling my leg) the shows are something real dynamic. The , real McCoy.

Now, is there any reason why I should not be heated up about the death of the Cultural Syndicate?

"Africa's Sweetheart"— Dorothy Masuka, now with Alf Herbert's "SHEBEEN" was star of first All African Music Festival. Lent glamour to the whole show, this one.

One thing, by the way, the show had brought us nearer to assesing the talent that abounds in the country. From it we have deduced the amount trash and sieved the cream for real first-class training. We could have produced real stars ,not just self-styled performers who could easily do very well with the Marx Brothers.

I can't place my finger on the snag itself. It's something I'm beginning to think, which 'cannot be solved as long as people like those who initiated the Cultural Syndicate don't make an appearance. Now, where are they? I've always said we have a lot of talent here, but the need is for someone who can do SOMETHING about this talent. Thats all.

zimbabwe township music

THE AFRICAN NEWS — Week-End Edition

Newspaper. SATURDAY, DECEMBER 13, 1958. PRICE 3d.

YOUR DAILY HABIT
LOBELS BREAD

THE Cool Fours of Bulawayo who "stole the show" yesterday at the first all-African Musical Festival. They were by far the best of the Jazz Groups.

150 Artists Arrive For The Big Festival

Music Festival Opens At Slow Pace

Salisbury, Saturday.

THE beating of drums in "The Call Of The Jungle", a number presented by a combination of singing troupes from Bulawayo, marked the opening of the All-African Music Festival in the Stodart Hall last night. The hall was packed to capacity, artistes in galore, and variety was provided to the over anxious audience that expected something out of the ordinary. But the show fell below expectations.

zimbabwe township music

THE ZIMBABWE FESTIVAL OF REGIONAL & INTERNATIONAL JAZZ

"Jazz Artists Making a Difference in HIV and AIDS"

- **FRI 24 Aug**
  - DOROTHY MASUKA
  - COOL CROONERS
  - MBARE TRIO
  - TOA HARID
  - DUDU MANHENGA
  - AVA ROGERS
  - SUMMER BREEZE

- **SAT 25 Aug**
  - RAY PHIRI (S.A)
  - OLIVER MTUKUDZI (ZIM)
  - COOL CROONERS (ZIM)
  - TANGA WEKWA SANDO (ZIM)
  - JAZZ INVITATION (ZIM)
  - UK ARTIST (UK)
  - THE AARON THURSTON TRIO (USA)
  - BRUCE CASSIDY (CANADA)
  - STEVE DYER (SA)
  - LOUIS MHLANGA (ZIM)
  - MANDEBVU (ZIM)
  - DETEMA
  - AMAGENTS

- **SUN 26 Aug**
  - COOL CROOONRS
  - SUMMER BREEZE
  - THE OTHER FOUR
  - JABAVU
  - MBARE TRIO

LIVE IN HARARE! 24-26 AUG 2001

- **FRI 24 AUG**
  7 Arts ($350) 8p.m.

- **SAT 25 AUG**
  Harare Gardens ($500) 12p.m.

- **SUN 26 AUG**
  Red Fox ($200) 2p.m.

7 arts Tickets on sale as from 6th Aug, 2001
Harare Gardens Tickets on sale at Jazz 105 and Sports Diner as from 20th Aug, 2001
Red Fox Tickets on sale at The Door

zimbabwe township music

programme

The first Zimbabwe festival of Regional & International Jazz welcomes all artists to the festival, sincere gratitude for the participation of each musician, and thanks to those who sponsored them - bringing people together through the power of music.

Fri 24 Aug
SEVEN ARTS THEATRE, AVONDALE
8.00PM Welcome & introduction
8.15-8.45 Toa Hand & Duduziie Mhenga (Harare)
8.50-9.20 Ava Rogers (Harare)
9.25-9.55 Mbare Trio (Harare)
20min Break
10.20-50 The Cool Crooners (Bulawayo)
11.00-midnight Dorothy Masuku (Zimbabwe/SA)

Sat 25 Aug
HARARE GARDENS
1.00-2.00 UK Artist with Detema (Harare)
2.10-2.55 Amagents (Harare)
3.05-4.05 The Aaron Thurston Trio (USA)
4.15-5.00 Mandebvu (Vic Falls)
5.10-5.55 Tanga Wekwa Sando (Harare)
6.05-6.50 The Cool Crooners (Bulawayo)
7.00-7.45 Jazz Invitation (Harare)
 & Prudence Katomeni-Mbofana

8.00-midnite :
Bruce Cassidy (Canada)
Steve Dyer (Sa)
Louis Mhlanga (Zimbabwe)
Ray Phiri (SA)
Oliver Mtukudzi (Zimbabwe)

SUN 26 Aug
RED FOX HOTEL, GREENDALE
From 2 pm
The Cool Crooners (Bulawayo)
Jabavu (Harare)
MbareTrio (Harare)
The Other Four (Harare)
Summer Breeze (Harare)

Jazz artists making a difference in HIV/AIDS
FIVE AIDS-related charities will receive a donation from this festival

the aaron thurston trio — usa

Aaron Thurston/dr, Kevin Louis/tr, Adam Scone/organ. The members of the Aaron Thurston Trio are once again happy to be touring on behalf of the United States as Jazz Ambassadors. Originating from Boston, Ohio and New Orleans, the trio have studied with some of the world's most famous jazz teachers and performed countless gigs in different parts of the world. Since 1999 they have been promoting Jazz throughout the world with the Jazz Ambassadors Touts, and performing as professional freelance musicians. Special Thanks to the US Embassy in Harare for their support of the art of Jazz in Zimbabwe Welcome to Zimbabwe!

ray phiri — sa
guitar/vo

Ray Phiri had his first break in 1962 when he danced for the legendary Dark City Sisters in Mpumalanga, his South African home. It earned him enough to travel to Jo'burg where he founded 'Stimola' a decade later, with whom he conceived several gold and platinum-winning albums. In the early 90s he was invited to join Paul Simon's Graceland project, and collaborated with him again on Simon's Rhythm of the Saints album, which saw him perform on stages such as Central Park and Madison Square Garden, and appearing on top television shows in the US

dorothy masuku — zimbabwe
vo

A warm welcome to our Auntie Dot-one of Southern Africa's most loved women of song. Known and loved by Zimbabweans since her early days in her home town Bulawayo, Dorothy Masuku has long won the hearts of Zimbabwean music-lovers with her warm, expressive voice which has carried her into the international arena with much success and such grace.

oliver mtukudzi — zimbabwe
guitar/vo

For twenty years, Oliver Mtukudzi has been at the heart and soul of Zimbabwean music. He has composed and recorded over forty albums and has toured, with his group The Black Spirits, extensively in North America, Europe and the UK. In Zimbabwe, all people love him, and he can be heard on every radio station, on every radio, in the most far flung corners of the nation. His albums 'Tuku Music' and 'Pavepo' are immensely popular and he continues to move people all over the world.

UK artist — uk

Thanks to the British Council in Harare who have once again shown their support of the arts in Zimbabwe by sponsoring a British jazz artist to this Festival. Welcome! The British Council have brought many fine artists to the Zimbabwean stage, promoting cultural exchange between Our countries

bruce cassidy — canada
trumpet/evi

Bruce is a trumpet player who worked extensively with jazz and jazz-rock bands in Canada and the US before moving to South Africa in 1981 where he writes music for film and TV. His playing credits include extensive stints with the groups Lighthouse, Rob McConnells Boss Frass and Bold Sweat & Tears. He plays extensively the wind synthasiser the Electronic Valve Instrument. He is regarded as one of the foremost proponents of the EVI in the world. Thanks to the Canadian High Commission for their support of Bruce Cassidy.

louis mhlanga — zimbabwe
guitar/vo

Louis Mhlanga is one of Zimbabwe's most celebrated guitarists, having achieved high acclaim both in South Africa and on the overseas music circuit, and he has collaborated with several and diverse musicians of the world, in the production of many recordings. Louis is well known to Zimbabweans - he's really done us proud. Welcome home, Louis!

steve dyer — sa
saxes,flute,keyb

One of Southern Africa's talented and creative musicians, Steve is no newcomer to Zimbabwean audiences. Whilst his musical ventures have been consistently expressed through his saxophone and flute for over a decade, Dyer's professional career has moved quite markedly in the last few years into the art of directing and producing music. Steve has produced sound scores for film and television, and has worked with Soweto String Quartet. He produced Oliver Mtukudzi's recent red hot album and currently directs Mahube, a dynamic collaboration with Oliver Mtukudzi and other Southern African artists.

valencia ferlito — sa
keyboards

Valencia Ferlito is also no stranger to this country. His first visit having been to the National festival in 1999. Ferlito's exciting keyboards have been supporting Southern African artists for years, and he is involved in several collaborations & productions

zimbabwe township music

INFLUENCES ON ZIMBABWE TOWNSHIP MUSIC

INFLUENCES ON ZIMBABWE TOWNSHIP MUSIC

The Mills Brothers

Zimbabwe Township music was mostly influenced by South African and Western Jazz forms, with limited impacts of other external modes. Thus "jazz", is used loosely throughout the text to be synonymous to "Township Music".

American Jazz had a significant impact on Township Music, because of Western movies which dominated the film screens of townships. Western Jazz was also played frequently on Voice of America broadcasts during the Federation days, for about two hours per week.

Jazz music from the USA, featuring Sarah Vaughan, Duke Ellington, Ella Fitzgerald, Louis Armstrong and The Mills Brothers; also dominated the radio scene.

Jazz and Western music records were a popular commodity in music shops. There used to be a jazz appreciation club, led by Sam Matambo, a member of the City Quads, which became a focal point for jazz enthusiasts. The topics of discussion at the club covered various jazz artists and their instruments.

Jazz music symbolises a lot of the African traditional music, as its origins can be traced to

Louis Armstrong

the continent. Slaves from Africa moulded the jazz we know today, which has returned to the motherland through the electronic media. Thus contemporary jazz is a result of several musical transformations and external influences upon the original African melody forms. Township Music as such, is a fusion of the indigenous musical modes and these externalities.

Some local forms of music among the Shona are "Shangara", "Mbakumba" and "Jiti", which involve instruments such as drums, "Chipendani", "Hosho"(rattles), "Marimba" and "Mbira" Among the Ndebele there exist the "Isitshikitsha", "Igquzu" and "Imbube" music; accompanied by drums, "umqangala" and "amahlwayi" (rattles). A typical singing style among the Zimbabwean people is a "call - and – response" rhythm, in which a group of singers responds to the vocals of a lead singer. It is characteristic of black peoples' religious sermons, jazz and Afro-American music archltypes. Both Shona and Ndebele music rhythms are amenable to dance, due to typical inbuilt tempos.

During the mid 30's and 40's local musicians sang mostly jazz copyrights, just as they sounded on records or radios. Other influences stemmed from the Negro Spirituals which were introduced into Zimbabwe partly by Mahalia Jackson and partly by The Golden Gate Quartet, both African- American performing artists, who toured the country in the late 50's.

The township comedians of the 40's often painted their faces black, and mouths white, to imitate American comedians or singing ministrels of the time.

The 40's witnessed musical groups being influenced by American big bands, of the likes of Duke Ellington, Countie Basie, Glenn Miller and Victor Sylvester. It was at this time that the De Black Evening Follies emerged. The Follies were more than twenty five in number, imitating the big band craze. These emerging groups sang mostly copyrights, although quite often they translated some English tunes into Shona or Ndebele. One such song which was a hit at the time is: "Kumadokero": a tune that Kenneth Mattaka adapted from the song: "Rumours are Flying".

"KUMADOKERO"
ON THE WESTERN HORIZON

Kumadokero kunemwoyo wangu
Where my heart belongs

Ndichifamba nemudikani wangu
Walking with my beloved

Shiri dzesango dzichibhururuka
The birds of the forest ululating

Dzichiti kwatiri rufaro rudo
Wishing us happiness and love

The song was later recorded

Ella Fitzgerald

Magavhu (leg rattles)

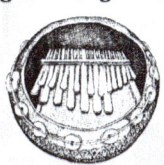
Mbira (Thumb Piano)

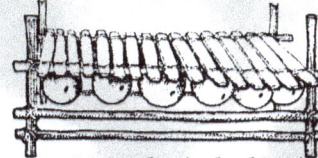
Marimba (xylophone)

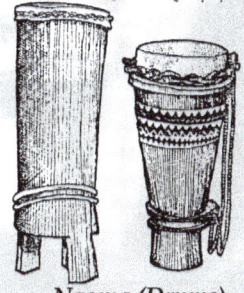
Ngoma (Drums)

The Manhattan Brothers

by the De Black Evening Follies, and became a favourite of the townships.

Township Music groups were gradually composing their own songs during the 50's, whilst retaining the jazz medium as their base for fusion. At the time, the Mills Brothers (USA) and the Manhattan Brothers (South Africa) had become popular. The visit of the latter to Zimbabwe triggered the formation of local groups, such as the City Quads (Harare), the Arcadia Rhythm Lads (Coloured band) and the Cool Four (Bulawayo). The Manhattan Brothers staged a show in the Mai Musodzi Hall, accompanied by Miriam Makeba, whose impressive tune, "Baby Tsware", attracted a big applause. The groups of the 50's often played fast jazz, mixed with traditional music such as, "Tsabatsaba" and "Marabi", which became a unique brand of the Cool Four.

According to David Coplan, "Tsabatsaba" was a working class urban dance, popular in South Africa in the 40's." Also, a versatile syncretic style of African melody and rhythm, the American Conga and Congo Rhumba, used to accompany the "Tsabatsaba" dance.

Women musical aspirants of the 50's mostly imitated Ella Fitzgerald, who often times sang with Louis Armstrong. Miriam Makeba was also an influential early inspiration. There was a string of other vocalists: Valerie Govenda,

Miriam Makeba

who sang with the Arcadia Rhythm Lads, Faith Dauti of the Milton Brothers, Mabel Bingwa, Joyce Ndoro and Dorothy Masuka.

Bulawayo's music had a significant South African linkage due to the common Zulu culture and the geographical affinity. Nonetheless, the city soon developed its own unique township music.

American Jazz influence came to Zimbabwe initially by way of the South African route. Thence, it would undergo transformations, initially in Bulawayo and finally in Harare. Eventually Zimbabwe Township jazz evolved into a unique jazz product.

An outstanding group of the 40's-50's was the Epworth Theatrical Strutters, whose music had church influence from Negro Spirituals and Shona traditional music. Their songs had a reformist message, such as: "Hwahwa Ndichazourega" (I shall stop drinking beer) and "Kudzidza Kwakanaka" (Education is so good).

The City Slickers were a popular musical group whose members belonged to the British South African Police Band. They were known for their popular tune, "Nhoro".

KWELA MUSIC

zimbabwe township music 71

KWELA MUSIC

"Kwela" music once had a big following. It was originally played on penny whistles, and it can be traced from the black South African Townships. The pioneers of Kwela were Lemmy Special, Spokes Mashiyane and Kid Marongrong (Albert Rarulimi). They would play in city street corners attracting both black and white passersby. The police disliked such gatherings in the city, which soon put the audience on the alert. The sight of police automatically triggered the dispersal of the audience.

Spokes Mashiyane and Lemmy Special visited Zimbabwe (Southern Rhodesia) in the early 60's, and played the pennywhistle and saxophone respectively. Their backing group was the Spokes Mashiyane Band. One of today's Zimbabwean prominent writers, Aaron Chiundura Moyo, attended Spokes Mashiyane's show when he visited the country. The show had an everlasting impact on him, as he got to play the pennywhistle, even to this day.

"Kwela" was originally associated with social outcasts who played cards on street corners, where crowds would gather around. At the sight of police people shouted "Kwela - Kwela", which in Zulu means "climb". The policemen would order those arrested to "climb" into police trucks, shouting "Kwela - Kwela." The word subsequently became a warning signal at the sight of police vans, for people to flee to safety.

"Kwela" music did not initially appeal to township jazz musicians, who felt superior to pennywhistlers. Recording companies preferred Kwela, as it was simpler and easier to exploit. Furthermore, they would deal with only one person or an individual. Timothy Ndaba, a South African Jazz musician believes that the recording companies' interest in "Kwela" was aimed at frustrating jazz bands. Eventually pennywhistlers were playing alongside the jazz artists, which resulted in further fusion of township music.

"Kwela" music was often played on local radio and on grammophones; and recorded as part of Zimbabwe Township Music. The pennywhistle thus became a popular instrument amongst young people, in both the rural and urban areas.

In the fifties Gallo recorded some Bulawayo "Kwela" musicians, whose tape has been rediscovered by their archivist, Rob Allingham. Unfortunately the recording musicians are not traceable, although the music is of high quality. Some Bulawayo "Kwela" musicians could be seen in the 90's playing for a small fee, mainly in the city's beer-halls. In 1992 promoter Sheila Cameron, organised a show of pennywhistlers, which had a highly successful reception. Sadly those pennywhistlers are now no more.

Spokes Mashiyane of South Africa

Jethro Shasha

Aaron Chiundura Moyo

Pennywhistlers made very little money in South Africa or locally, despite the fact that "Kwela" records sold much more than other types. The music somehow appealed to white people, especially the younger ones.

A contemporary pennywhistler in Zimbabwe is Emlot Ndlovu, who used to play at a local hotel. He also plays flute and saxophone simultaneously, which blends into a rich melodic township jazz. One Harare pennywhistler of note was Rufus Nkonde, who recorded popular tunes with the Rhodesia Broadcasting Corporation on vinyl records.

Emmloty Ndhlovu and Robbie Kroeger

Penny Wistlers: Isavutha

THE INFLUENCE OF ZIMBABWE TOWNSHIP MUSIC ABROAD

THE INFLUENCE OF ZIMBABWE TOWNSHIP MUSIC-ABROAD

Zimbabwe Township Music was partially influenced by South African and American music forms. However, Zimbabwe music conversely influenced South African music. The local music industry then was not as well-developed as that of South Africa, which explains why the country is not keeping pace with developments in countries where music is held in high esteem. Josaya Hadebe, generally credited with having introduced Ukuvamba Music, which involved a unique strumming (vamping) of guitar chords, was popular in the late 40's. He travelled to South Africa where he played his guitar on street corners, attracting a large following, as his music was so novel. George Sibanda and Sabelo Mathe were other Ukuvamba Music pioneers. The mode of guitar playing is still popular in Southern Africa, as typified by the popular musician Phuzutshukela.

The South African musician Miriam Makeba in her book

Dorothy Masuka and August Musarurwa

"My Story"; writes about how she idolised the Zimbabwean Dorothy Masuka. In the 50's Masuka was a jazz queen based in South Africa. She also wrote some songs for Miriam Makeba.

August Musarurwa's tune, "Skokiaan", has been recorded widely by South African artists, American, Jamaican and German musicians. Local musicians of the 50's and 60's travelled and played in neighbouring countries such as Zambia, Malawi, Ethiopia, Kenya and Uganda. The music emissaries at the time included Dorothy Masuka, Simangaliso Tutani, Sonny Sondo, Shelly Mazoe, Andrew Chakanyuka and Jacob Mhungu.

Louis Armstrong, one of the finest jazz musicians, had earned the nickname Ambassador "Satch". His music has had a tremendous influence in Zimbabwe and in neighbouring countries.

THE VISIT OF LOUIS ARMSTRONG

Louis Armstrong and wife arrives at the Harare (Salisbury) airport in 1961

Armstrong visited the then Southern Rhodesia in December 1960. Earlier on he had travelled to Ghana where he was the guest of Prime Minister Kwame Nkrumah. His itinerary included Lagos (Nigeria), Nairobi (Kenya), and Blantrye (Malawi), before proceeding to Harare, Bulawayo and Kitwe (Zambia).

Louis's visit was facilitated by the United States Information Service (USIS). Among the local music lobbysts at the time, was Pat Travers. Jazz enthusiasts were excited when the USIS brought Louis Armstrong to Zimbabwe, as part of a cultural exchange programme. Armstrong's visit is still fresh in the memory of many jazz lovers who witnessed the show. Professor Stanlake Samkange had also invited the maestro musician to help fundraise for Nyatsime College. Some local musicians participated in the historic show, with the greatest role performed by Louis himself.

On arrival at Harare airport, Armstrong was welcomed by several fans, some of whom had travelled from South Africa. They included August Musarurwa, who became popular for composing "Skokiaan", which Louis later recorded in the United States. On arrival Louis was accompanied by composer Musarurwa, who played "Skokiaan" all the way to the city in an open lorry. Armstrong became passionate for "Skokiaan" such that when he played it, one would wonder if at all he had taken a swill of the "Skokiaan" concoction! Louis could not play in South Africa at the time because of the Apartheid system. The Rhodesian racism at the time was relatively more relaxed.

Louis Armstrong ant the Pine Tops a band from Arcadia Harare

Louis received a resounding welcome, befitting a "king". There was much jubilation and dancing to accompaniment of traditional drums. Some placards were dubbed; "We need the release of high notes", "Welcome SATCHMO".

Peter Rezant was a notable South African jazz musician, who travelled from South Africa to join in the welcoming of Louis. The Jazz Appreciation Club led by Sam Matambo partly organized the welcome.

"Satch" was delighted to have visited Africa: "Im so happy to be in Africa, after all it's home you know," he remarked.

Louis Armstrong played at the Harare's Glammis Stadium, which was packed to capacity. His entourage comprised of Velma Middleton, the female vocalist who sang alongside another great, Ella Fitzgerald, Trummy Young on trombone, Billy Kyle on piano and Danny Barcelona on drums.

Popular promoters who facilitated the great show included the late Mike and Eileen Haddon, who struggled hard to arrange chairs and a stage with minimum assistance. Mike and Eileen belonged to the Inter Racial Association, which had been tasked by the USIS to organise the show. Eventually the association also benefited from the proceeds of the show.

In addition to the Haddons, Rodger Brickhill, who worked for Rothmans as a public relations officer, also played the role of organising and managing the show.
Incidentally, Louis Armstrong became the late Pat Travers son's godfather, rather against the Catholic church, as the trumpeter was not it's member.

After Harare, Louis travelled to Bulawayo where he performed at Ikhwezi. The young Paul Lunga was in the forefront of the welcoming party, as had happened in Harare. It was an

zimbabwe township music

overwhelmingly popular reception. Those present at the time still have a vivid memory of Louis' eventful visit to Bulawayo. Thereafter, Louis headed for Lusaka, Zambia, where his trumpet music excelled as expected.

The legendary maestro died in 1970: his music relives the man who introduced New Orleans Blues into Africa, the original home of his ancestors.

Louis Armstrong being recieved at the (Salisbury) Harare Airpoprt.

RECORDING HISTORY

zimbabwe township music

RECORDING HISTORY

The recording of music in **Zimbabwe** started in 1929 in Masvingo, then Fort Victoria. Hugh Tracey's fear then was that the music would disappear into extinction if measures were not taken to preserve it. In a way, he did preserve the music but not for the majority population then, who were not given enough airplay. The colonial masters depicted the indigenous African performing arts generally as "uncivilised", and encouraged adoption of Western styles of music and ideas. The music which was recorded by Hugh Tracy from 1929 –1940 benefited mostly researchers and those who had an interest in African Music. The author freely used Tracey's recordings in her research findings. Traditional music, like cultural beliefs, was passed on orally from generation to generation. Today, Hugh Tracy's recordings can be found in the archives of Rhodes University (South Africa) International Library of African Music, ILAM, where his son Andrew supervises.

Hugh Tracey

In the 1940's Gallo became interested in recording Zimbabwean Music. Some of the first musicians to be recorded were Josaya Hadebe, George Sibanda and Sabelo Mathe, who unfortunately signed their royalties to the recording company. The music of Josaya Hadebe did not get much airplay as it consisted of vulgar verses often-times. Most of his songs were eventually destroyed by the Federal Broadcasting Corporation (FBC). His music was mostly promoted by live shows, as he used to perform in halls and in streets. He was more popular in South Africa than in Zimbabwe. Josaya was the first to introduce a certain style of guitar playing, involving strumming of a few chords (ukuvamba) or vamping. These early musicians died poor as they ceded their royalties to Gallo. Gallo is currently reissuing some of the songs by the early musicians and honouring

politically conscious, authorities banned gatherings of Township Musicians, as they attracted a wide spectrum of personalities. The demise of the Federation of Rhodesia and Nyasaland thus heralded a new era on the musical country's scene.

During the 40's –70's the Broadcasting Corporation deployed technicians around the country to record mostly traditional music in rural areas. Township Musicians were also invited to the studios to record their music on reel-to-reel tape. The recordings are still with the ZBC, and some with the National Archives of Zimbabwe. The material was later re-recorded onto "acetatic" discs (breakable records) for home use. The discs and the grammophone, which needed winding and frequent replacement of the stylus or needle, constituted a popular form of home entertainment in the African communities.

Eventually, some well-established companies produced plastic (vinyl) records which were bendable and not easily broken.

In the 40's the Ministry of Information recorded live bands for entertainment in the rural areas via Mobile Cinema. Thus the style and perfomances of the 40's-50's, were captured on tape and film. Today these recordings serve as rich historical resource and entertainment material. The films also helped in publicising the groups, and hence contributed to popularisation of music throughout the country.

In time, with increasing numbers of Africans finding themselves able to acquire radio sets, the fortunes of many musicians became brighter, as music record sales also increased significantly.

During the 60's the Zimbabwe

royalties to the artists' families. In the 50's Gallo recorded August Musarurwa, composer of the popular "Skokiaan". He was the highest paid Zimbabwean musician from the 50's, whose family is still receiving royalties.

Troubador and **Trutone** recorded Dorothy Masuka in 1953; the masters of the recording are with Gallo, which has reissued some of the songs including "Iyo IPata-Pata" and "Imali Yami Iphelele Eshabhini".

Another company to record in the 60's besides Gallo, was Polydor which did the first Long Playing disc in the country, by the City Quads. It was during the peak of political dissent and one of the tunes: "Lizofika nini Ilanga", (When Will The Day {Of Freedom} Come?) led to the virtual banning of the record. As people became more

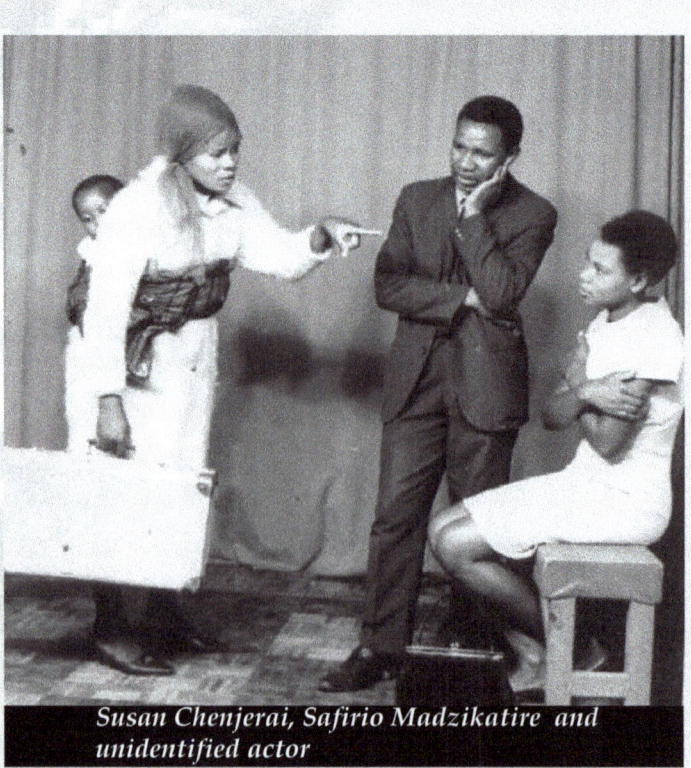

Susan Chenjerai, Safirio Madzikatire and unidentified actor

zimbabwe township music

music industry took a new twist due to the changing political climate. Recordings disappeared, as creativity of local musicians was compromised with the upsurge of South African and DRC music, which was flooding the market. South Africa had several recording companies then; Gallo, Trutone, Troubadour, to mention a few. They brought artists to Zimbabwe, as a way of promoting their bands/music, and to take advantage of the newly found lucrative market. Their music also got a lot of airplay on the radio, as a way of marketing. South African music was not "political," but purely entertainment. Some of the musicians sang in Shona to attract audience. Rhumba too got a lot of airplay, and was largely recorded by companies based in France.

Rhumba, like Simanje-manje, became the in-thing, such that several local groups were compelled to copy the styles to survive in the music business. The Broadway Quartet and Harare Mambos occasionally experimented with Rhumba styles, as exmplified by the hits "Iwe Maggi," and "Zvanhasi Ndezveduwo" respectively.

Gradually, local groups began to reassert themselves as Simanje-manje and Rhumba became less dominant by the end of the 60's. Thanks to the efforts of Jordan Chataika, Susan Chenjerayi and Safirio Madzikatire, who played a significant role in restoring local music to a position of honor and pride. At times they sang comedy tunes to make people laugh and dance away sorrows.

The 70's were a hectic phase during which local popular music reached its peak. Recording companies which had disappeared during the 60's came back, including Gallo and Teal.

Local music had blossomed again, also as a powerful medium for championing the revolutionalry cause of the black people. Rock, Blues and Soul, being music already embraced by African-Americans, became a legitimate sound tool through which political messages were passed on to fellow Africans. Groups such as Eye of Liberty, Pied Pipers and Wells Fargo, among others, were at the forefront in this particular brand of music.

Suddenly Mbira, which had been confined to rural areas and ignored by the younger generation, burst onto the Zimbabwean music scene. Gifted and

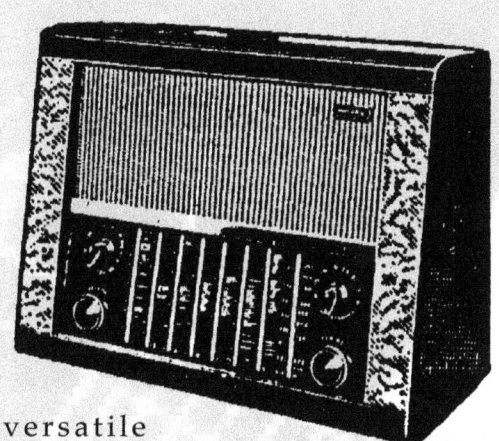

versatile musicians duplicated the sound of mbira to electric guitars and modern instruments; composing, rearranging and singing traditional songs reminiscent of the resistance movement of the 1890's, evoked ancestral spirits to rise and guide the course of liberation. The fusion of Mbira tunes with contemporary styles was the last straw that broke the camel's back. Both the old and young had come together, speaking the same musical language, playing identical tunes. Musicians who excelled in this form of music included Tineyi Chikupo, Thomas Mapfumo, Oliver Mtukudzi and Zexie Manatsa.

A remarkable and appealing aspect of the 70's music was the supreme mastery of language use and traditional idiom displayed by the artists. The subtlety of political messages conveyed through music, evaded white Rhodesians who never bothered to learn vernacular Shona or Ndebele.

The music was given adequate airplay on radio as some of the producers and DJs were part of the salient revolution, including Webster Shamu, who recorded "Calling Your Name by the Eye of Liberty", in the 70's. An exemplary tune was "Maybe Tomorrow (I will be there)", which lured young people to cross the border and join the liberation struggle.

zimbabwe township music

The first LP by an African Band the City Quads produced by Polydor in 1961 entitled; Music In The African Townships.

SONGS ON THE ALBUM:

1. Lindi — Mtunyane
2. Lizofika Nini Ilanga — (Arranged by Sondo)
3. Dhalala kece — (Folk arranged)
4. Kunembaravazi — Matambo
5. Lamulela — (Folk arranged)
6. Hakuna mumwe — Matambo
7. Nyathel'Uqihile — (Folk Wedding rearranged-Matambo)
8. Chipo mwana wababa — Sondo
9. Abazali Bami — Rearranged-Sondo
10. Zonki Insuku — Mtunyane
11. Wacithu muzi — Matambo
12. Ndafuna funa   Sondo

zimbabwe township music

Besides radio, the music spread throughout the country through juke boxes at shopping centres or in beerhalls, hi fi (fidelity)/stereo systems, cassette players in motor vehicles, and at night spots where DJs and live bands entertained crowds. The trend helped to conscientise people via entertainment, and also contributed to the growth of the music industry through record sales.

When Zimbabwe attained independence in 1980, the music industry accordingly boomed due to sensational and local interest. A variety of deals were sealed which enabled local musicians to perform and record outside the country. Township music gradually regained ground and found its way into the mainstream recording industry.

New and small recording companies sprung up to take advantage of the musical revival. Subsequently, township musicians resorted to financing their own studio recording facilities and marketing of products.

The 75% stipulated local content in TV/radio broadcasts has effectively liberalised the music industry. Radio music is easily available in the record shops, which adds to the popular promotion of local artists.

The advent of video production has immensely promoted the marketing of music. Videos as such, enhance both the recorded songs and visual performances tremendously. Music awards such as NAMA (National Arts Merit Awards) and ZIMA (Zimbabwe Music Awards), have also gone a long way towards greater facilitation and development of local music, by way of competition and creativity incentives.

POPULAR GROUPS/ MUSICIANS AND THEIR MUSIC

The Bantu Actors

POPULAR GROUPS/ MUSICIANS AND THEIR MUSIC

The Bantu Actors/The Mattaka Family

Kenneth Mattaka, a multi talented entertainer, singer and magician, led and championed township showbusiness in Zimbabwe. Mattaka's legacy can be traced to the year 1922 at The Golden Valley Mine, where his father was a compound manager, having migrated from Malawi. The owner of the mining/farm, John Meck, used to give Christmas presents to children, and thus Kenneth Mattaka got a mouth organ. He played his new instrument to various audiences, as some would go dancing. In 1925 he went to Musami Church School {Murewa} to start (ABC), which is the equivalent of early primary school grade. During those days there were types of tunes called Sunkee Songs, such as "Umbolidwa Tidzaimba". Kenneth used to be invited to entertain at parties or weddings.

He later went to Domboshawa School, which had been built specifically for black people. Whilst there, he demonstrated a high aptitude in both music theory and singing sessions. With other interested friends, Kenneth formed a singing group in1932, with leader, Cephas Hlabangane.

The whole Mattaka Family was eventually involved in music and acting, achieving some remarkable fame. In 1959

Kenneth Mattaka

they were featured in a 13-week radio programme: "Meet The Mattaka Family," produced by Ephraim Chamba. The backing group was The Talent Band, led by son Eddison.

The Bantu Actors

In December 1936 Kenneth Mattaka formed the

The Three Bantu Actors

Expensive Bantus with his former Domboshawa schoolmates. His colleagues joined The British South African Police (BSAP), whilst he opted to work for The Herald. The group met every Saturday for practice as they had done at school. They rehearsed in the open, and people would gather around to listen. Mattaka began his musical career by translating English songs into Shona equivalents. The tunes were at the time contemporary, and easily appealed to people. One such hit was "Rumours Are Flying." Mattaka's equivalent was: "Kumadokero".

The same tune was recorded and popularised by The De Black Evening Follies, a breakaway group from the Bantu Actors, led by Moses Mpahlo-Mafusire.

Kenneth Mattaka did not like recordings, as he felt that the technology often distorts the originality of a song.

In 1936 one Rashid Mlenga, a member of the Criminal Investigating Department in the BSAP, and a Methodist Church goer, used to hold concerts for fundraising. He requested Mattaka and his group to perform for the church's fundraising show. The performing group was nicknamed the Expensive Bantus, as the shilling they charged was too expensive. The singers later changed their name to Bantu Actors; it was then the only group which performed variety shows on stage. In 1958 The African Daily News ran weekly articles on early musicians, entitled: "Following the History of Showbusiness". The articles portrayed The Bantu Actors as undoubtedly the first well-organised choir in Central Africa.

In 1939 Moses Mpahlo, Samuel Gotora, Elisha Kassim and Ernest Gwaze joined the group, until 1943, when Mpahlo, Gotora and Kassim broke away to form The De Black Evening Follies. This latter group became the second largest in Harare. Mattaka then brought in brothers Austin and Lawrence Mapemba, as well as commedian Charles Chikoja. Several musicians who became popular in the 50's, passed through Mattaka's hands, among them Jeremiah Kainga, Moses Mpahlo-Mafusire, the late Safirio Madzikatire and Thomas Mapfumo. In 1944 Lina Mattaka joined the Bantu Actors, as a musician in her own right.

At one time in musical competitions, sponsored by a company Fereday and Sons, The Bantu Actors came first in three successive years. In the third year Mattaka decided to take back the trophy to the sponsors.

The Bantu Actors travelled throughout Southern and Central Africa; singing, entertaining and charming a variety of audiences.

Today the Bantu Actors are almost forgotten; they were once the shining star of early showbiz. "The older order changeth, yielding place to new" – Tennyson.

Lina MATTAKA

Historically black women sang only in church choirs or

Lina Mattaka

at traditional ceremonies. Anything outside the traditional context seemed to raise society's eyebrows, if not ire. Lina Mattaka was brave enough to confront prejudice against women performers, and to set jazz aflame in the African Township. Ultimately she got resounding acceptance by several audiences. Lina was also a refined Soprano and a fine tap dancer. Furthermore, she taught young women singing and tap dancing. "For a decade tap dancing was chic, it really dominated the music scene to be replaced by jazz music in the 40's, and who was at the forefront? None other than Lina Mattaka and the women who followed in her footsteps," read The African Daily News (1958).

Lina Mattaka's musical career began in Bulawayo in the 30's, where she was born and bred. As a young girl, she sang for her church and in Sunday School. She once visited Simonstown in the Cape Province of South Africa with a group, where they staged shows for the church. Upon her return the desire to sing became even more paramount.

The first professional choir in which Lina Mattaka sang was the Bantu Glee Singers, led by a Mr. Sipambaniso. Other singers were Willie and Fazo Shandavu, and Mauta Matshazi.

Whilst working at The Stanley Hall, Lina formed a choir in which she was nicknamed Queen of Soprano.

In 1944 Kenneth Mattaka performed in Bulawayo with The Bantu Actors, where he met the attractive Lina at the Stanely Hall. They instantly fell in love and got married. Lina eventually settled in the then Salisbury where Kenneth Mattaka was based. She joined the Bantu Actors, and subsequently brought in more female singers: Challote Phiri, Thandi Sheba, and Rennie Jones

Lina featured in the movie

Bertha and Eddison Mattaka in 50S

zimbabwe township music

Mattaka's Money (or Mattaka Buys A Bicycle), with daughter Bertha and husband Kenneth, who played the major role.

When The Bantu Actors disbanded, she continued to sing, with the family grouping: Kenneth and children, Bertha and Eddison.

Eddison "Nunusi" Mattaka

Eddison Mattaka had a nickname Nunusi. He was born in Harare on the 7th November 1949 and died on the 21st February 1963. He went to Harare's Chirodzo School and died a year before completing his primary education. Eddison was a brilliant lad, always in the top two of his class.

Being multi-talented, he started playing piano and guitar at the tender age of 6. Eddison could also play drums and sing tenor. He led his father's band which accompanied some musical groups that had no instruments, especially those based outside Harare. Often he would back a group which travelled all the way from South Africa. Eddison featured in two films, namely, a comedy, "Mattaka and Son" and a musical, "Mattaka Family." He also appeared in a film produced by the Ministry of Information, in which he played piano for a South African group, The Theodora Sisters.

Bertha Mattaka-Msora

During the early days of Zimbabwe's popular music in the 1930's, women were also at the forefront, blazing a trail for the youth who were to succeed them. Bertha Mattaka-Msora was a young female musician/entertainer of the 1950's, who followed her parent's footsteps. Lina Mattaka, her mother, was a pioneer musician who confronted gender prejudice in the musical arena.

Bertha started singing at the age of five alongside her parents, and featured as a member of the Mattaka family in the musical programme; "Rufaro Mumba", produced by Ephraim Chamba in 1959, for the Federal Broadcasting Corporation (FBC). In the film: "Mattaka Buys a Bicycle," her father was the main actor. She also appeared in a 15-20 minute film, with brother Eddison on piano. At the 1969

Bertha Mattaka Msora

Neshamwari Festival, Bertha won a first prize for soprano solo. She is a playright and actress, and won an award for her play: "I Will Wait", which was sponsored by the Zimbabwe Publishing House in 1982. "Nyasha", a TV Series on baby dumping, was scripted by Bertha.

Besides her musical and acting career, Bertha has made great strides as an educationist, tutor and trainer. She studied for a Diploma in Adult Education (UZ) 1972, B.Sc in Sociology (UZ 1982). She is a Doctoral candidate with the University of Califonia. She won the International Student Leadership Award in 1995, and in the following year; the Graduate Recognition for Scholarship Leadership and Community Service Award. Before she embarked on her studies in California, Bertha worked as a Lay Women's Trainer, Adult Educator, Market Research Executive and Sales Representative for an adult educational institution.

Bertha's current ambition is to re-record some of the sentimental tunes she used to sing with the family.

THE Merry MAKERS

The Merry Makers, formed in the 1930's, was a pioneer musical group consisting of Remmington Mazabane, Simon and Evelyn Juba, and Ernest Sithole. Emma Moyo, Gladys Mazabane and Agnes Zengeni joined later. The singers all lived in Bulawayo's oldest township, Mzilikazi.

The group initially performed in streets or in the open, until the Stanley Hall was built. They used to do their rehearsals at Juba's house, and often they would stage concerts at the same venue. At a later stage, their concerts took place at the Roman Catholic Church Hall.

To publicise themselves, the Merry Makers sang in an open lorry that would be driven around the townships. The popular "ditty" would go thus:

"Go and tell your mother that the Merry Makers are staging here tonight."

They staged variety shows, which was the practice of all groups at the time. Such shows involved singing, interspaced by comedy acts or sketches. The Merry Makers most known tune was; "Elokitshini" (In the Location)

The Merry Makers

NDEBELE	ENGLISH
ELOKITSHINI	**IN THE LOCATION**

Elokitshini, Elokitshini
In the location
Oh!Maye asibunzima bayilokitshi

Oh! It's difficult
Ikhonenku, Bekisiningi ezisehlela elokitshini It is difficult to live in the location
Omaye asibunzima

there are problems
bayi lokitshi that we face in the location
Its difficult to live in the location

The song is a narrative of township/location life; the hardship strains and family dislocation; brought about by rapid urbanisation. The township{location} was a creation for black people only, and had its unique attendant problems.

zimbabwe township music

The late Dr Joshua Nkomo

Remmington Mazabane was a multi-talented composer/conductor, who was conversant with dancing styles, which he freely imparted to the group.

The Merry Makers travelled throughout the country, and often to Harare where they held joint shows with The City Quads and De Black Evening Follies. At Christmas time they would be invited to sing for the sick at Harare Hospital.

In later years they travelled to Botswana where they staged shows in Gaborone, Serowe and Francistown. They were received and hosted by Chief Tshekedi as his guests. Some people and patrons travelled on horse-back to centres where The Merry Makers were staging concerts.

At one time the group sang with the late Joshua Mqabuko Nkomo.

Entertainment in the early townships was initially non-existent, especially for the young. However, the concerts of the 30's-60's were geared to provide entertainment for the whole family.

The Merry Makers gradually faded out in the 60's, as the majority of members joined The Bulawayo Choral Society, led by Maklema, who apparently made it into a top flight choir.

Female members of the group used to dress smartly, with black dresses, decorated with a white flower and pleated hair. The singing queens were Evelyn Juba, Emma Dube, Alice Bonkwe and Martha Ndebele.

The Merry Makers staged their shows at fully-packed halls in Bulawayo; be it at The Stanley Hall, The Jewish Theatre, or The City Hall {Bulawayo City Centre}. They pioneered stage performance in the City Hall, which was previously reserved for whites. Permission to perform had to be granted by the Native Commisioner, a Mr. FitzPatrick. The show was eventually a big success, as it sent tremors around the city.

Evelyn and Simon Juba

AGNES ZENGENI

Agnes started singing as a young girl, leading the choir at the United School, where she was a pupil. She also sang in the church choir. At an early age, she was a self-assertive and confident personality.

When Agnes teamed up with the Merry Makers, her mother would discourage her from frequenting concerts, where she would be alone with male company. Her brothers would often intervene to persuade the mother to allow the young girl to perform at concerts. Agnes feels that women musicians ought to assert themselves in a society which is often dominated by male chauvinism. To her, music is a broad arts field that offers innumerable challenges to the girl-child and to the community as a whole.

EMMA MOYO

Emma Moyo teamed up with the Merry Makers in 1953, having been nicknamed Judy Garland ("Wizard of Oz" fame), the Queen of Jive. At the time, local musicians aspired and liked to be identified with American actors or singers whom they adored. As Emma grew up singing, and later qualified as a school teacher, she was eventually conducting the school choir.

Whilst with the Merry Makers, Emma learned strict stage discipline and to be respectful of the audience. " When we were going on stage we wore shoes which did not make any noise," recalled Emma. She feels that contemporary musicians are often not well - disciplined when performing in front of an audience.

Moses Mpahlo-Mafusire/ The DeBlack Evening Follies

Moses Mpahlo- Mafusire

Moses Mpahlo-Mafusire was born in 1923 in Harare. Waddilove School offered Friday social evenings for pupils; which prompted young Moses to form a singing trio: "The Mysterious Three," which included Weston Chakachadza and Samuel Gotora. The trio became the major entertainer at the school, as they sang popular copyright versions, especially by famous musicians, which attracted large audiences.

On leaving school Mpahlo worked in Harare, where he joined Kenneth Mattaka who was leading the Bantu Actors. Earlier on, he had attended a concert by the Bantu Actors at Mai Musodzi Hall, where he had come into direct contact with Mattaka. He joined the latter with his friends

zimbabwe township music

Gotora and Chakachadza. The Bantu Actors specialised in jazz and church music, with interludes of comedy acts and sketches.

Moses had a passion for traditional music blending, but his friends were not supportive as they favoured Western-type tunes. He was thus labelled "old fashioned."

Macloud Chitiyo

" I should have done what Thomas Mapfumo did long time back, but my friends discouraged me," lamented Mpahlo. Somehow at the time, his friends were correct because the market-place demanded Western/modern – type music. Traditional music was often displayed at Mbare Musika, where various tribal dancers held their shows at weekends.

Mpahlo stayed with the Bantu Actors until 1943, when he formed The De Black Evening Follies, with Elisha Kassim and Samuel Gotora. As young people, their dynamism influenced them to do things differently from the Bantu Actors. He is, however so grateful to Kenneth Mattaka who ushered him into the professional music world. The Follies generally sang Shona songs, often fused with Western jazz and Indian rhythms.

When Moses Mpahlo formed The Follies he was working in the police force. He used to cycle from the Police Depot (Dhepa) to Mbare Township, where the group met for rehearsals. There were no commuter buses at the time.

The Follies initially sang without guitars; rather, they used their footsteps to accompany musical rhythm. Their inspiration came from the Mills Brothers, as well as from South African groups such as the Ink Spots and Manhattan Brothers. Once they held a combined show with the Manhattan Brothers, which was facilitated by Stanlake Samkange, to fundraise for Nyatsime College.

At a later stage Jonah Mbirimi played guitar for the group, after which he switched to clarinet and saxophone. Nicholas Chidhuza, who later belonged to the City Slickers, once played clarinet for The Follies. Just like the Bantu Actors, the De Black Evening Follies became a training ground for several musicians who later went their separate ways. Themba Mandizha, who in the 60's-70's teamed up with Safiriyo Madzikatire and Susan Chenjerayi, was one of the youngsters who joined the group in the 50's. He also sang with the Star Gazers, led by Bill Saidi. Macloud Chitiyo, now a medical doctor, played guitar for the De Black Evening Follies in the 50's. When he was studying medicine in South Africa, he would purchase instruments for the group. His guitar style was influenced by Josaya Hadebe, and American guitarists Barney Kessel and Les Paul. Dr. Chitiyo still reminisces the musical past with his guitar and old-type grammophone. Another musician who joined the Follies in the late 50's was Patrick Msengezi.

Initially The Follies sang copyrights, but later on, were composing their own tunes. Mpahlo-Mafusire did some compositions of which one was: "Dai Ndirimuumbi" (If I was a Creator).

zimbabwe township music

Sonny Sondo, who sang with the group during 1943–1953, composed some memorable tunes. After a show in Mutare the group was travelling to Harare when Sonny, from a distance, saw local girls climbing mountains. He remarked "Do you know why these girls are short? It is because they climb high mountains." He was inspired to compose a tune; "Makomo EkwaMutare" The (Mutare Mountains).

SHONA   ENGLISH

"Makomo EkwaMutare"
(Of Mutare Mountains)

Ndayenda KwaMutare
I visited Mutare
Ndadzoka nemushure
I have turned back
Ndawona zvandinetsa
After I have struggled
Zvokukwira makomo
To climb the mountains
Hamusati mazviona
You have no idea
Zvinoitwa KwaMutare
What takes place in Mutare
Vanokwira mumakomo
They climb mountains
Vasina manera
Without using ladders

Mpahlo reminisces on how he misses the late Sonny Sondo, whose rich vocals coupled with unparalleled charisma, made him the show-man of the day.

The Follies initiated beauty contests, as they had been always innovative when it came to entertaining. They held the contests and dressing competitions in major urban centres, with finals being dubbed "knockout." The first Miss Rhodesia was Marceline Dzvowa, who later married the late Jonathan Chieza, a member of the group. As Townshic Music/ Entertainment brought people of different races together, Peggy and Keith Heally helped with beauty contests, as judges and sponsors.

Moses' desire to sing traditional music, compelled him to introduce tribal dances on stage, with such themes as "Jerusarema" and "Muchongoyo", which added flavour to the variety shows. On Sundays they would visit the market place, which was a hive of activity with tribal dancers from different parts of the country. There, they would look, listern and learn. Tribal dances as such, did not feature prominently in the variety shows.

As the order of the day dictated, the Follies had women singers, of which the first was Rennie Jones.

Subsequently, other females joined the group, namely, Mabel Bingwa, Margaret Pazarangu, Christine Dube and Joyce Ndoro, who ultimately sang with the group for a longer period. At one time Joyce Ndoro was crowned Miss Harare. She was also a good dancer who often song - duetted with Jonathan Chieza on stage. Joyce popularised the tune "Goli Goli", a song which she learnt at an Indian cultural festival. Zimbabwean women musicians were highly influenced by their counterparts in the U.S.A and South Africa, who were featured in movies and on radio. In their heyday, The Follies sang to fully packed halls, with big applauses from the audience. They used to charge 1/- (one shilling) for their shows, going up to 5/- (five shillings), when demand was high. At the time, the artists' goal was to entertain

The De Black Evening Follies

zimbabwe township music 95

the audience, not so much money-making.

The Follies used the proceeds of gate takings to purchase fuel, staging uniforms and musical instruments. Their blazers were inscripted with the words: "Pro Bono Publico", meaning "for the good of the public." The uniform consisted of blazers with black and white stripes, matched with cream trousers and black shoes. They held a bank account, underscored by

Moses Mpahlo-Mafusire

trustees, for accountability of the group's finances. One of the trustees, Sam Matambo, went on to form the City Quads with Sonny Sondo. Through Sonny Sondo, as secretary for the Follies, a charitable fund was estblished by the group to offer school bursaries for under-privileged children.

The De Black Evening Follies numbered more than twenty five, and were thus able to stage more than one show at different venues simultaneously. Once the group split into two, so that one half of the ensemble staged a show at Runyararo Hall, whilst the other half performed at Mai Musodzi. These concerts were dubbed; "Double Header". The audience of the day were amazed at how the group staged two shows at different locations, at the same time.

A highlighting event of the group in their musical career, was when they were honoured to play at the wedding of Sally and Robert Mugabe, in 1961. The Follies used to hold Christmas Parties for young children, in search of talent; be it playing an instrument or singing. That's how guitarist Zacharia Gwaze was discovered. The group made some recordings for a flat fee of six pounds, the highest money they were paid being eighty pounds. Their recordings included: "Ewe Dudu", "Sono Sami", "Makomo EkwaMutare", "Dai Ndirimuumbi", "Chaminuka" and "Kumadokero".

Eventually they threw in the towel in the 60's, when some singers left the country mostly for political reasons. The government of the day had introduced a State of Emergency, which barred people from gathering in groups.

The Follies had a significant impact on Zimbabwes's musical history, having pioneered big band music, original compositions and fusion of indigenous rhythms with other forms. They sponsored beauty contests and talent shows; recognising music beyond the narrow limitation of just entertainment. They felt obliged to assist the underpriviledged pupils with bursaries, and to fundraise for the needy in general.

Robert and Sally Mugabe in 1961, wedding blessed by the De Black Evening

zimbabwe township music

OMASIGANDA

The solo or one-man band musicians sang and entertained township folk in the streets. "Omasiganda" is derived from an Afrikaans word for musician. The Zulu twisted the term to mean a musician who sang traditional lyrics on guitar. "Omasiganda" performed in townships where there was lack of entertainment. They sang in the streets, in trains, at beerhalls and tea parties. Because they performed mostly in the open, patrons paid very little for the entertainement. Token money was often thrown to them by the enthusiastic audience.

In the 40's the popular "Omasiganda" in Zimbabwe were Josaya Hadebe, George Sibanda and Sabelo Mathe, all from Bulawayo. Eric Gallo recorded them in 1948. For their recordings, they were given a flat fee, and no royalties for sales of their records; hence they died poor men. The Omasiganda were the first artists to popularise an early mode of strumming a guitar called "ukuvamba", involving strumming all strings simultaneously (vamping).

Josaya Hadebe recorded more than 15 songs with Gallo. His favourite tunes tended to be derogatory or vulgar in meaning. A song like, Pendeka (Prostitute), is typical of Josaya's compositions. He grew up in Ntabazinduna, close to the Bulawayo - Harare main road, amid the growing industrial area, where the surrounding population was gradually getting urbanised. Hadebe sang about the deteriorating social values, which were a reflection of emerging city life: drunkeness, prostitution and crime. The decline of moral standards, and family values provided interesting material for his songs. Some tunes were satirical on women, although nevertheless, he was popular with females.

A contemporary "umasiganda" of Josaya was George Sibanda, who also recorded with Gallo in 1948. In all, George recorded 15 songs, of which the most popular was "Gwabi-Gwabi Kuzwa". His lyrics differed slightly from those of Hadebe. Mention must be made of Sabelo Mathe, another "Umasiganda" of past repute.

According to **Jacob Mhungu**, people loved "Omasiganda" to the extent that they would track him down to his home

Josaya Hadebe

in the event of a brief disappearance from the streets. After playing and by the time he returned home, he was already a richer man. In the beginning Jacob Mhungu played at tea parties, and in the 50's, he focused on rural areas, often performing the whole night. He played for five shillings, which was on the expensive side; but his music was on demand. The tea parties/concerts took place mostly after harvests, when people had relatively more time and money to entertain themselves. Mhungu moved to Gweru and later to Bulawayo, where he played behind curtains, to avoid sensitivities of the white audience. On one occasion a curious white man went behind the stage, opened the curtains and remarked loudly: "I thought there was recorded music behind the curtains!" Eventually, a few whites began to appreciate Jacob's music and to admire his artistry.

Jacob Mhungu recorded with the Federal Broadcasting Corporation (FBC), as well as with Trutone Records, which was based in South Africa. He lived in Bulawayo when he recorded the songs: "Chengeta VaBereki" and "Kushaya Amai". Bulawayo's by-laws were more relaxed than Harare's; hence the predominance of *"Omasiganda"* musicians there. According to him music was serious business; he would punish group members who absented themselves from rehearsals or concerts without good reason.

Jacob Mhungu

John White an albino, was a popular "Umasiganda" of the 50's, who used to sing and play guitar for train passengers. Travelling by train, thus became an exciting pastime. His guitar style was "Hawaian", whereby he used a thumbing bottle on the guitar. At a party in Sarahuru (Mwenezi), he was rated the best; people had thronged to the occasion in such great numbers that some had to climb up trees to listen to him. A local businessman later persuaded him to play in an open lorry for easy viewing by the audience. Patrons soon swelled around the lorry. A white policeman who had witnessed John's instant popularity, surprised people by giving the musician some money, which was unusual in 1952. Some of the tunes which John played were variants of George Sibanda's songs. However, subsequently he played mostly his own compositions. As happened to other musicians, John White was invited to play in Kariba for the dam builders, at which he met another invited "Umasiganda", "Chigonamubhawa"; whose show was completely overshadowed by that of John White. In 1953 John,

zimbabwe township music

unknowingly, was hired for a token fee by a policeman to perform near a jail close to a railway line in Bulawayo, apparently to trap and arrest people who did not have colonial identity cards (stupas).

with such tunes as, "Bhurukwa Rako Rinechigamba." (Your trousers are full of patches).

Another celebrated "Umasiganda" of the 50's was Ali Vintuale, a migrant from Mozambique. His guitar

John White

Just before his death, John White was no longer performing in passenger trains, but in beerhalls where he charged 50c for a song.

Daniel Mukonorwi was yet another unique "umasiganda" who used to advise people against laziness,

music resembled that of John White, in which he used a bottle to produce (Soulful) Hawaian-flavoured tunes.

zimbabwe township music

August Musarurwa

August Musarurwa

August Musarurwa is world-famous for his tune Skokiaan, recorded by Gallo in 1951. Musarurwa was born in 1920, at Musarurwa Kraal, in Zvimba Reserve, Chinhoyi (Sinoia). He went to Marshall Hartley School (now Moleli) near Makwiro, from where he left for Harare in search of employment. He got a job in a tobacco company as a clerk, an assignment that was not so challenging to him. In 1942 he joined the police force as a district interpreter. He was a conscientious worker such that he impressed his superiors, who transferred him to the Criminal Investigation Department Branch. The country's economy was gradually expanding and opening up opportunities in the entertainment arena. Soon a police music band was formed, whose players were all blacks. The band inspector, a Mr.Sparks auditioned Musarurwa and found him suited to be saxophonist. This signalled Musarurwa's first step into the world of Township Music.

Musarurwa had bulging lungs and shapely lips, suited to "make a saxophone speak". Ill-health forced him to leave the BSAP in 1947. He had to revert to clerical work, this time at Rhodesia Iron and Steel Corporation (RISCO) in Kwekwe. Being a born-musician, he played in his spare time with a small band he had assembled. Kwekwe was not challenging enough, and after three years he migrated to Bulawayo, which was his ideal city. There, he joined the Cold Storage Commission Band. As the germ of music was biting hard, Bulawayo became a fertile ground for socialites and entertainment galas. Musarurwa eventually formed the Bulawayo Sweet Rhythm Band, later to be signed on by Gallo.

When the band played their key tune, the recording technician asked August the name of the composition, to which the latter responded: "Skokiaan".

Thus, Skokiaan was born, which has become a famous hit locally as well as far afield.

When he recorded Skokiaan with the Cold Storage Band, it became an instant hit, making Musarurwa a household name. Louis Armstrong, the acclaimed jazz trumpeter, recorded Skokiaan in 1961. When Armstrong visited Zimbabwe he requested

P. Rezant, L. Armstrong and A. Musarurwa

Musarurwa to be a supporting musician. Upon arrival at the airport, Louis played Skokiaan with backing of other musicians, all the way to the American Embassy.

When Louis visited Bulawayo just like in Salisbury, he was welcomed by August Musarurwa once more. Ivy Mupungu, daughter of Musarurwa has vivid memories about the visit. "At the airport Louis Armstrong gave my father a cream jacket with black stripes, and it was written at the back: "August Machona Musarurwa, famous composer of Skokiaan."

To date, Skokiaan has been recorded by various arstists the world over, which include Nico Carsten, Robert Delgado, James Last, Sam Klair, Joe Carr, Nteni Piliso, Herb Albert and Tanhatumarimba. The Hugh Masekela version of the 70's became highly popular. Skokiaan was a big hit to the young people of the 70's, who could hardly contemplate on its humble Zimbabwean origins. In contemporary times it relives its popularity and composer.

Nteni Piliso did a version of Skokiaan in 1992, and planned to bring out yet another version. In 1991 Paul Lunga of Bulawayo had his alternative of Skokiaan. Paul grew up in Mzilikazi Township, admiring and aspiring to Musarurwa's prowess. Today he is a highly distinguished contemporary trumpeter and flugelhorn player. Some fifty three years after the Musarurwa original recording, Jabavu Drive has come up with their own innovation: "Ndipe Chikokiaan".

Skokiaan is a highly intoxicating alcohol brew which was a favourite of the township folks, and which Musarurwa eulogised in song.

Skokiaan alcohol concoction was in its heydays claiming the appetites of several adherents in the townships. In what was dubbed, "Tea Parties" in the townships of the 50's, patrons were served Skokiaan instead. The drink became also, popular at "birthday parties" or "mabhavadheyi", even though there was no birthday

The Cold Storage Band

zimbabwe township music

CELEBRATING SKOKIAAN

Louis Armstrong: USA

Hugh Masekela: SA

Paul Lungae: ZIMBABWE

Ephat Mujuru: ZIMBABWE

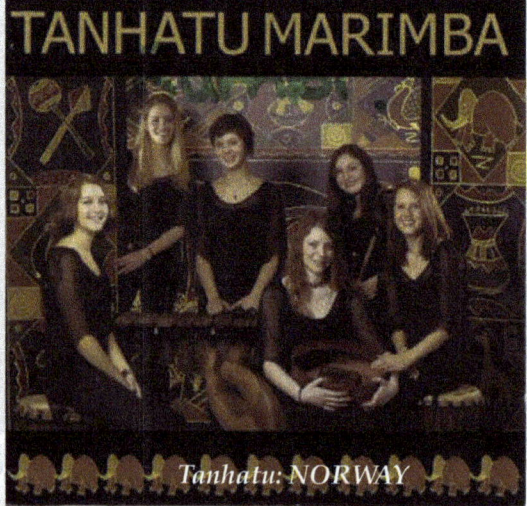
Tanhatu: NORWAY

Spokes Mashiyane: SA

Jabavhu Drive: ZIMBABWE

party being celebrated. These terms in reality were gimmicks to attract people to liqour houses or "shebeens". At the time black people were banned from the city centre after 7pm; hence shebeens were more like entertainment night clubs. Further, clear beer was solely for the "whites," which indirectly led to popularisation of home-made Skokiaan.

The government authorities were eager to ban "Skokiaan", but uncoordinated police raids proved fruitless. They made a serial film called; "Mr Tea and Mr Skokiaan", which potrayed the former as leading a better and healthier life than the latter, in an effort to educate the public on the dangers of drinking such alcohol. Nevertheless, Skokiaan brew remained persistently popular, even today. When Skokiaan was played on the loud speakers people would take to the streets in crazy dances. Some eulogised Skokiaan: "Skokiaan is a devil - a beloved devil".

Louis Armstrong exported the tune to the United States where it gained high popularity. Thus, Skokiaan goes down as an internationally acclaimed composition, with its humble and modest origins in Zimbabwe's Mzilikazi-Makokoba Township.

August Musarurwa performed most of his shows at the Stanley Hall, in Mzilikazi Township of Bulawayo. The township is one of the oldest in the country where Skokiaan drink reigned "tops" in the 50's. Besides "Skokiaan" August Musarurwa recorded 15 other numbers with Gallo Africa.

When August wrote "Skokiaan", he was working for the Cold Storage Commission, where he also stayed with his family. He later moved to Pelandaba Township. The family intended to settle in the United States at the invitation of Louis Armstrong, but unfortunately Musarurwa's wife Tandiwe fell ill and died. Musarurwa then went back to his original home in Zvimba.

August died on 27th September 1968 at Musarurwa Village. On 28th September, The Herald reported: "Rhodesia's famous African composer of the songs Skokiaan and Limpopo, Mr. Musarurwa, died at his home yesterday morning. He was one of the first Africans to join Performing Rights Society ..."Skokiaan" is a hit throughout the world, attracting large sums of foreign currency into Rhodesia by way of the royalties." His children are still receiving royalties from the evergreen composition.

August Musarurwa was buried at the family cemetery, with the inscription: "Here lies August Machona Musarurwa, great singer and music composer, renowned the world over."

EPWORTH THEATRICAL STRUTTERS

The Epworth Theatrical Strutters became popular for their social commentary songs, which were a mixture of traditional Shona and Church music. They had a Christian background, having been brought up at The Methodist Misson in Epworth. Their music was

Peter Kanyowa and Herbert Simemeza

zimbabwe township music

Andrew Kanyowa

influenced by Negro Spirituals, American jazz and South African Township Music. In time they came up with their own brand of music which had these traits, whilst retaining the Shona originality.

A lot of their musical inspiration, including dancing styles, was inspired by the Manhattan Brothers of South Africa, and De Black Evening Follies.

The Strutters were a family singing group composed of the Kanyowa brothers and their nephews. They were mostly from the teaching profession and consisted of Andrew, Peter, and Nesbitt Kanyowa; as well as Herbert Simemeza and Gilbert Chimbarange. In the 50's Andrew had formed the Merry Andrews and Swing Stars, a group which comprised of female musicians.

The name Strutters arose after they merged with another group called Strutters. The earlier Strutters comprised of John Marvie, Sam Kali, Isaac Chiremba and Luke Konde. Later on, they were joined by Isaac Chamunorwa, Douglas Marova, Winston Kanyere, Curtis Maromo and Chiremba Muzambwa; all residents of Epworth Mission.

The group composed and arranged several tunes during the 50's, some of which were "Kudzidza Kwakanaka," "Uridenga Rangu Mwanawe," "Hwahwa Ndichazourega," "I wish I could fly," "Ndinoda Mangwiro Mkuwasha," "Tambai Mose," "Chimwemwe Chmulungu," "Dombo Guru raMwari," "Gomo Guru Rembire," "Tave Munyika Itsva" and "Mhere Yarira."

"Kudzidza Kwakanaka," encourages the youth to go to school; "Hwahwa Ndichazohurega", discourages alcohol drinking, "Ndinoda Mangwiro Mukuwasha", persuades a son in-law to pay bridal price to in-laws, "Dombo Guru raMwari" tells of the sacred Balancing Rocks at Epworth. "Rudzi Rwevatema", is a political satire which bemoans the suffering of black people under colonial rule. "Tambai Mose", encouraged people to be involved in sporting activities. "Chimwemwe Chamulungu", was the only Nyanja song, and was arranged by Douglas Marova, of Malawi origin. It had a Rhumba bit.

The group leader was **Nesbitt**, composer of many tunes, and an able vocalist, who worked for the railways. His brother, Peter would often coin words for the tunes, and teach dancing styles, which often matched those of the Bulawayo Cool Four. Both Nesbitt and Peter are late. **Andrew Kanyowa**, the youngest brother, would fine-tune the lyrics on the piano. He was a teacher, and later a journalist, becoming one of longest serving in the profession before retiring in 2000.

Nesbitt Kanyowa

zimbabwe township music

In the 60's the Strutters were phasing out of action, as was happening with other groups.

In 1997, they featured in a video documentary; Township Music (The Epworth Theatrical Strutters); produced by the author. Those who participated were Douglas Marova (late), Herbert Simemeza, Isaac Chamunorwa (late) and Norman Kali. The few members who are still active are contemplating to record some of their old music.

The Epworth Theatrical Strutters' salient messages, through song and dance, are still relevant today, at a time when the community seeks both ethical and a moral re-armament.

Epworth Theatrical Strutters 1950s

EPWORTH THEATRICAL STRUTTERS

EPWORTH THEATRICAL STRUTTERS 1997
L to R: Herbert Simemeza, Samuel Kali, Douglas Marova and Isaac Chamunorwa

zimbabwe township music

DOROTHY MASUKA

Dorothy Masuka is a celebrated female musician of

Dorothy Masuka

unique experience and maturity, having been in the music scene for some 50 years. She began singing professionally in South Africa, where she went to school. Dorothy became popular as a jazz singer in Sophiatown, where she staged shows with the likes of Dolly Rathebe, Miriam Makeba and maestro Kippie Moeketsi. The Harlem Swingsters teamed up with Masuka and toured Cape Town on a series of musical shows lasting seven months. Masuka's popular tune was; "Hamba Nontsokolo", which has since become an all-time household hit. The tune was recorded in South Africa by Trutone and became a popular single during the 50's. Other numbers were "Imali Yami Iphelele Eshabhini","Unolishwa" and "Isono Sami", which were recorded by Troubador in South Africa.

Back home, Dorothy Masuka performed with major musical groups of the 50's; the Cool Four, Golden Rhythm Crooners, City Quads, De Black Evening Follies, August Musarurwa, as well as the Gay Gaeties. She taught the latter group on the finer points of vocal production and stage performance.

Masuka's musical shows were filled to capacity, as her music style and rich vocals were unique. Parade Magazine at one time remarked on one of her shows in Sakubva, Mutare: "half of the residential houses must have been empty", as all roads led to the Sakubva Beit Hall. Several groups aspired to stage shows jointly with Dorothy, whose jazz/blues offering became so excelling.

In 1953 Dorothy performed at the Rhodes Centenery Exhibition in Bulawayo. She also participated in a few multi-racial music events, which were fairly successful, an endoorsement that music can be a vehicle of racial integration.

Dorothy Masuka starred and held a press conference at the 1959 First All Africa Music Festival, held in Harare and organised by Daniel Madzimbamuto, then leader of The Cultural Syndicate. The festival had a high and brisk attendance, and indeed Dorothy was the star dominating the scene. She travelled to Britain where she appeared on BBC shows, as well as at the West End London Clubs.

Dorothy featured in the "Ready Steady Go Show", produced by UK's Independent Television. It was a crowning moment for her, since only big names appeared on this show: Beatles, Rolling

Masuka advertising "Miss Wonderful"

Stones, Dotty West: those were the times. One of Dorothy Masuka's spectacular moments was when she sang at the General Election Campaign, at a fully packed London Wembley Stadium. The event was momentous; it was aired on live television.

Dorothy gave shows in Malawi {Nyasaland} in 1961, on behalf of the Malawi Congress Party. Eventually she became popular throughout Malawi, where she later formed a trio with two local girls; Helen Kapesi and Matilda Bandawe.

In middle life Dorothy Masuka spent some time in Zambia, where she often teamed up with Jacob Mhungu and the Broadway Quartet {led by Simangaliso Tutani}. She also found time to record her own songs.

When Zimbabwe attained independence in 1980, Dorothy returned home, still with a feeling that her musical dream had not been fulfilled. She decided to settle in Johannesburg, to revive her musical career. For her, this is where it all began. Oftentimes she sings with old friends: Patience Africa, Abigail Kubeka, Letta Mbuli and Miriam Makeba. She has since bought a house in one of Joburg's affluent suburbs. Dotty is currently doing well, singing and performing in concerts and popular clubs. In the mid 80's she featured with Letta Mbuli and Caiphus Semenya on a tour called BUWA. Most of her songs have been recorded by Gallo, which offer her some royalties. Recently she has visited Zimbabwe to participate in Jazz Festivals and as diva in celebrated galas.

Dorothy has also held shows in Botswana with the Jazz Impacto, led by Zimbabwean Paul Lunga.

Masuka, popularly known as Dotty was once married to Dusty King {Freddie Gotora}, a one-time Zimbabwean star footballer of the 50's. She still sentimentalises that some day a local football stadium be named after her former husband, (Dusty King) Freddie Gotora.

She is now based in South Africa, still charming township music lovers. Most of her music of the 50's has been reissued by Gallo.

Dorothy Masuka in Botswana

THE CITY QUADS

The City Quads: left to right: Steven Mtunyani, Titus Mukosanjera, Sonny Sondo and Sam Matambo

The City Quads group was formed in 1953 by Sonny Sondo, and were later popularly known as the "Boys". Sonny had broken away from The De Black Evening Follies. His new group had Sam Matambo, Steve Mtunyani and Titus Mukosanjera. Sonny, Titus and Steven grew up together in Mbare (Harare). Sonny and Sam had been together in The Follies, when Sam was Treasurer/Secretary. Steve and Sonny used to sing together at school in Masvingo in 1945. Their group; "Follow Me Boys", was the main source of entertainment at the school social evenings. One of Sonny Sondo's early compositions was thus, "Follow Me Boy." Although the City Quads had full-time jobs, they made it a point to rehearse daily after work, often up to 10.00pm. They would commute back to their homes after rehearsals, often on foot, as there were hardly any buses after 10.00pm. It was straining especially for Mtunyani, who had to travel back into town where he was temporarily residing.

The "Boys" became a prolific singing group within a short period of their staging history, particularly at Mai Musodzi Hall, which always got filled to capacity. Their music was initially jazz copyrights, mixed with Negro spirituals and Mills Brothers ballards.

Starting with simple songs, they eventually mastered complex rhythms, which they readily copied from published sheet music or gramophone records.

As their music evolved to maturity, the City Quads fused traditional lyrics with American jazz forms.

The Quads were the first musical group to produce a Long Playing Record (LP) in the country, entitled: "Music In The African Township". The LP which had 12 songs, was engineered by Klaus Kruger, a representative of Polydor Recording Company (Germany) in the then Southern Rhodesia. The songs were recorded at different locations, and were eventually mixed in Germany. The group never received royalties for the record, despite a signed contract with Polydor. The LP was subsequently banned because of a track: "Lizofika Nini Ilanga?" - (When Will The Day {of Freedom} Come?).

NDEBELE   ENGLISH

"Lizofika Nini Ilanga Lenkululeko"
When Will The Day Of Freedom Come

Lizofika nini Ilanga Lenkululeko
When will the day of freedom come

Lizofika nini Ilanga lenjabulo
When will happiness come

Abantu abensundu bayshlupeka
Black people are suffering

Kudala, Kudala, Kudala
It's been long, It's been Long, It's been long,

Sam Matambo, whilst working for the Federal Broadcasting Corporation, was taken to task by the authorities each time he played the controversial tune. His other duties involved arranging Ndebele/Zulu traditional songs mixed with jazz, for example: "Nyathelu Ugqihile", "Lamlela" and "Dalala Khece".

A popular Chewa mourning song: "Ndafunafuna", was rearranged for fast tempo by Sonny Sondo, after which the City Quads made it into a big stage hit. The tune was later recorded by a series of artists, which include Molly Banda, Virgina Sillah (with Harare Mambos) and Prudence Katomeni-Mbofana (with Jazz Invitation). In fact, Sonny was fluent in spoken Chewa, Ndebele, Shona and English. His other popular number was, "Chipo Mwana Wababa".

Stephen Mtunyani composed, "Lindi" (Urimwana Wakanakisisa) (Lindi You Are a Beauty}, a love song which had a high audience appeal. The backing group for the City Quads included Andrew Chakanyuka (guitar), the late Simangaliso Tutani (bass), Athur Xahe and Duncan Achulu. The police band also backed the group on particular occasions.

The City Quads never made much money from singing, which was the order of the day. Music was then a part-time hobby, essentially meant to provide entertainment to the community. Entertainment groups were registered under the Social Welfare Department, as non-profit making entities. Any net profit after expending on overheads was channelled to charity. Consequently, the City Quads and several other performing groups assisted a number of charities. The "Boys" paid their backing artists well compared to other groups of the time, despite the fact that concert entrance fees were also minimal.

In Bulawayo the Quads staged concerts to fundraise for The Jairos Jiri Centre. They travelled as far as Kariba to sing for the dam builders, as a form of moral support. A particular show was sponsored by the Women's Volunteer Service (WVS), led by activist Muriel Rosin, then the only female member of the Federal Government Parliament.

The Quad singers also fundraised for a childrens's nursery: The Sister Barbara, a well- organised creche in Mbare Township, which also trains nursery teachers; and for a fund to assist flood victims in Hungary. The latter show was held at the Palace Theatre during the Queen's Command Performance, where the City Quads was the only black group. A complementary group was the coloured Arcadia Rhythm Lads, which often held

The Quads And Short-Gun Boogie

combined shows with The Quads at Mbare's Mai Musodzi Hall. Other beneficiaries of The Quads concerts were the Athenium Hall and Nyatsime College. Louis Armstrong had also participated in the fundraising of the college. The "Boys" were among other musical groups that welcomed Louis Armstrong on his historic visit to Zimbabwe.

The secretary of the Jazz Appreciation Club was then Sam Matambo. The club was active in popularising jazz, and in its membership recruitment. Deliberations of the club included topics covering familiarization with musical instruments, stage performance and vocal mastery.

Aside of music, the City Quads were active members of The Runyararo Drama Group, led by Mornica Marsden. Stephen Mtunyane and Pat Travers were actors in a play by Ken Marshall: "Poised in the Sun", a political satire, staged at the Reps Theatre. Adrian Stanley, then director of the Theatre, produced Macbeth, which had Sam Matambo, Ruth Mpisaunga and Albert Chaza as the main actors.

Matambo's acting career has persisted for long; as he has featured in recent films: Steve Biko and Neria, including the television soap drama; "Reflections". He is the only surviving member of the City Quads. At 80, Sam Matambo has seen it all in the entertainment industry.

The "Boys" had a number of women singers from time to time, and held joint concerts with female groups, such as the Gay Gaeties, led by Victoria Chingate. Some female musicians who sang with The Quads included Valerie Govenda, Faith Dauti and Molly Justin.

The group unfortunately disbanded in the 60's, due to the mounting political unrest and volatile tension prevailing in the country. Their leader Sonny Sondo, died tragically in Zambia. He was stoned to death by a drunken mob from a nearby beer-hall who mistakenly thought he had run over a child as he drove home. Apparently the child was only slightly injured, and was alive after all. Thus, spelt the death of a great singer and actor in Central/Southern Africa. Sonny's colleagues travelled to Zambia and brought his body home, whereupon he was solemnly buried at the Harare Beatrice Cottages Cemetery.

He never lived to witness the country's independence which the "Boys" yearned for, when they sang: "Lizofika Nini Ilanga?"

The late Sonnny Sondo

Sam Matambo

PAT TRAVERS

The late **Pat Travers** was a musician, actor and sportsperson. He led the Arcadia Rhythm Lads, a musical group formed in 1953. Arcadia is a resident suburb, which was then reserved for persons of mixed race or "coloureds".

Other members of the Arcadia Rhythm Lads were Albert Nathenson (Jomo), Stanley Williams, Frank Johnson and Valerie Govenda. Initially the group had one guitar and one microphone. They were a hardworking lot, as they practised from Monday to Friday afterhours. They based their repertoire on the African-American groups of the era; Mills Brothers and Ink Sports. Thus, the group combined influences from contemporary rhythms with African-American jazz paradigms, to articulate their artistic identity. The 50's were known for trios or quartets, and similarly The Rhythm Lads was a relatively small group.

Pat Travers

Pat's group often held combined shows with the City Quads led by Sonny Sondo, at Mai Musodzi Hall. This did not augur well with the then racist regime. Mai Musodzi Hall was nevertheless the hub of entertainment in old Harare.

Pat Travers grew up in the Harare Old Bricks section, which was just behind Mai Musodzi, before moving to National, which was another suburb reserved for indigenous Africans. Finally he was forced to

Pat Travers with The Ambassadors

zimbabwe township music

reside in Arcadia reserved for coloured people. By then he had found a job earmarked for coloureds, as fire-fighter at the airport

sang with the City Quads at a whites-only night-club, against the wishes of the proprietor who had to bend the regulation.

involved in a play called Ishe Komborera Africa (God Bless Africa); which was the vernacular title of the National Anthem.

The Arcadia Rhythm Lads: L to R: Frank Johnson, Pat Travers and Stan Williams

His mother welcomed the situation, as Pat had become the family's breadwinner. He thereafter endeavoured to use musical shows to discourage the colour bar. Often he would organise multi-racial concerts with performers and audiences drawn from the Blacks, Coloureds, Indians and Whites, without permission from the authorities. "Music has no bounds, and there is no vehicle in this world which can bring people of different races together like music," remarked Pat Travers, in a 1992 video clip on Township Music, by the author.

On an occasion, Pat Travers

He also participated in a play, Poised In The Sun, by Jack Watson, a journalist with the Herald newspaper. The play was produced by Ken Marshall, at the Reps Theatre and also featured the late Steve Mtunyani of the City Quads. Pat and Steve were the only non-whites in the cast, before a whites-only audience. Blacks, Coloureds and Indians were then forbidden to attend the Reps Theatre. However, the attendees apparently enjoyed the play, although some disgruntled whites disapproved the style of Pat's acting. Travers was also

On realising Pat's talent, Marshall introduced him to Ted Heath, who led a reputable orchestra in London. Subsequently, Travers travelled to London in 1960 and found himself playing with The Ambassadors. The group made musical tours in London, Paris and Stockholm, before Pat returned back home in 1962. He featured on Rhodesia television in the 60s, in Cy Jaffey's musical, Let's Go Show, with the City Quads, The Kay Jays Kombo and Simangaliso Tutani. When Louis Armstrong visited Rhodesia in 1960, the legendary trumpeter became godfather to Pat Travers' son.

As a social service, Pat Travers entertained prisoners on Boxing Day, by staging separate concerts for white, coloured and black inmates. Realising that his music was on demand, he later insisted to perform only to a mixed audience or to political prisoners. Eventually his conditions were met, and in a particular show he performed for, among others, Robert Mugabe and Eddison Zvobgo.

Travers is often remembered for his contribution, at sponsoring and facilitating sporting activities. He acted in response to changes in the social, political and cultural environment of the colonial period. His zeal and foresight moved him beyond the limitations of racism and colour prejudice, from which he recovered his artistry and musical identity.

He was born in Zvimba in 1934, to a black mother and white father. He died in 1998, having left this world a better place, believing in music as a vehicle "which can bring people of different races together".

The Milton Brothers and Faith Dauti

The Milton Brothers was a family group who provided entertainment by enganging in Township Music. They made a mark on the music scene in 1957. The group consisted of family relatives; Reuben and Faith Dauti who were brother and sister, **William {Bill} Saidi** and Chase Mhango (their cousins). At Regina Mundi School near Gweru, Reuben, Chase and Bill had formed a musical group, "The Swing Jazz Brothers". Apart from offering school entertainment, the group sang jazz music at social functions. Their performance standard improved with time, says Bill Saidi. He was born in 1937 in Marondera, and grew up in Harare's Old Bricks. He used to accompany his mother to Mai Musodzi shows, where his musical talent became evident.

When he left school he sang with the Kid Brothers led by Sherry Mazowe, who also taught the group some dancing styles. They imitated the De Black Evening Follies. With friends Willy Sondai, Willy Dzara and Chase Mhango, they sang in the Star Gazers. At a later stage, the group included Reuben Dauti and Themba Mandizha. Gibson Mandishona and Andrew Chakanyuka played guitars for the group. It later fell apart after which Bill Saidi, then formed The Milton

Bill Saidi

zimbabwe township music

Brothers led by his uncle Chase Mhango.

The Milton Brothers and Faith Dauti believed that a family group would last long, as the chances of breaking up were slim. They started off with one guitar. In those days an adequate group needed a string bass, drums and guitar.

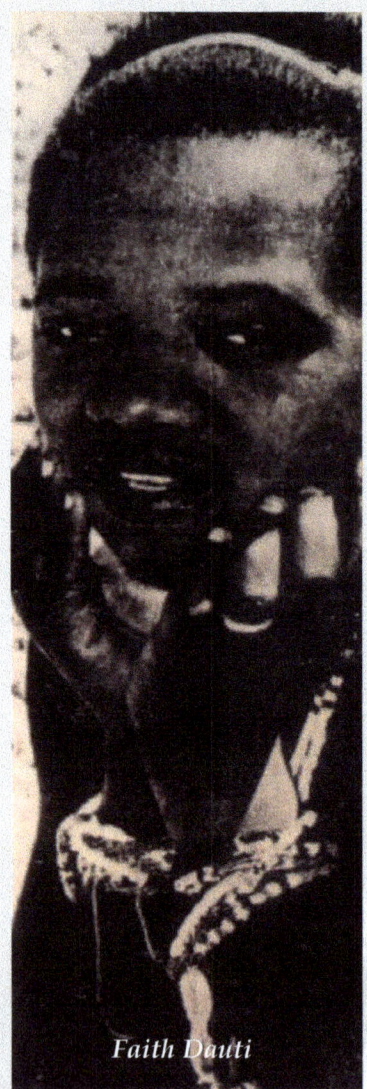

Faith Dauti

They bought instruments using a finance company specialising in funding musical equipment. Their first guitar was not electric, but just a box guitar. They initially sang copyrights, as Saidi aptly remembers the tune: "Put Another Chair at the Table", by the Mills Brothers.

The Milton Brothers performed Township jazz, often with a South African flavour. Their famous recording was "Hama Neva Bereki" (Relatives and Parents). Another popular tune was *"Tarasikirwa Nevabereki"*, which recalled the great influenza that once ravaged the country. "Rosvika Zuva", was played on the General Service Radio (European Service) during the general/bus strike of the 50's. It was about love; aimed at persuading black workers to abandon the strike and go back to work. Faith Dauti was the lead singer, who was popular during 50's-60's, and commonly mistaken for Dorothy Masuka's sister, as their vocals were similar. The

The Milton Brothers: L to R: Chess Mhango, Bill Saidi and Reuben Dauti

African Daily News of the time reported:"Faith must have been born when the allocation of voices to creatures was still fresh!" Faith Dauti would team up with the City Quads, Golden Rhythm Crooners, or DeBlack Evening Follies, though she permanently belonged to the Milton Brothers. Musical groups were elated to share the stage with Faith, as she had rich vocals and a sweet personality. Her short stature won her the nickname "Shot Gun Boogie", which became a trademark in her shows.

Faith Dauti attended Chitsere School, the oldest government primary school in Harare (Mbare), where she completed her primary education. Thereafter, she partly trained as a nurse at Harare Hospital, which she abandoned as she could not stand the sight of a corpse. She teamed up briefly with Victoria Chingate's Gay Gaeties; music was to be her ultimate career.

The Milton Brothers performed live shows at the African Services Radio in Harare during 1956. The show was hosted by Benjamin Chipere, a popular presenter of the time. Bill Saidi, a journalist with The African Daily News then, introduced his group before the start of singing sessions. Chase Mhango and Reuben Dauti were also full-time employees at the time.

The Milton Brothers and Faith Dauti had their model mentors such as, The De Black Evening Follies. At the time it was commonplace to form smaller trios or quartets. Prominent quartets of the 50's were, Golden Rhythm Crooners, Cool Four, City Quads and Arcadia Rhythm Lads.

The Milton Brothers and Faith Dauti disbanded in 1960, when the political situation became untenable and volatile; when musicians were unable to perform freely. Bill Saidi fled to Zambia, where he worked as a journalist. Faith Dauti also left for Zambia with the Golden Rhythm Crooners where they sang for United National Independence Party (UNIP). She later returned to Zimbabwe, where she died in 1970.

Bill Saidi is still a journalist, coincidentally with the new Daily News. He joined the former African Daily News in 1957, when he promoted township musicians through media coverage of their performances. With friends, he wrote under pseudonym: "Socialite".

Bill has worked with various media houses, being one of the longest serving journalists in the region. Chase Mhango is into advertising in Botswana; and Reuben Dauti works in Harare.

The Gay Gaeties

The Gay Gaeties singers were formed as a group in 1954, by the first batch of trained nurses at Harare Hospital. They were led by Victoria Chingate, a nursing sister who had trained at The Baragwanath Hospital in South Africa, which was her original home. She settled in the then Rhodesia, due to her marriage to a Malawian (Mr. Schotting Chingate) who was resident in the country.

As nurses, The Gay Gaeties felt that, over and above their profession, they also had to entertain the patients and the community at large. People were surprised to note that educated females would take up musical entertainment, which had always been associated with low - class women.

After the Gay Gaeties staged a successful show at the Mai Musodzi Hall, women patrons emulated what their counterparts could do on stage. One woman patron remarked to Victoria Chingate: "You know there is nothing wrong with singing on stage, you are still as respected as you were before."

The Gay Gaeties: from left standing: Tetiwe Solani, Dorcas Fry, Tabeth Kanyowa, Ruth Jero, Martha Mabhena and seated: Grace Mandishona

The Gay Gaeties were formed by nurses who felt some boredom at the hospital. The white nurses used to have their own entertainment, at the exclusion of black nurses. The Gay Gaeties line-up comprised of: Tetiwe Solani, Grace Mandishona, Dorcas Fry, Martha Mabhena and Rose (Mrs Samkange). The formation of Gay Gaeties partially destroyed colour bar at Harare Hospital, because soon the white nurses were attending the "black" nurses shows. The all-female group became popular because of their unique music, and the grand Christmas parties they used to organise for the community. They often raised money for the Christmas party by staging plays at The Runyararo Hall. One memorable play was about a woman who refused to be operated upon. The Hospital Superintendent watched the play at Runyararo Hall, and anxiously encouraged it to be repeated at the hospital for the benefit of a larger audience. The Christmas parties subsequently attracted other groups to perform, sing and play instruments. The Gay Gaeties later performed with the City Quads, at which Victoria Chingate did a duet with Sonny Sondo: "Have I Told You Lately That I Love You". The group also performed with Dorothy Masuka, Faith Dauti, Simangaliso Tutani and police bands, as back-ups.

The glamour girls had to disband when Victoria Chingate left for the UK to further her studies in nursing. Furthermore, the remaining nurses where eventually outposted to different locations, making it impossible for them to perform together.

The Gay Gaeties were an epoch-making event.

ALICK NKHATA

Alick Nkhata was a popular singer/guitarist of the 50's, whose unique music appealed to both the young and old. The Manchester Guardian regarded him, "as a bridge between the old and the new African music." Alick played a fusion of traditional folk and jazz music. In 1948 he toured Southern and Central Africa, researching and recording indigenous songs. He was thus a foremost scholar in the field of Ethnomusicolgy. He once worked with Hugh Tracey, who recorded African traditional songs during the 30's-50's. Nkhata also recorded with the Gallo Company, mostly in Bemba; producing such hit songs as: "Makokoba", "Imbote", "Nekweba","Kanonkope", "Chiperoni" and "Maggie".

Alick was a self-made man in the musical profession, having taught himself guitar. As the norm of the 50's, he had a full-time job, with music as a part-time hobby. He joined the

Alick Nkata

zimbabwe township music

Central Broadcasting Corporation with headquaters in Lusaka (Zambia), which was also his home base. During the Federation he was transferred to Harare, then the Federal capital. In the mid-50's Nkhata was rated top broadcaster cum musician. Whilst working for the Federal Broadcasting Corporation (FBC), he recorded songs whose themes derived from contemporary social events. He also composed tunes of a political nature during the 1960's, which were never recorded.

Alick was characterised as a fast music composer; he produced an album at short notice for Zambia's independence in 1964. The album was an assortment of tunes comprising calypso and traditional songs. His music was later featured on BBC, including a contribution to the coronation for which the Queen Mother was grateful, when she toured the then Southern Rhodesia. Musical films for mobile cinema produced by the Central African Broadcasting Corporation and Ministry of Information, also featured Alick Nkata. These shows were in high demand in rural areas and in the townships of urban centres.

During his broadcasting days in the 50's, Nkhata formed the All Stars Group, comprising himself, Sam Matambo and Eliah Banda, who was relatively young at the time. Eliah later formed the Springfieds during the 60's. Nkhata eventually performed with Matthew Chinhoyi, Jonah Marumahoko and the late Simangaliso Tutani, who openly admitted that he learnt a lot from Alick. When Zambia attained independence in 1964, Alick was appointed Director General of The Broadcasting Corporation and Cultural Services, an acknowledgement of the immense role he played in shaping and developing African Broadcasting at the time. Above all, and apart from his other contributions, Alick Nkhata was the great broadcaster/ composer/ musician, for which he will be dearly remembered.

On October 19, 1978, Nkhata died tragically in crossfire, when a ZAPU camp close to his farm was bombed by forces from Rhodesia. His music still lives on, his recordings are alive, which portray the multi-talented musical giant of Southern Africa.

JEREMIAH KAINGA

Jeremiah Kainga was introduced into the music scene by his uncle Edwin Kachisi, who taught him how to play the guitar. In 1947 uncle Edwin who used to play banjo for the Bantu Actors, facilitated Jeremiah to join the group, led by Kenneth Mattaka. Kainga played the part of tap dancing which he had learnt from Samuel Mhlanga, a known expert at the time. Jeremiah and the Bantu Actors travelled and performed shows in the then Democratic Republic of Congo, (Belgian Congo), Mozambique (Portuguese East Africa) and Malawi, (Nyasaland). They also used to sing in the Bulawayo's Stanley Hall. The early group consisted of

Jeremiah Kainga

Kenneth Mattaka- as leader, Lina Mattaka, and her young sister Judith, Safirio Madzikatire, John Madzima {teacher and football administrator} and Domingo Chatula. The ensemble sang without microphones, yet their voices could be heard from afar. At the time, audiences were highly disciplined, and would remain quiet during a singing session. Popular tunes included jazz songs, Jita Bag, and calypso. Today's Jiti is a modified form of the 50's Jita Bag.

Ruth Mpisaunga

Apart from Lina Mattaka and her young sister, other women musicians in the Bantu Actors were Susan Chenjerai and Susan Sithole. Jeremiah Kainga had a high impression of these women, who apparently displayed unparalleled staging and singing skills Kainga's music was influenced by the Hawaian guitar style with which he played; "Imi Munosara nani Ndaenda," in 1952. He later recorded the popular tune with other singers, which included, Ruth Mpisaunga and Dorothy Gutu. It was subsequently recorded by various artists, including The Mahotella Queens of South Africa and Fred Zindi. Kainga's other songs were: "Kune Muti Unonzi Muwonde", "Ndakanga Ndichi Famba", "Baba Ivai Nemwoyo Muchena", and "Bromley" (Spanish flavour). He recorded the latter tunes on his own, after he had left The Bantu Actors.

Jeremiah apparently never received any royalties from the recordings, and somehow felt that the recording studios took advantage of the fact that he had left popular music and become a church pastor. He stayed with The Bantu Actors during 1947–1953, and left the group when Mattaka was getting more involved with Magic shows. On leaving The Bantu Actors, he formed The Menton and Sisters, which included, Ruth Mpisaunga, Peter Muchawaya, Dan Manyengere, Dorothy Chidzanga (Gutu) and Jean Machingura.

During his tenure with the Menton and Sisters, Jeremiah was working as a clerk, for The African Weekly. He stayed with Menton and Sisters for five years, after the group disbanded. He nevertheless continued on a solo career as a one-man singer-guitarist. Jeremiah did not make much money in music business, as entrance fees for shows were low and royalties were not operational.

In 1959 Jeremiah Kainga left the music scene on personal religious grounds, after listening to a sermon by pastor Nicholas Bhengu of South Africa. He consequently became a full-time pastor, before he died in 1998.

RUTH MPISAUNGA

Ruth Mpisaunga (Muchawaya) was born in Mbare in 1939. Her first parents' house was in New Line Section of Mbare (Manyuline), near Mai Musodzi Hall, then the hub of entertainment. She had easy access to musical activities performed at the

Ruth Mpisaunga - 1950s

hall, because of the close proximity of her home. Being musical-minded, she soon found herself involved with the Menton and Sisters musical group, led by Jeremiah Kainga. The group was specifically to raise funds for the independ church which was the first African church founded in 1946 by Solomon Chada Machingura. When Jeremiah recorded his hit song *"Imi Munosara Nani Kana Ndaenda"*, Ruth was one of the backing vocals.

She left music to pursue further education and trained as a teacher. Thereafter she worked in Harare, where she was also involved in drama. In 1960 she acted in Macbeth (Zulu version), which was produced and directed by Adrian Stanley. The play drew a lot of audiences from both blacks and whites, as the latter were curious to watch a Zulu version of Macbeth. Blacks were equally delighted to witness Macbeth modified into an African context. Despite the racial segregation of the day, the event was a mixed audience, due to the popularity of the drama. Ruth Mpisaunga played the part of "Nowawa" the wife of Macbeth and Joseph Chaza played Noluju- Macbeth.

In 1988, Ruth wrote a booklet on entertainment in the home, inspired by her exploratory experiences.

She now looks back to her contribution in music and the arts, and feels fully contented for the role she has played.

ALBERT NDINDA

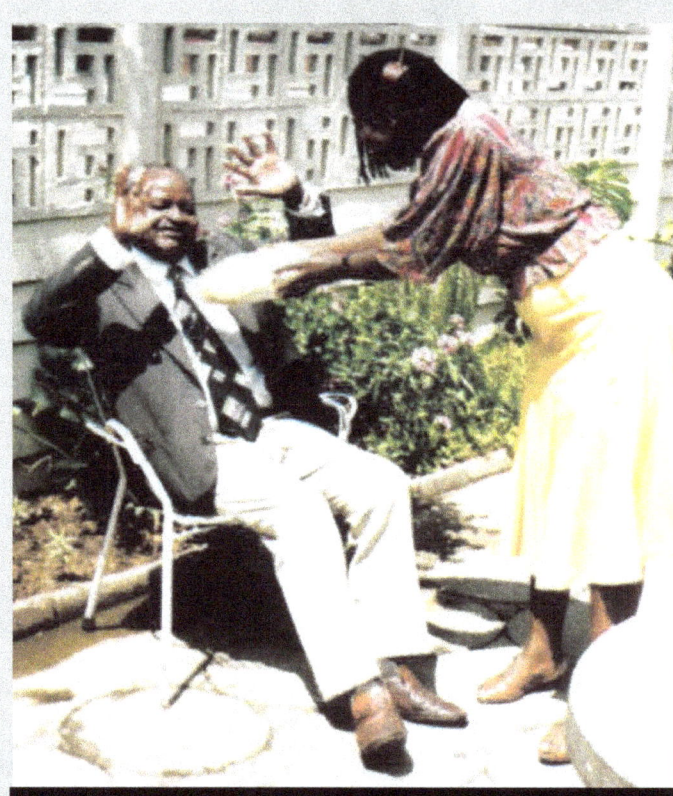

Albert Ndinda and Joyce Jenje Makwenda

Albert Ndinda was a unique comedian, as he did not stage a talk-and-act show. Instead, he would consume on stage three loaves of bread in 5 minutes, after which he gulped a family size coke or fanta. This act got him the name Magaisa No 2. He would say Magaisa No 1 was "floating" in the air. Magaisa was a member of a musical group called the Mashonaland Melodians, which included Flora Dick, Herbert and Wilson Munangatire. During the 50's, staging groups held variety shows, whereby the singing session was interspaced by a brief interlude of comedy and sketches. Magaisa's act was meant to advertise bread baked by Wonder Bakery, as the band played the tune:

SHONA/	ENGLISH

"Wonder Baker *Chingwa chinonaka*

Ndakati huya tisangane"

"Wonder Bakery, You have nice bread,

I said come lets meet".

At the end of the song Magaisa would commence devouring the bread. For the act to succeed, he would eat nothing on the day until showtime. He made a considerable amount of money, as he pocketed all the proceeds of this particular act.

Magaisa toured the country with the Mashonaland Melodians: Mutare, Masvingo, Gweru, Plumtree and Bulawayo. In 1955 he went on a regional tour, to Malawi and Zambia, lasting for six weeks. In Kitwe, Zambia, he became ill and fell unconscious, due to ill-prepared home-made bread. He remembered a faint voice in Zambian Bemba saying, "Katuwi afa, katuwi afa", or the greedy bread-eater is dead. After Magaisa's recovery, the singing group travelled to Lusaka where

Albert was reluctant to perform the "bread-act" as he no longer trusted Zambian bread. On reaching Victoria Falls, Magaisa was at it once more, as he was on home-ground. The Mashonaland Melodians and Albert Ndinda charged 2/6 (two shillings and sixpence) as an entrance fee in Harare; 3/- (three shillings) in Mutare and 4/- (four shillings) in Bulawayo.

Ndinda was employed full-time as a newspaper vendor by the African Daily News. He was a part-time commedian, which also facilitated his newspaper sales. Often-times he was a boxer, aspiring to be Duli No. 2; this sport did not go very well for him. He soon quit boxing to become a football referee, where he could be paid ten pounds per big match. The footballers who were around those days were; A.B.C. Rusike, Chigoma Brothers, Buns Chiwareware, Square Mutare, Nathan Shamuyarira and Freddie Gotora {Dusty King}, who was the ace sportsman of the time. There were teams such as Red Army (Bulawayo) and Yellow Peril (Harare). There was not much football in Mutare and Gweru. Besides being a referee, Magaisa also played the fullback part for the team Coronation.

Albert was abreast with almost all township activities. He was into Trade Unions as a member of the Reformed Industrial Union; he also belonged to the Southern Rhodesia Youth League, which amalgamated with the African National Congress of Bulawayo, to form the Southern Rhodesia African

Albert Ndinda (The Bread Eater)

National Congress {1957}.

Due to political involvement, Albert fled the country in 1959, before an imminent arrest. A friend had given him five pounds and a police car to drive. Bystanders asked: "Magaisa, when did you join the police?" "I have always been in the force," was his sombre response. Magaisa dumped the car on the border of Mutoko and Mozambique, and ended up in Germany, where he spent several years. He got married there and had five children, before returning to post-independent Zimbabwe.

The days of "bread devouring" were over, as Magaisa, upon his return, could now make do with only two slices of bread. He was born in 1925 and died peacefully in Harare in 1994. He will be remembered as a unique commedian: "bread eater par excellence."

CITY SLICKERS

David Matereke

The City Slickers played in the then Rhodesia Police Band, which was at the time forbidden to play in African townships. Band members thus decided to form private groups to offer entertainment in the townships. Such bands included the Hot Shots, The 12 Bar Blues, The Volcanos and the City Slickers, which was he joined the police band, as clarinetist, which was his passionate quest. His desire was to be a stage actor, as he had admired such groups as the De Black Evening Follies, City Quads and the Jazz Revellers. Being a member of the police band, he was forbidden to perform with private groups without Harare" and "Nhoro", which is a popular tune. The City Slickers once competed with other groups at the Stodart Hall, and came first because of, "*Nhoro*".The group was relatively better equipped than other groups, as their instruments which consisted of saxophones, piano, string bass and clarinets, were

City Slickers

formed in 1959 by Nicholas Chidhuza, Reginald Matiza and **David Matereke**.

Matereke's musical career can be traced to 1952, at the then Old Mutare Mission, in Standard Three, watching the police band play at the Agricultural Show. This was his initial inspiration, and later he was selected for the senior school choir. On completing Standard Six, David moved to Harare where official permission.

Matereke was tempted to join the De Black Evening Follies, as he greatly admired Sonny Sondo and Moses Mpahlo-Mafusire. Ultimately with encouragement from colleagues and permission of Mr. Sparks, the police band leader, was allowed to form a private musical group.

The City Slickers recorded such songs as, "Kana Usingandide", "Nyika ye government-owned. On stage Nicholas Chidhuza and Reginald Matiza were partly dressed in traditional attire of leopard skins, while others wore maroon blazers.

As the norm of the 50's, the groups performed with a female;Una Chipere, who later composed the song: "Kana Usingandide Nditaurire". Thomas Mapfumo popularised the same tune later with his own version.

Safirio "Mukadota" Madzikatire

Safiro Madzikatire will be remembered for his comedy acts which sent audiences into hysteric laughter. He carried on with the tradition of the 50's, where comedy was used to break the monotomy of music, becoming a top class hits as "Ndatemwa Negogo" and "Dai TirikwaHunyani". Occasionally he performed with Ernest Kachingwe. With Susan Chenjerayi they were a prolific duet, in the radio programme: Mhuri YavaMukadota of the 70's, carpenter. Music was always his forte, as he eventually became a full-time actor-performer. He was once with the Bantu Actors, which had become a training ground for musicians of the time. He left the Bantu Actors for The

Safirio "Mukadota" Madzikatire

comedian during 60's-90's. The "Mukadota" TV comedy show mimicked the 50's Township Music (shows) at which comedy drama complemented music. When Township Music briefly faded away Safirio was one of the few musicians to continue with the tradition. In the late 60's he paired with Susan Chenjerayi to produce such based along the lines of Mattaka Family of the 50's-60's. Safirio was "Mukadota" and Susan Chenjerai was "amai Rwizi." During the 80's-90's Mukadota Family was featured in a much acclaimed TV series.

The legend was born in Rusape, and grew up in Mbare, where he was educated and trained as a

Modern African Stars, before he formed The Safe Brothers. When the group split, he purchased instruments to establish The Safirio Madzikatire and Sea Cottage Sisters, which was a hit up to the 70's.

Later he formed The Rich Maize which comprised Andrew Ngoi, former group leader and guitarist of the OK

zimbabwe township music

Safirio Madzikatire

YavaMukadota". Safiriyo died in 1996, after a short illness. He contributed immensely both to Township Music and comedy drama.

SUSAN CHENJERAYI

Susan Chenjerayi often featured on radio, jukebox, in concert halls and in trendy magazines. A multi-talented artist, who entertained the township folks-people, and now retired; Susan's career spanned over a period of four decades. As Amai (Mrs) Mobape, she remains a foremost musician - actor. During the heydays, she was affectionately known as Amai vaRwizi, which contrasts with her present status as a born-again Christian, married to a pastor Mobape. Together they spend much time in evangelical work. She cannot stage popular shows anymore, which would compromise her vocational duties.

As she grew up in Mbare, Susan used to sing with friends in the streets. The city council police would disperse them and discourage the young girls from making noise in the neighbourhood.

Susan Chenjerayi drew her musical inspiration from Kenneth Mattaka's Bantu Actors, Sonny Sondo of the City Quads, De Black Evening Success Band, and Alan Mwale, former bassist of same group. Maize was a popular outfit of the 70's. Son Elijah Madzikatire was also in the band, which he left for the Ocean City Band, then a junior group to the Rich Maize.

In the 90's Safirio's career climaxed when he sang duets with Elizabeth Taderera (Katarina), and popularised the tunes: "Ndinemusikana Wangu" and "Ndatenga Mota". Both were star actors in the comedy "Mhuri

From left: Safirio Madzikatire, Pat Chimbwido,

zimbabwe township music

Follies, Dorothy Masuka and Faith Dauti. She never sang with Dorothy in the 50's, but they were later to team up in the 80's in the television series Mukadota Family, in which Masuka acted as a second wife of Baba vaRwizi. In the drama Dorothy was unable to prepare traditional meals, except American goulash, which she learnt during her long stay in the U.SA. In the 50's Susan Chenjerayi used to watch Dorothy sing with the Manhattan Brothers of South Africa. Quite often, she sang with Faith Dauti at the Presbyterian church, which they both attended.

Naturally, she got early guidance from Kenneth and Lina Mattaka, when she was still at school. She sang with the group in the evenings and staged shows at Mai Musodzi, which was close to her parents' home. "We had a nice uniform with streaks of black and red, which was very innovative of Mr Mattaka;" Susan recollects the good old days. With Sylvia Sondo, they had a group in the 50's; the Bush Babies. Later, she supervised young women musicians; Sea Cottage Sisters, from experiences she had mastered with Bush Babies.

Susan had a desire to record music, and was only delighted when Safirio Madzikatire requested her accompaniment after the latter heard her singing; Hondo Yechindunduma. At that time Madzikatire was performing with Temba Mandizha and Willie Dzara. The Rhodesia Broadcasting Corporation could not record "HondoYechindunduma", as it was a political lyric. Her determination to record was finally crowned, when she recorded "Ndatemwa Negogo", a Madzikatire composition; and "Isaac Hawuchandida Here", her

The Sea Cottage Sisters: L to R: Christine Nyandoro, Arbigail Dhliwayo, Junior Mtenda, Molly Moyo, Susan Chenjerayi and Safirio Madzikatire.

zimbabwe township music 125

Jane Chenjerai

origination. The numbers were on "the top ten" for quite some time in the early 70's. Her other compositions were "Fungai Mudiwa", "Tingachate Here", "Kwa Hunyani" and "Dhali Iwe", which were duets with Safirio. Subsequently she recorded with the Pied Pipers accompanied by Pius Makore, on hits "Mwedzi Muchena" and "Unondiroora Rini". A popular tune which she unfortunately did not record, "Ana Amai Vane Rugare"; was later to be recorded by Thomas Mapfumo. "I wrote the song "Ana Amai Vane Rugare" for my mother, who was very supportive of my musical career," remarked Susan.

Susan Chenjerayi was a talented drama actor; who became popular in Mhuri YaMukadota, a television series first produced by Webster Shamu, and thereafter by Patrick Bajila (Bra Pats). The serial proved to be a source of entertainment, for both young and old. Other actors included Elijah (Madzikatire's son) and the late Petronilla (Chimbwido), Susan's daughter. Yet, there was a film; The House of Hunger, in which Susan also featured.

As a versatile artist, Susan has great respect for her audience and society at large. She is held in high esteem by, the musicians she worked with. According to her, a performing artist must be highly professional, and abstain from alcohol when on stage.

In retirement, she delights in watching her children perform along her footsteps: Jane had a 70's hit: "Usandimirire Pagedhi"; Daisy composed "Zai Regondo" in the the 80's, and grand-daughter Meline dances with the Tumbuka Ensemble. Township Music culture and drama could not have been revered as such without Susan's forte and singular dedication.

The Marshall Brothers

The Marshall Brothers began singing as a group in Bulawayo in 1956. All the members hailed from Chegutu (then Marshall Hartely), hence their name. Although the group had halted singing some 40 years ago, they recently regrouped and performed at the National Hunger Concert (2002), bringing back memories of old Township Music. Indeed, they crooned the memorable: "Kure Kwatinobva Makwiro Shamwari", their 1956 recording at the Luveve Studio, then run by the Federal Broadcasting Corporation (FBC). They sang about Makwiro, their distant rural home, which was several kilometres away from Bulawayo, where they had migrated for employment. The tune encouraged people to work hard for a brighter future.

At the Hunger Concert, they were just as vibrant, with Ava Rogers belting in, as her father also hailed from Makwiro.

The Brothers comprised of Joshua Pedzi, Mathew Nyikadzino, and the late Albert and Ernest Soka. The Marshall Brothers other hits were, "Ruvimbo Mwanawe", "Tiki Yangu", "Ngatimbofunga Nguva Yeucheche" and "Zvino uno Voruzhinji". Pied Pipers had a popular version of "Kure Kwatinobva" in the early 80's A young musician, Mateo (Matthew Kaunda) has improved on "Ruvimbo Mwanawe".

As happened to musicians of the 50's, the Brothers stopped singing, having found out that music did not pay. They never got royalties, except a small flat fee. They now yearn to record most of their old tunes. Having made their mark in Township Music, and back to it they should now excel in the Jazz
Craze currently on the charts.

The Marshall Brothers: L to R: Joshua Pedzi, Andrew Costa, and Mathew Nyikadzino

zimbabwe township music

Simangaliso Tutani

Simangaliso Tutani was born in 1942, of a modest family, in Marirangwe, about 50 km South of Harare. He began his musical career at the age of nine whilst at school. He grew up in Mbare Township, where good music was played, and home to several township jazz musicians. Harare was typified by such groups as the Bantu Actors, De Black Evening Follies, City Quads, Epworth Theatrical Strutters and Gay Gaeties.

Simanga, as he was popularly known, used to listen to music, played on the Welfare Club radio. There were loud speakers which beamed music at popular centres, in addition to regular film shows featuring American jazz artists at Mai Musodzi Hall. These influences impacted positively on Simangaliso's love of jazz and on several of his contemporaries. He was thus a product of Mbare's Boys' Club.

Crazy Kids: L to R: Simangaliso Tutani, Chris Chabuka, Charles Fernando,

Rhumba music or "Cha-cha-cha" was of considerable influence on Zimbabwean artists. During the Federation days, Zambia used to house the broadcasting service, and its proximity to the Democratic Republic of the Congo made "Cha-cha-cha" music a household theme.

Tutani's original group was the Big Three, which comprised himself, Faith Dauti and Chris Chabuka. He later formed the Shelton Brothers with Charles Fernando, Chris Chabuka, Jerry Masauso and Andrew Chakanyuka. The group won a musical competition in 1956, which was organised by the Coca-Cola Company. Then followed the Crazy Kids which was a support group of the City Quads in the 50's. Simanga's Crazy Kids were popular at birthday parties, in addition to performing at concerts in and outside Harare.

Tutani's thirst for musical diversity led him to experiment with the Pine Tops, a coloured band which performed at the Goodwill Centre, and the Arcadia Community Hall. Alick Nkhata also imparted to the young Simanga unique musical knowhow. Together they were active on radio commercials in eight languages, which included Shona, Ndebele, Chewa, Bemba and English. Commercial advertising was a then source of stable income.

Tutani backed several bands and groups of the 50's, including the Gay Gaeties, an all female group of nurses, led by Victoria Chingate. As a musical "jack of all trades", Simanga could play lead/bass guitar, saxophone and piano. Above all, he had admirable

zimbabwe township music

ETHNOMUSICOLOGY PROGRAMME

Simangaliso and author Joyce

While the Broadway Quartet was playing in Zambia, Simangaliso Tutani with facilitation of Gibson Mandishona, a boyhood friend, went to the Berklee College of Music in Boston, USA, to further his musical expertise.

At independence the Broadway Quartet returned to Zimbabwe, only to discover that local music had undergone several transformations. There was reggae, funky and you name it. The Broadway Quartet and other musicians of the 50's made an effort to revive township jazz music. Success can only be partial in a society enlivened by musical diversion. Nevertheless, township jazz relives its vibrant past.

The Broadway Quartet was to split up with players going their separate ways, and with Simangaliso regrouping a quasi-jazz group; Body and Soul.

Simanga's passion for passing on music to young generations made him the first administrator of the Ethnomusicology Programme, where he lectured on guitar, piano and saxophone. Upcoming contemporary jazz musicians, such as Dumi Ngulube went through Tutani's tutorials.

Simanga is credited to have formally launched the Zimbabwe National Jazz Festival. After his death jazz enthusiasts have regrouped to continue with the festivals, which have become focal points for local, regional and international jazz artists.

Simanga passed away quietly on September 11, 1995 after a prolonged illness. His contribution to the Zimbabwe Township Music will always be remembered. In the orbituary which appeared in The Manica Post of November 17, 1995; Gibson Mandishona wrote: "Always a notch ahead, and like a radar sent down to probe the jazz depths, Simanga goes down in Zimbabwe's history as a true musical hero."

leadership qualities and supreme vocals.

Simangaliso eventually formed the Broadway Quartet with Andrew Chakanyuka, Jonah Marumahoko and Zacharia Gwaze. Timothy Sikova was a late addition. The group recorded jazz instrumental tunes with the Federal Broadcasting Corporation (FBC) in the 60's, of which one was "Chelete"

Tutani left the country for Zambia in the mid 60's, when The Broadway Quartet was invited to perform during the United National Independence Party campaign. They did not return to Zimbabwe due to the unfavourable political environment prevailing then.

Simangaliso at College of Music

zimbabwe township music

The Broadway Quartet

From left to right: Simangaliso Tutani, Henry Peters, Johnny Papas and Jonah Marumahoko

Andrew Chakanyuka

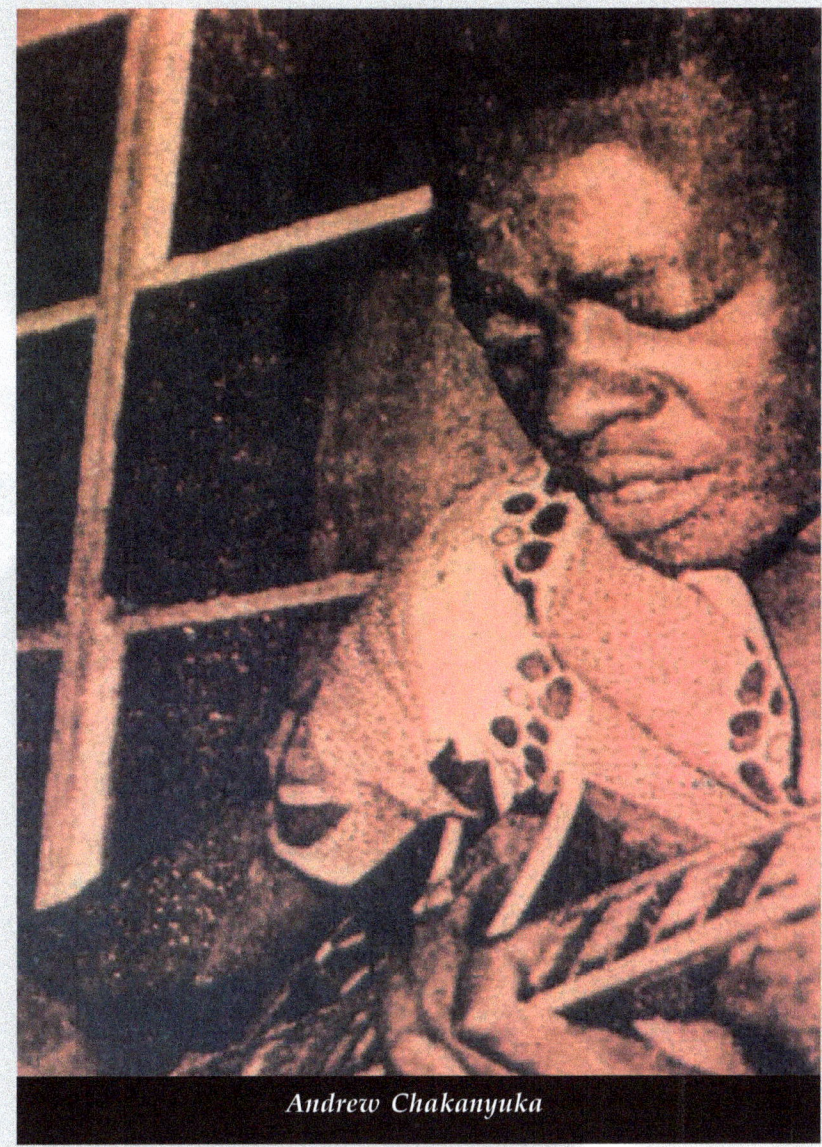
Andrew Chakanyuka

Andrew was a talented guitarist, who would make the guitar "talk". As the trend then, Mai Musodzi was the cradle of his musicianship. He was in touch with Kennneth Mattaka, who had a variety of instruments. Andrew eventually chose the guitar as his pet instrument.

A refined guitarist, Andrew was overwhelmed by invitations to back up artists as lead guitar. He often played for the City Quads, which was a leading singing quartet then. The City Quads recorded their LP, a first in the country, with Andrew as background guitarist. He later joined Safiriyo Madzikatire's Safe Brothers in the mid 60's, which he left for the Trio State Boys, with friends Charles Fernando and Chris Chabuka. With burning ambition he left the country for Zambia where he formed a duet with a night club artist. Simanga, Timothy and Jonah came to Zambia with Alick Nkata as musical promoters of the UNIP Party. They immediately invited Chakanyuka to play in the newly-formed Broadway Quartet.

Andrew and Simanga left the Broadway Quartet to join Churchill Jolobe (once Miriam Makeba's drummer) at the Woodpecker Inn, in Lusaka. When Jolobe left for Europe, Andrew and Simanga rejoined the Broadway Quartet, together with a "white man" Keith Clarke, on drums. They were involved in festivals; in Bulawayo they won a shield award as the most original group. Eventually drummer Timothy Sikova joined the group.

The Broadway Quartet were now playing at the Harare's Federal Hotel. The group participated at yet another Jazz Festival and won again, with Andrew prized as best guitarist. Andrew returned to Zambia and stayed there until 1966, when he was invited by Jolobe to join him in Dar es Salaam, after which he left for Kenya. Andrew's place in the Broadway Quartet was taken by Zacharia Gwaze. Afterwards he played with bands in Uganda, Ethiopia and Djibout, until 1975, when he moved to Switzerland.

There he joined a new and enterprising music group, which toured Germany, France, Italy, Austria, Poland, Tunisia and Luxembourg. The band was quite resourceful in that it managed to make some musical videos.

At the time of Zimbabwe's independence Andrew Chakanyuka returned home, only to discover so many

zimbabwe township music

transformations on the musical scene. Andrew stuck to his old jazz, and later infused it with a funk beat to win the hearts of young people. He contributed immensely to the Township Music jazz movement that is surviving today. He taught guitar at the Zimbabwe College of Music, passing on his talent to the younger generation.

As contribution to Township Jazz, he had planned to record tunes he arranged in the 60's. In his final days Andrew was strumming progressive jazz; going back, as it were, full circle.

The maestro guitarist is no more; but his sounds still ring in people's hearts.

L to R: Simangaliso Tutani, Sonny Sondo, Faith Dauti, and Chris Chabuka

Chris Chabuka

Chris Chabuka

Chris Chabuka was a brilliant all-round musician and talented pianist. He was a strict musical arranger who made certain that no one was off beat even by a second. Chris emulated the keyboard style of Jimmy Smith and Oscar Peterson. Because of his versatility and ability to read musical staff notation, he played keyboards in the Clint Eastwood movie, King Solomon's Mines, which was shot in Zimbabwe.

Chris tasted a variety of instruments: drums, bass and lead guitar, and finally settled as Township Music jazz pianist.

Like several youngsters of his time in Mbare, Chris' music can be traced to the Boys' Club. He teamed up with, Simanga Tutani and Faith Dauti under the leadership of Sonny Sondo, to become the Crazy Kids, which was City Quads' junior group. Together they toured Malawi in the 1950's. He then went on to play with the Capital City Dixies which included Friday Mbirimi, William Kashiri and Samuel Shonhiwa. The Ministry of Information made a film of the group. The Dixies became a popular group amongst the youth of the time. Later on he joined the Springfields where he played with Manu Kambani, before moving to the Zebrons, then to the Harare Mambos led by Green Jangano, where he doubled on keyboards and drums. Having made a name for himself he went to venture in Mutare and played for a "whites only" band. On returning to Harare he left his drums in Mutare, which incidentally became the learning tool of Jethro Shasha.

Back in Harare he was to gang up with John Nyathi and Johnny Papas, as he exhibited his prowess on guitar, drums and piano. In the 60's Chris was a founder member of the Broadway Quartet with Simanga Tutani, Charles Fernando, Jonah Marumahoko, Andrew Chakanyuka, and Timothy Sikova.

In the 70's Chabuka was with Movement, and later played at the Skyline Motel with Jonah Marumahoko and Lenos Mutariyana. In the early 80's he studied for a Jazz piano diploma course with the Boston-based Berklee College of Music, through distance learning correspondence.

In his later days he was performing with John Nyathi, whilst also teaching piano at the Zimbabwe College of Music. He also graced the Zimbabwe Jazz Festivals as an exemplary piano maestro.

Chris was born on 28th February 1943; he died on 3rd December 2002. He left an indelible mark as a jazz pianist and teacher. Indeed he was way ahead of his contemporaries.

Eliah Banda

Eliah Banda persisted playing township tunes in the 60's, when the country's entertainment scene was dominated by music from neighbouring countries. He performed with popular groups of the time; Great Sounds (of "Anopenga Anewaya"), and Springfields led by Thomas Mapfumo, to mention just two. Although he was popular in the 60's, his musical career had begun in the 50's when Simangaliso Tutani invited him to join Alick Nkata in The All Stars Group.

Banda sang a mixture of Rhumba, traditional music and rock, with a fusion of jazz. Rhumba was dominant as was the order of the day.

SimangalisoTutani discovered Eliah when the latter was singing with his schoolmates; Edward Shimulambo, Peter Sango and the late Petros Kazipe. They emulated the City Quads and the De Black Evening Follies. At the time Simanga was playing bass guitar for Alick Nkata's All Stars, before introducing Eliah to the group in 1961.

Nkata would have wished to take Eliah along with him to Zambia to help UNIP's election campaign in 1962, but he was still at school. Banda later joined the Springfields led by Thomas Mapfumo; which also included Susan Mapfumo, Elijah Madzikatire and Ernest Kachingwe, who led the Jazz Revellers in the 50's. After splitting from Springfields in 1968 he formed the Great Sounds with the late Jethro Shasha, John Chibhodhoro, and Moses Bhekilanga Kabubi.

Dominic Mandizha, a producer/presenter with the Rhodesia Broadcasting Corporation, was kind enough to buy musical instruments for the band. They recorded, "Connie", "Mupfuhwira", "Nherera" and the famous "Anopenga Ane Waya". Some of the tunes are reminiscent of gambling and amusement games, once played by men and women in old Mbare township.

Eliah Banda

The Great Sounds disbanded in the mid 70's, as Eliah Banda quit music, which was then not financially rewarding. Royalties for a single recording was one cent. Eliah was a foremost pioneer musical composer of the 60's.

He left the Township Music scene, having enabled younger musicians to gain from his first-hand experience as a professional pace-setter.

zimbabwe township music

George Sisimayi

In the mid 1960's Township Music and Cha-Cha reigned country-wide. **George Sisimayi's** real name was Gideon, but the recording company in South Africa mistook his initial G for George. His popularity rose through the song "Ndapera neChacha Amai"; recorded by the Rhodesia Broadcasting Corporation (RBC). Once he visited a music company with the aim of recording Jazz and Kwela songs, during the Spokes Mashiyane famed era.

The recording company reminded him that jazz tunes were not a priority, unless it was Cha-Cha-Cha, which was then highly marketable.

Back home rather depressed, he created a tune "Ndapera neCha-Cha-Cha Amai" (Cha-Cha-Cha has destroyed me mum). He practised the song on guitar all night until the tune and words blended together.

He then finally recorded the hit, with the Zonk Recording Company. "Ndapera Ne Cha-Cha" stayed as tops on radio for six months, until it was overtaken by a Rhumba tune, "Julieta Uko Wapi", played by some East African band. Another of his hits was "Bibi Uya Kuno".

George's group was called 'The Crazy Five,' and it included Ephrage Sithole, James Gandari and Alan Amatayi. At the time, he was a full-time school teacher in Highfields, with music as a part-time hobby. In the mid 1970's he quit music to pursue further education, since a guitarist was looked upon as a social misfit.

"I decided to study in order to prove to people that a musician/guitarist is not a social deviant, as perceived at the time."

George Sisimayi left the country to study in England, where he subsequently read Social Sciences and Education at Nottingham University.

He later studied at Bristol University where he obtained a Masters Degree in Education and Development. He is currently a civil servant as an Educationist in Curriculum Development.

George's song "Ndapera Nechacha Amai", will go down as the best locally composed Cha-Cha-Cha/Rhumba of the 60s.

George Sisimayi

WOMEN SET THE BALL OF JAZZ ROLLING

WOMEN WHO SET THE BALL OF JAZZ ROLLING

Lina Mattaka

Exerpts from the African Daily News 1958 (by Socialite)

The column "Women Set The Ball of Jazz Rolling" appeared in the African Daily News in 1958, and was meant to trace women who had contributed to Township Music/Jazz from the days of Lina Mattaka to Faith Dauti.

Lina Mattaka and Evelyn Juba set the pace in the 30's. The 40's are characterised by Rennie Jones (Nyamundanda). Zimbabwe's popular music of the 50's ushered in Dorothy Masuka, Mabel Bingwa, Joyce Ndoro and Faith Dauti. Miriam Yafele and Margaret Pazarangu had their contributions, but to a less extent. The mid 50's also witnessed the emergence of Victoria Chingate's Gay Gaeties, a female ensemble of nursing sisters. Zimbabwe's women who set the ball of jazz rolling, braved their way against the odds of gender prejudice and racial discrimination.

"When the Bantu Actors toured Northern Rhodesia and the Congo border four years ago, audiences everywhere mobbed and heaped praises on the troupe's slim, vivacious and elegant looking leading female singer-Lina Mattaka. To them she was all and all that show biz could give Southern Rhodesia troupes who had visited the Copperbelt before. Many had received thunderous welcome, but none of their stars had been so warmly received as Lina Mattaka. As the old Mashona proverb aptly puts it, "it was the sound of a drum about to crack." And indeed it was the last Northern Rhodesia saw of Lina and a life so full of gaiety and splendour. On returning to Salisbury Lina quit the stage to look after her family of four.

…….. She very well deserves being termed the greatest of the women pioneers. For it is Lina in those stale curtain-laced years, the late thirties, who alone championed the women's cause.
In the larger cities, there were times, so she tells me, when a woman was not so readily welcome on the stage. But Lina and jazz came rolling and was among the first few women who joined to set the ball of Jazz-O-Africa Townships rolling." (4, February 1958).

Lina Mattaka

Mabel Bingwa

"The year 1953 had its uniqueness. While politicians saw the Federation become reality, socialites attended the centenary of Cecil John Rhodes. It was in Bulawayo, 22 miles away from Matopo, where they laid his remains in 1902. There were delegates of all kinds and from all nations. But it is at this time that the attention of the country became focused on "16- year old" Mabel. The Follies were the only Rhodesian group invited to entertain people, and Mabel was with them. She sang side by side with the Manhattan Brothers, competing with Dotty Masuka and Miriam Makeba. Throughout the three weeks she remained at the Centenary African reserves and townships." (25, February 1958).

Victoria Chingate

"..........There appeared yet another young woman who was to make big news in show business. This was Mrs Victoria Chingate or Vic. For a long time she sang with the City Quads until early 1955, when she formed her own outfit, which she had appropriately named the "Gay Gaeties", which was an instant success. It was an all - female group of nurses just like herself.

…..Vic was an impressive entertainer, with highly stylised voice, and charming personality.

The Gay Gaeties' exploration into the musical unknown territory, made them secure a permanent place in showbiz." (11 February 1958).

Victoria Chingate 1991

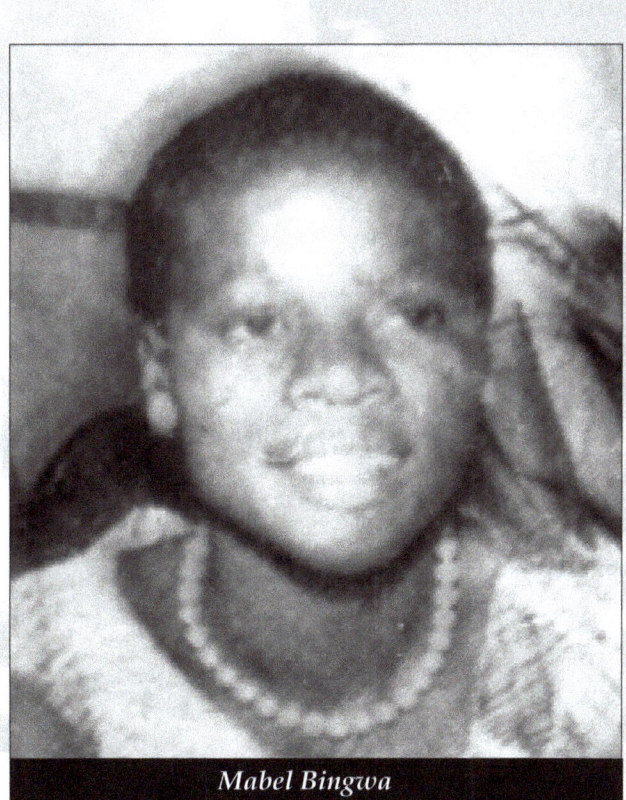

Mabel Bingwa

City she drew large audiences to herself. She jived and mimicked the sorrows of the

zimbabwe township music

Sylvia Sondo

"There is a moment, brief though it may be, in the history of Jazz - O- African

Sylvia Sondo

Townships when women led the men. We can fix this period somewhere during 1954 to 1955. There was a memorable occasion when Vic Chingate's Gay Gaeties jointly staged a concert with another All - Female troupe Sylvia Sondo's "Yellow Blues." It all happened at the Runyararo Hall. Young women leapt and wriggled in fantastic dance-styles.

The Yellow Blues, although short-lived, owe their existence to the untiring energy of Mrs Sylvia Sondo, wife of showman Sonny Sondo." (11 January 1958).

Flora "Zonk-Girl" Dick

".....Flora was not just a simple jazz woman, but a singer of rare merit. In her mezzo-soprano voice she provided the then Rhodesia with some of the best ever recorded pieces. Listeners of the African Service of the Federal Broadcasting Corporation ranked Flora's "Sesse-ture" highly as it capture the minds of many Zimbabweans.

...When she invaded Malawi (Nyasaland) in 1954, so enthusiastically was she received that the audience still have a vivid impression of the dark Mashona jazz beauty.

...Flora is to be remembered as an audacious woman who influenced the course of jazz." (22, February 1958).

Flora Dick

Tabeth Kapuya

"She was smallish at the time, but swift and sure-footed; the self voice characterised Tabitha Kapuya. Wherever she sang audiences would quickly recognise her unique talent. She crooned and jived to the joys and sorrows of her people.

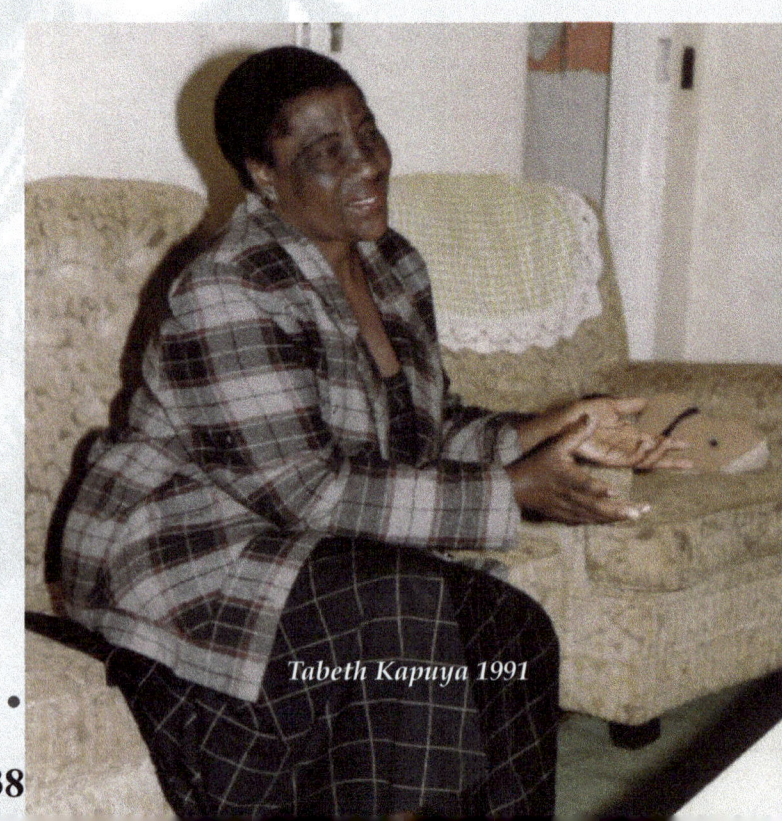
Tabeth Kapuya 1991

Tabitha was born and bred up in Harare. She went to the same school as Faith "Shot Gun Boogie" Dauti. Together they witnessed the emergence of township jazz. Flora was popularly known as "Zonk Girl". Up to the time of her joining Vic Chingate's Gay Gaeties, her talent, as a singer had never been known to anyone, except to herself and close friends." (22 March 1958)

●

Florence Modikwane

"Florence Modikwane was perhaps the most "diminutive" artist ever to tramp the African Musical Hi-way. A daughter of the Rev. Modikwane of the African Methodist Episcopal Church, Florence was born in the Golden City (Johannesburg).

In 1955, Florence, better known to her friends as "Tiny", settled in Harare (Salisbury), where her pastor-father had been transferred. Her fame as a musician and tap-dancer had preceded her arrival in the Federal capital. Florence's overall contribution on the stage was marginal, yet she took a bold stand. Like the other women before her, she knew the risk she was undertaking as a staging artist, being daughter of a pastor. For even as late as the middle fifties, there still prevailed a dominant conception to look down on women who took part in stage performances." (15 February 1958).

Christine Dube

"**Christine Dube** made her debut into show business in 1956, when she signed with the Milton Brothers.

Her lithe and shy figure, when posing on the stage, resembled a ballet dancer in the "Swan Lake". Many a fan clamoured for more of her rich romantic voice.

Christine, on the whole, had an endearing and gentle personality."
(5 April 1958).

●

Joyce Ndoro

"Joyce made her mark with the De Black Evening Follies, as she oftem serenaded with Jonathan Chieza. She was an active participant in furthering the cause of Townhship Music, and jazz in particular.

Another aspect of Joyce's life, was her glamour and alluring appearance on stage. No wonder, hundreds of Harare concert fans hailed her when she was crowned "Miss Harare 1955." (1 March 1958).

Christine Dube and Joyce Ndoro

zimbabwe township music

Faith "Shot Gun Boogie" Dauti

"From the dark confines of Harare Township, at the onset of Zimbabwean jazz, emerged a young girl, who claimed her place amongst the already well-known cluster of musical dames. She was short, shy and stage- wise vivacious.

Faith "Shot Gun Boogie" Dauti, received glittering commendations for her clear singing voice, from her teachers while at the Salisbury African School West (now Chitsere), Her deep and sophisticated mezzo-soprano vocals had made lovers curdle into each other's arms.

With the Milton Brothers, Faith was immediately crowned "Queen of the Blues", as fans were overwhelmingly calling her the Shot-Gun Boogie." (15, March 1958)

Evelyn Juba

"Concert-goers of the early 1936 would focus on the name; Evelyn Juba. Eve, as fans in showbiz knew her, held sway in musical showbiz until 1952,. long after the advent of the old jazz era. She soon retired from active stage work to give more attention to her growing family, having been active for more than 16 years. Such an achievement is her singular

Evelyn Juba

honour and memorable contribution..

Evelyn Juba made her debut in Bulawayo during 1936, at the newly built Stanely Hall with the Merry Makers." (8 March 1958).

Grace James

"Scores of African women have tramped the Rhodesian stage over the past ten years. Some played a prominent role for years, that their names will ever be remembered. Others too, in a small way, would never be overlooked. These could be classified as small time singers; such is a characterization of great stars who had a humble beginning. In this category we place Miss Grace James of the Show Down Quakers.

Over the past few months Grace has been rising high up the ladder in showbiz. Critics and concert fans have noticed in her a tremendous wealth of undeveloped talent. I was startled when I attended one of her recent concerts in Highfield. So well did she sing; her jazz style was so fine that it was all like a dream. When I heard her present "Farayi Mose", my blood warmed up. She sang it with the ease and accomplished poise of a master. Her clear soprano voice rang like a skylark on a warm summer morning.

Yes to this day Grace, together with several other African women have helped to set the Ball of Jazz Rolling in the African Townships." (19 April 1958)

Dorothy Masuka

"**Dorothy Masuka** played a onerous and outstanding role in the evolution and development of Zimbabwe Township Music.

Dorothy Masuka

Today,"Dotty" as a star of Showbiz, has risen to the top of artistic excellence. She is the foremost recording star and acclaimed Jazz Woman in Southern Africa. Dorothy Masuka, the girl who grew up in the township, is one of the unique women Who Set The Ball of Jazz Rolling." (15 March 1958).

Rennie Jones

"Fifteen years ago, as Miss Rennie Jones, the bright young singer and star of the stage, Mrs. Nyamundanda made a terrific debut in Salisbury's Harare African Township. That was her first appearance on the stage. She was singing with a young group which had just been started by leader and singer Fancy Mpahlo. It is Fancy and Rennie who made that wonderful two-some. Together they tapped, danced and crooned the music of the African setting. They mixed ancient with old, and sang in the mines, schools as well as in towns. Whenever they sang they were hailed by packed houses. She *was* thus the first woman to sing with the Follies.

During those two eventful years she sang with the Follies she won for herself the title of Harare's most popular female stage artist. But ....., how shortlived her glory was!

...so much did she do during those two crowning years that now, many years after she is gone posterity still remembers her as one of the few bold women who paved the way for the African woman on stage. But how far those days seem to be from the present Jazz Era? Yes they were all heralding the coming of JAZZ-O-AFRICAN TOWNSHIPS." (8 February 1958).

Miriam Yafele

Margaret Pazarangu

Margaret Pazarangu

Margaret was discovered as an able vocalist by the De Black Evening Follies, as they went around on their talent search in the township. She then proceeded to join the African Melodians, which also included Flora Dick. Margaret was popular for her song: "Handidi kuenda kuTanganyika" With the African Melodians she recorded "Ekhaya Baya Ngibisa". Margaret started singing in 1945 when she was aged seven. Her musical career ended in 1955. (interviewed by author).

Miriam Yafele

Although she did not stay for a long time in stage shows, Miriam Yafele made her mark in Township Music. She teamed up with a group Mubvumbi Brothers who she stayed with for two years, with her husband as band leader. Subsequently she stopped singing township music, for the church choir. (interviewed by author).

zimbabwe township music

TOWNSHIP MUSIC/JAZZ: A GREAT REVIVAL

TOWNSHIP MUSIC/JAZZ: A GREAT REVIVAL

The Jazz Survivors Band: L to R: Jonah Marumahoko, Virgilio Mutare, Jethro Shasha, Cookie Tutani and Christopher Chabuka.

Zimbabwe Township Music/Jazz has emerged from survival to revival in a musically turbulent environment, despite a brief respite in the colonial era. Its reappearance then did not appeal to the younger generation, as is the case today. Musicians/supporters and promoters who witnessed the peak of Township Music in the 50's have now been at the forefront of reviving the tradition.

Conveying the beauty, potential and richness of township jazz, the survivors persisted even when some other types of music were dominating the stage. Township Music has gone through different phases, with the mid 80's, characterised by a cliché which was mostly around during the 30's-60's, as well as teenagers whose parentage witnessed those hectic melodic times.

In the 90's a new breed of young Township Music followers came onto the scene, initially as fans, and later they were flying the flag of the unique musical experience. Today the young jazz survivors are extremely motivated and raring to go; to inform the world of the untold story of Zimbabwe's rich heritage. Jazz world is symbolic with interacting experiences; as Jazz Festivals also created continued interest in Township Music in the country. It is interesting to observe how the continuity of past music blends into contemporary structural forms.

Township music revisionists include Dorothy Masuka, who is currently a force to reckon with in South Africa, where she still performs jazz.

Basil Kumpeu (left)

Elisha Josamu

plays guitar for Musik Ye Africa (Axemen), which also included the late Jethro Shasha and James Indi. Louis' musical career started in the 70's; he lived briefly in London, where he played with Zimbabwe's Fred Zindi. In the 80's Louis was with Southern Freeway, with late brother Willie (drums) and popular jazz artist Steve Dyer.

Drummer Jethro Shasha was popular in the 70's, when he was part of Movement and Tutenkhamen. In the 80s he toured with Caiphus Semenya and Letta Mbulu in the musical BUWA, which was a success in itself. He rearranged the song; Alois naJane, a mixture of Rhumba and jazz. In South Africa, Muzik Ye Afrika played alongside Ray Phiri and Hugh Masekela. At Sun City they featured at the Afro Jazz Orchestra Band festival in 1995. James Indi, another member of the group, is a brilliant bass guitarist of the 80's who composed and recorded "*Ndoenda*".

Andrew Chakanyuka, a one –time member of the Broadway Quartet in the sixties and guitarist – composer, was one of the jazz survivors. In the sixties he was in Zambia with the Broadway Quartet, before he left for

She often teams up with old colleagues; Miriam Makeba, Letta Mbulu and Dolly Rathebe. Other artists in the survival process are; the late Jethro Shasha who was top drummer, Andrew Chakanyuka an ace guitarist - composer, Eric Juba, the Cool Crooners baritone, and parents Evelyn and Simon, who pioneered township music in Bulawayo. Basil Kumpeu, will be remembered for his solo trumpet sounds of the 70's, especially when he played the "*Skokiaan*" tune.

Louis Mhlanga's musical artistry mainly arose from family influence, of aunt Sara Mabhokela, an able jazz singer. Now based in South Africa, he

Checks Tavengwa

Terrence Mapurisana with South Africa's Jazz maestro Jimmy Dludlu.

Ethiopia and Switzerland, where he played with a variety of bands. When he returned home at independence, he was linked to different groups of which the latest was Mhepo. At the time of his death, Andrew was a guitar tutor at the Zimbabwe College of Music.

During the 70's Elisha Josamu appeared on the Township Music scene. He played with the Tutenkhamen Band, with the late Johnny Papas, another Township Jazz survivor. Elisha later played with Two – Plus- Two, alongside Checks Tavengwa, former Tutenkamen player. Josamu banded with the Harare Mambos in the 60s. A brilliant musical career was cut short when he died suddenly in 2001.

The Harare Mambos of the 60's, led by Green Jangano was a jazz outfit, which also trained some of today's finest musicians.

In Bulawayo Paul Lunga formed Jazz Impacto which had Jacob Ncube, with a history of the 50's bands, including the Kenneth Mattaka Talent group. The late Bezel Kumpeu featured as a jazz survivor of the 80's-90's, although he performed from the 70s.

A number of jazz artists who revived Township Music are Cookie Tutani, Chris Chabuka, Checks Tavengwa, Elisha Josamu, Jonah Marumahoko, Ernest Tanga wekwa Sando, Clancy Mbirimi, Virginia Sillah, Paul Sillah, Friday Mbirimi {Mbare Trio}, Moses Kabubi, Bonface Takadiyi, Jonah Mutumha, Sam Mataure, Bob Nyabinde, Paul Brickhill, Chris Kuruneri, Gibson Mandishona, James Indi, Austin Zvoma, Biddy Patridge, Pablo Nakapa, Blessing Muparutsa, the late Sanchez Allen, Jimmy Buzuzi, and Filbert Marowa.

Contemporary jazz craze has produced diverse musicians such as Summer Breeze, Jabavu Drive, Africa Revenge, Colour Blu, Too Open, Duduzile Manhenga, Patience Musa, Prudence Katomeni-Mbofana, Jazz Invitation, Prince Edward Jazz Band, Harare Drive, Churchill School Jazz Band, Dumi and Amagents, Overdrive; we can go on and on.

The Cool Crooners, a group of the 50's, have made waves on the musical scene, locally and abroad. They are Ben Gumbo (Pula-Pulani), Lucky Todlana, Abel Sithole and Eric Juba.

Media broadcasters have also facilitated the perpetuation of Township Music; Ishmael Kadungure pioneered a jazz programme on popular radio; Hilton Mambo through radio and performing, Comfort Mbofana was a joy to listen to on Sunday mornings, as he played selections of township Jazz.

The print media played a vital role in reviving and creating interest in Township Music. Terrence Mapurisana is one such scribe, who has his Jazz Column in the Sunday Mail, which has generated zeal and interest among lovers of Township Music. Through attendance of the Jazz Festivals

Prince Edward Jazz Band

Tinashe F. Mukarati

Churchill Jazz Band

organised by Simanga, Terrence Mapurisana was inspired to write about Township music. The festivals attracted several fans; audiences and performers of the 70's to the 90's. Terrence, a musical scribe, was able to document this unique experience for popular newspaper readership; which had been neglected by the media in the past. He trailed Township Jazz from the dull days to the present hectic times. He also assisted in the organisation of the National Jazz Festivals in 1996, with Sam Mataure, Penny Yon, Gibson Mandishona (Patron), and Rowland Nindi, to mention a few. At a later stage he facilitated at the Jazz Revival Rock Blues Show, where Chris Kuruneri, Austin Zvoma, and other artists performed.

Performance venues played an equally contributory role in promoting Township Music, with their numbers increasing since 1980. To date some of the popular jazz spots have folded down or are poorly patronised. In the 80's there was the Manhattan, annexed to the Crowne Plaza Monomotapa Hotel in the city center. Other popular jazz spots of the mid-80's were The George Hotel in Harare's Avondale suburb, Skyline Motel, Oasis Hotel, Job's Nite Spot; and The Alabama and Basement at the Bulawayo Sun Hotel.

From the 90's to the current period, there has been a mushrooming of Township/Jazz venues; Ikon, Jazz 105, Red Fox Hotel, Smokeys, Mannenberg, Sports (Thamies) Diner and The Book Café.

Donors and corporate establishments have had a pivotal role in the promotion of Township Music; for through their support successful festivals and concerts were realised. The African Banking Corporation has supported the Zimbabwe International Jazz Festival; BAT funded other festivals; Interfin put up the National Hunger (Jazz) Concert in 2002. Other sponsors are African Distillers and Rex Kabwato (Universal Jazz Label), who supported the Veteran Jazz Artists at the Sports Diner. **Oliver Hawadi's** company, Sparks Distributors, has supported jazz shows. He feels "obliged to support the movement," as he grew up in Mbare, where it all started. Mention must also be made of: Peter Chikwanha, Ray Mawerera, Moonrise (Francis Hamadziripi) The British Council, IGI Insurance (Minos Mudukuti), Alliance Francais, Zimbabwe Music Corporation, Gramma and RTP.

THE COOL CROONERS

The Cool Crooners are a

Oliver Hawadi

The Cool Crooners

L to R: Ben "Pulapulani" Gumbo, Eric Juba, Abel Sithole, Lucky Thodlana

Township Music group with musical careers that go back to the 50's. Despite age, their dancing styles/ choreography and creativity are both inspirational and compelling. They want to be different, yet outstanding and popular even among the youthful audience. They have staged on the international scene where they left audiences wishing for more. Their vocal harmony is as good as it was fifty years ago. The Crooners have produced a classic album *Blue Sky*, a jazz masterpiece with such numbers as: "*Ibhulugwe Lami lilezigamba*" and "*UmaDhlamini.*"

The singing quartet is an amalgamation of two Bulawayo-based musical groups of the 50's; The Cool Four which excelled in footwork styles, and Golden Rhythm Crooners, who were masters of the vocal sound. Even today, these two attributes of their earlier staging glory are glaringly visible.

Their early inspiration came mainly from the Mills Brothers, Manhattan Brothers, Ink Sports, Woody Woodpeckers, Dolly Rathebe and Miriam Makeba. The two groups were an audience-puller during the 50's, as entrance fees went up when they performed. They sang and danced, from a fusion of Mbaqanga and Township Jazz.

By coming together, the two former groups integrated and fine -tuned their talents. They are: Ben "Phula Phulani" Gumbo(72), Lucky Thodlana(65), Abel Sithole (67) and young Eric Juba(52). Eric's unique baritone adds to the vocal mastery of the quartet. Timothy Selani (formerly of Crooners) has replaced Ben Gumbo, who recently died. Abel was the man behind the integration of the two singing groups. Like other nationalists of the sixties, he joined the liberation struggle, was initially sentenced to death, and later to 18 years imprisonment by the colonial regime. He gained his freedom

The Cool Crooners

in 1980, at Zimbabwe's independence. The song, Blue Sky, pays tribute to Abel's long incarceration in prison. "Blue Sky" was at one time a notorious high security South African prison, where inmates could only gaze at the "blue sky" above, as a symbol of cherished freedom.

The Crooners have performed abroad at The Montreal Jazz Festival, New York's Central Park, San Sebastian (Spain), Cannes (France) and Palco Festival (Nyon, Switzerland).

The song Baleka Mfana (Runaway Boy), signifies running or escaping from a hell-like prison. A visiting filmmaker, Patrick Meunier, did not regret abandoning an original plan to shoot a film on Zimbabwe for the challenging option to produce a forty-minute documentary of The Cool Crooners. Zimbabwean film maker, Jackie Cahi, is also the promoter of the singing group. The Cool Crooners are a glowing example of how past concert styles can blend into contemporary music.

A recent press statement had this to say of the ageing quartet: "It's clear that the Cool Crooners are happy about their new-found popularity. Their record, Blue Sky, is their pride and joy as well as the ambassador of a long overdue and well-deserved recognition".

instilling discipline in musicians, and allowing them to play a wide spectrum of music. Township Music/Jazz dominated their programme. When most township groups had folded up in the 60's, he carried on with the township music trend up to 1999, when

family sang before bed-time, Green's love for music grew.

Before embarking on music, he worked as lorry driver in Gweru, after which he left for Zambia where he was a mine driver. He was able to buy a truck, that he used for casual

The Harare Mambos Band with Green Jangano

Harare Mambos Band

The Harare Mambos made its mark in the music circuits of the 50's-90's; being the longest surviving and most consistent musical group. They also served as a training ground for many latter musicians; Tanga wekwa Sando, William Kashiri, Paul Sillah, Virginia Sillah, Clancy Mbirimi, Chris Chabuka, Newman Chipeni and Elisha Josamu. Greenford Jangano who started the band in 1957, was known for

the outfit finally disbanded. Green, as a professional musician, realised that serious showbiz should be approached not just as mere entertainment, but a business-like venture.

Green Jangano fell in love with music at a tender age, at The United Methodist, where his father was a reverend. He would volunteer to clean the church, to give him time to learn the piano. His destiny was since shaped with the piano as his favourite instrument. He was then ready to take on music as a full-time career. Each time the

business. With the proceeds, he bought a set of musical instruments, which he hired out to bands. When the famous Afro Cubans performed in the country, they hired his equipment. In the 50's he teamed up with a friend, the late William Chigoma and recorded "Sarura Wako Kadeyadeya", produced by West Nkosi who named the two musicians - Harare Mambos. They later signed a contract with British American Tobacco (BAT), after which they changed their name to Players Gold Leaf. Soon they reverted to the old name Harare Mambos.

zimbabwe township music

In 1965 Green lined up other musicians; Elisha Josamu, Mike Joseph, Jimmy Chavanga and William Kashiri, who later stayed with the group for a long time. The Mambos became famous and were contracted by big hotels in Harare. They also played at weddings, beerhalls and exclusive night clubs.

Virginia Silla Jangano

The group performed at Federal Hotel, Mutanga Night Club, Machipisa Beer Garden, Elizabeth Hotel, Las Vegas (Bulawayo), Beatrice Cottages Bar, Club Tomorrow, Stones Bar, Castle Hotel, The Ardbennie and Monomotapa Hotel. They later moved to the Victoria Falls Elephant Hotel.

In the 70's the group recorded the 50's hit Ndafunafuna, which topped the charts. They also recorded Tamba Suzana. Their 80's favourite recordings were: Mbuya Nehanda, Iwe Neni Tine Basa, Buhera and Kudendere.

As chairman of the Union of Musicians, Green lobbyed relevant ministries to make music instruments, easily available to artists. "Music is not a luxury, it is a priority," he reaffirmed. Government has of late, made it possible for musicians to import instruments duty-free.

William Kashiri, stayed with the group for a long time before it disbanded, having joined it in 1956. Like youngsters of his time, he trained with Kenneth Mattaka's group before moving to the De Black Evening Follies.
With the group Kashiri composed, "Josephine", "Nhasi Ndezveduwo", "Siya Waitanda". William is now with Mbare Trio, a singing group that also includes Friday Mbirimi.

Another musician who outlasted with the Mambos was **Clancy Mbirimi,** bassist, who started off with the junior Harare Mambos. His interest in music was realised at 19, when he played with the Groovey Union Band, a youthful troupe of the 70's. Some of his compositions include: "Rufaro MuZimbabwe" and "Buhera". Clancy plays for the group Detema, and is a producer with Metro Studios. He has produced Bob Nyabinde's first album, "Pane Nyaya," which is going rounds on the musical scene.

Virginia Sillah was a senior vocalist of the Mambos, and the only female member. The Mambos performed Township Music for four decades.

VIRGINIA SILLAH JANGANO

Virginia Sillah -Jangano, or sisi Vee, or the Queen, hammered Township Music since the 1960's. Born in Bulawayo, she followed the footsteps of Lina Mattaka, Evelyn Juba, Faith Dauti and Dorothy Masuka. Her father, David Sillah, was a jazz singer/pianist, attributes which Virginia so affectionately emulated.

Virginia Sillah

Additional encouragement came from aunt Ethel Jaya, who looked after Virginia as an orphan girl. Ethel was herself blind, who taught Braille at the Jairos Jiri Centre.

In the 70's, when Township Music was temporarily on low-key, Virginia kept the revival pace of the 80's, being in the forefront.

She left school in 1965, where she had been involved in music, and opted for "pop and the blues," thereafter.

She sang with the Jairos Jiri's "Sunrise Kwela Kings Band" in 1966, for a year, after which she was with The Keynotes Revellers, a junior band of the Kings. In 1969, she converged to Harare, and signed up with the OK Success. Green Jangano immediately spotted her, and in 1972 she was with the Harare Mambos. Other members of the group were: Paul Sillah (Virginia's cousin) on lead guitar, Clancy Mbirimi, on bass, Basil Kumpeu, on saxophone and Daramu Kalanga, on trumpet. The group was at the time the Rhodesia top "African" Band. A few years down the line Virginia married Green, and together they were with the outfit for 25 years.

In the 70's with the Mambos, Virginia recorded *"Ndafunafuna"*, a tune originated by the City Quads, she later sang "Mbuya Nehanda", which became the Mambo's trade mark. Sillah and the group had rearranged the tune, which derived from a traditional lyric sung during the liberation struggle. Her velvet voice contributed to the exuberance of this high-spirited ballad. With the same zeal she later recorded and popularised "Amainini Handeyi Kumusha".

Now retired from active performance, Virginia brightened the musical arena in difficult times, as role model and champion of the Township Music revival.

FANYANA DUBE

Fanyana Dube was a brilliant saxophonist who saw it all in music. Although blind, he has performed to ecstatic audiences as if he had no visual impairement. Township Music was not separated from his life as he grew up listening to his father play Amarabi, Kwela and Omasiganda tunes. His father was quite involved in music that the family named the sister Marabi. He grew up during the grand era of Josaya Hadebe, George Sibanda, Jacob Mhungu, Edward Khanda, and Sabelo Mathe, who were his father's colleagues. When Fanyana was 12 years old in 1958, he formed Sunrise Kwela Kings with a group of friends. They were a prolific group during the 50's-70's. In 1969 the Kwela Kings toured Mozambique.

In 1974 Fanyana moved to Vic Falls and joined Combination (Submarine) for a year. He went back to Bulawayo where he played with the Cantos Quartet led by Never Nevado Ndlovu (of the 50's Cool Four).

He was on the move again with brief stints in Gweru and Triangle. In 1978 he was

The late Fanyana Dube (left) and Summer Breeze

zimbabwe township music

performing with The Elbow, led by Bheki Khumalo. The group played at the Federal Hotel, a social focal point of the 70's. When they disbanded Fanyana formed Jobs Combination which hightened his popularity. He made compositions which were popularised by Lovemore Majaivana. The Jobs Combination climaxed in the mid 80's attracting spectacular audiences. When Lovemore Majaivana left the group Fanyana performed as vocalist, guitarist and saxophonist. He recorded the hits "Ngidhingi Imali", "Isimamnga", "Inyama Yembongolo" and many others.

Always on the move, Fanyana was with Champ at the Federal Hotel. In 1989 he travelled to Canada to perform alongside other disabled musicians. It was a great moment for him, as he met several and diverse artists. He bought himself a house from the proceeds of the trip. Back home, he teamed with Andrew Chakanyuka (a guitarist of note), and Tony Makwavarara at the Southerton Night Club. He then moved to Dete and paired up with a renowned musician of the 80's, Solomon Sikhuza. In 1992 he settled in Mutare where he performed in a hotel. Fanyana decided to make Mutare his home. He occasionally visited Harare to perform at Jazz Festivals, where he was popular with fans.

Fanyana fought odds to stay in the music business. "Blindness is not a disability, I can do anything, it's only my eyes which cannot see," he once remarked somberly. Sadly Fanyana is no more.

PAUL LUNGA

Paul Lunga is a contemporary jazz survivor who grew up in Bulawayo's Makokoba

Paul Lunga

township, the cradle of good music in the 50's. He saw it all in this sprawling and exciting township. Paul attended the so-called tea parties, as well as the concert shows. He became familiar with George Sibanda, Josaya Hadebe and Sabelo Mathe, the solo musicians then known as "Omasiganda". They would play guitar music past Paul's residence, and as a young man, he would throw coins to them. Paul was lucky to watch August Musarurwa perform, and admired how the maestro musician handled the saxophone. Musarurwa, the composer of "Skokiaan" was a great inspiration to Paul Lunga, who later recorded his own version of the tune in 1991; forty years after Musarurwa's original recording.

Currently Zimbabwe Township Music is re-emerging and being revived by the likes of Paul Lunga and other contemporaries. It had died down during The Unilateral Declaration of Independence, when the State of Emergency was declared by the Smith regime, and people were forbidden to be seen in large groupings.

Lunga showed his talent early at school, where he first tasted musical instruments. The instruments at school were few and restrictive; he would then visit the Boys' Club, which had a larger variety of instruments. He started off by playing the guitar, then piano. Later he became interested in the trumpet because the Boy's Club had an abundance of under-utilised trumpets. Furthermore, the trumpet proved to be a difficult instrument to most young people, and Paul took the challenge. Drum-playing did not inspire him.

Whilst at Mzingwane School, Paul performed student gigs with a friend Clifford Mataya. Later, he joined a band "Pirate of the High Seas", which performed in public halls, such as the Macdonald and Stanley Hall. In his search for challenges, Paul formed the Jazz Merchants with Henry Thodlana and Isen Phiri; after which he banded with Lucky Thodlana and the late Never Nevada Ndlovu (former Cool Four). They established the Jazz and Pop Band, later known as Jazz Impacto. Paul still plays with Jazz Impacto, although over a period of time the band has often been manned by different players. Despite being a renowned trumpet/flugelhorn player, Paul believes in intensive rehearsing for his shows, which are a mixture of Amarabi and Afro-Jazz.

Jazz Impacto recorded a long playing record entitled "Zimbabwe Jive" in 1991. The title track is by Jacob Ncube {former African Talent Band/ Kenneth Mattaka}, with Davis Munemo on drums, Richard Mutendevure on bass guitar, and Eric Juba on percussion. Eric later formed his own group; Jacaranda. He is the son of Evelyn and Simon Juba, the pioneers of township music in Bulawayo, and currently sings with the Cool Crooners.

Lunga was present and played at the welcome party of Louis Armstrong, at Thabiso Boys' Club, when the famous trumpeter visited Bulawayo in 1961. Louis impacted upon Paul an even greater musical inspiration for the trumpet.

Paul believes that the Boys' Clubs played a crucial socio-economic role in early township history. They provided supplementary feeding facilities and recreation; kept kids off the streets, besides scouting for arts talent, in particular music. Popular musicians: Simangaliso Tutani, Chris Chabuka and Jonah Marumahoko, are an offspring of the Boys' Clubs. As Paul relates sorrowfully, the disappearance of the Clubs has contributed to the increase, in juvenile crime and delinquency as well as the attendant mushrooming of urban street kids.

Paul was a train driver for more than 25 years; but found joy and solace in playing music during his spare time. Currently he is full-time in the vocation he loves most: Afro-jazz. He plans to spend time producing and recording popular township music.

FRIDAY MBIRIMI/ MBARE TRIO

Friday Mbirimi enjoys his singing and when on stage, he dwells whole-heartedly on Township Music. Music has been at the center of his life, and

The Mbare Trio: Friday, Lovejoy Mbirimi, and William Kashiri

zimbabwe township music

in the early days he nearly abandoned school to pursue a musical career. He quickly learnt how to pursue both, music and school in a complementary manner. "If I can remember anything, I remember being a musician, and I think I am just naturally a musician."

Growing up in Mbare exposed Friday to a hectic musical environment. He was educated in Harare, Goromonzi Secondary School and at the University of Zimbabwe, where he read for an honours degree in English. He recently worked as Senior Registrar Officer at the same university, before currently taking upon the full-time post of Registrar at the Zimbabwe College of Music.

Born in 1943 on a Friday, he got his befitting name from a social welfare officer of Mbare, Edith Operman.

It is befitting that he named his vocal group Mbare Trio, to honour the township which groomed and nurtured his musical artistry. The trio consists of; William Kashiri, Friday and Lovejoy Mbirimi.

Friday remembers friends at Mai Musodzi Boys' Club, who influenced his musical appreciation: Danny Bakasa, William Chigoma, Chris Chabuka and Simanga Tutani. He treated the latter as big brother who taught him a variety of topics in the musical field. Some members of the De Black Evening Follies worked with his father, who was also a singer. An uncle, Jonah Mbirimi, played saxophone for the police band and often backed the Follies group.

Friday's first group was Shelton Brothers, which imitated black American musicians; Joelson Brothers, Louis Armstrong, South African groups, including some Zimbabwean popular artists at the time.

Mbirimi was good at imitating, as he could sing in different roles. He later joined Capital City Dixies, then led by a white man, Eric Williamson. They were fifteen in number, and often sang and danced to large audiences.

The Dixies included Chris Chabuka, William Kashiri and Sam Shonhiwa. Friday later featured with the Presley Kids, which was made up of Misheck (Doctor), Clement Gatsi, and Mabel Pindurayi.

Friday Mbirimi

He remembers Mabel well, a serious musician who tragically died in a car accident. He later performed with the Crazy Kids, which was a junior counterpart of The City Quads. They sang at the Stodard Hall's opening inauguration, including fundraising for the Zimbabwe African People's Union (ZAPU). Friday featured with almost all local eminent artists, including Dorothy Masuka, at the Rainbow Theatre. When Louis Armstrong visited Zimbabwe in 1961, he was in the welcoming party with the Capital City Dixies. It was a momentous event for Friday, as he recalls shaking hands with the great trumpeter. Later, they attended Louis' show at the Glammis Stadium, where Friday was part of the exclusive audience. He remembers too the Cliff Richard/Shadows concert, which attracted mostly young people, in contrast to the Armstrong show, which brought crowds of people of all ages, sexes, creeds and colour.

Whilst at school, Friday jammed with the Broadway Quartet, and would often appear on local TV. His father encouraged him, otherwise to concentrate more on school work, and not on music.

At Goromonzi Secondary School, he belonged to a staging group. During his University of Zimbabwe days, he regularly performed with the Harare Mambos, which was then based at the Art Gallery – in the basement. The Director then was McEwen. Simanga Tutani played bass, Jonah Marimahoko (guitar), and Green Jangano (keyboards). The same group would also perform at Machipisa Night Club in Highfields.

After graduating from University, Friday went to teach at Mazowe Secondary School in 1970. He became a regular entertainer at Mazowe Hotel. Rock had climaxed into popularity in those days, but Friday persistently stuck to his Township Music/jazz. During his tenure as Chairman of the Zimbabwe Union of Musicians, parliament passed the minimum wage bill for musicians.

Friday Mbirimi has contributed tremendously to Township Music, as entertainer, singer and drummer.

BASIL KUMPEU

Basil Kumpeu carried on with Township Music during the 70's, when most local musicians had gone into exile, and there was almost a vacuum on the township scene. In his shows he often featured "Skokiaan", Hugh Masekela's version, of the tune originally composed by August Musarurwa in 1950. It was through musicians such as Basil Kumpeu, that the seventies' generation, which was hit by rock and soul, got

Bezel Kumpeu in 1970's

the feel of Township Music. Basil's trumpet-blowing moreso thrilled the rocky teenagers. He excelled on saxophone and trumpet playing. Although the groups that he played with fancied soul music, he was never the less focusing on township jazz.

Basil took up after his father who played jazz music with the African Writers' group, especially Mura Nyaruka, an early township musician. He was also a product of Father Davis, a one-time principal of St Paul's Mission, who was well known for music and football promotion. Initially in 1966, Basil played with the St. Paul's Blues Band, which comprised of Peter Tamburai, Sylvester Gano and Christopher Matanhire. Later on, the veteran guitarist Timothy Makaya, now with Jabavu Drive, joined the band; as well as composer of the time, Arthur Chipunza, of "Mvura Ngainaye" and "Gona raMachingura" fame. The band thus became highly in demand and moved to Harare. Later musicians were Fanuel Chikukwa, Francis Chakanyuka, and Matthew Chinhoyi. In Harare they played at the Mbare Vito Tavern. Eventually they grew bigger, acquiring more instruments in the form of horns, guitars and drums. Soon they were contracted to play at the Federal Hotel. Subsequently Basil was offered a contract to play at Club Flamingo in Blantyre, Malawi. Upon his return to Zimbabwe, he played at Marisha with the St. Pauls Blues Band, before moving to Happy Valley Hotel in Bulawayo, then owned by Jerry Vera. There he played with Richard Makore (late), Francis Sabeta (late) and Paul Lunga. During 1969-70 Kumpeu was based in Victoria Falls. He got an offer to play in Portugal, with the likes of Henry Peters, Hilton Mambo, Ricky, Timothy and Robert Moore. The tour took him to Switzerland where he met old pal Andrew Chakanyuka, who was temporarily based in that country.

Back home Basil joined the Harare Mambos, led by Green Jangano, where he stayed for five years, (1970-1975). The band became a popular outfit at the city Elizabeth Hotel. Being a roving musician, he left the Mambos to join Soul and Blues, led by Ricky Moore, renowned musician, of the 70's In 1978, Basil was a founding member of Happily, which included Elisha Josamu, Clement Chinyawo, Sam Banana; and later on; Paul Lunga, Bradshaw Muchirahondo and Nelson Mapango. They recorded the famous traditional "Chamutengure", when they were based at the Skyline Motel. On the move once more, Basil was with Happening, joining hands with Thomas Mapfumo in1979.

When Zimbabwe attained independence in 1980, Kumpeu enrolled at the Zimbabwe College of Music to further his expertise, after which, he played in the Army Band for five years. In 1985 he was with the Militia Army Band, up to 1989, before going solo and becoming a session musician. Basil Kumpeu's saxophone featured prominently in Fungai Malianga's "Jesus Saved My Soul". He also participated in the Aids Campaign music, with Virginia Sillah-Jangano, Louis Mhlanga, Jethro Shasha and Kelly Rusike. With Jazz Impacto led by Paul Lunga, he was involved in the recording of "Catch Up", for which he composed two numbers.

Basil died in 1999. He was an ace saxophone/trumpet player, and Township Jazz survivor, who kept jazz aflame in the 70's, despite his apparently high mobility among music groups.

MHEPO/ BIDDY PATRIDGE

Mhepo was formed in the early 80's when Township Music was gradually re-emerging. Early members of the group were Biddy Patridge, (trumpet and keyboards) and husband Nigel Samuels (leader, trumpet and keyboards). The line up included, Stan Zimi (bass), Dave Moyo (drums) and Mike Mokone (guitar); with contributions from - Marcello Maishe, Joe Kgasi, Andrew Chakanyuka, Richie Lopes, Agrippa Kambarami, Penny Yon, Tsitsi Vera and Kenny Marozva. In 1992 they produced a long playing album; entitled Made in Zimbabwe, a first independent production by a local musical group. It had six jazz tracks which include; "Kuraura", "Bata Mahuhu", "Edge City" and "Corner Boys". The group disbanded in 1999.

Biddy moved to London, but returned to launch the album "Mapapiro" in Harare in 2001, with Mhepo. In London she is involved in various music/

Mhepo: L to R: Penny Yan, Ritchie Lopez, Biddy Patridge, Ronny Kambarami, Vaughan French and Nigel Samuels.

educational projects, and promotional work on arts, jazz and photography.

Patridge's musical career had its origins in South Africa, where she grew up. Her upbringing in "white suburbs" as opposed to the 'Townships', did not deter her onward march to musical fulfilment.

Biddy's first understanding of jazz dawned on her when she accompanied her father to a Brotherhood of Breath concert: "I thought, I saw - how it works - all the musicians are in conversation with each other, and the solos are about someone having a lot to say". This was her first taste of Afro-jazz, which was a breath-taking experience.

Listening to Abdullah Ibrahim, Hugh Masekela and Letta Mbulu in the 70's while she was in the UK, further spurred her love for Afro Jazz. When she returned to South Africa in 1980, a playwright Matsemela Manaka lent her a saxophone, until her father donated one. She enrolled at Federated Union of Black Artists, (FUBA) to consolidate her passion for music. Apart from casual gigs, the students participated in practical shows. Their tutors were eminent musicians; Barney Rachabane and brother Martin, vocalists Sophie Mgcina and Sithembiso Khumalo, and guitarist Alan Kwela.

In Zimbabwe she was one of the few to revive Township Music. She witnessed its rebirth and the countrywide craze for Afro-jazz.

In 2002 she was involved with UK-based Zimbabweans and formed a group, Pamwechete, which included Bryan Paul, Paul Lunga, Grant Hannan and Tich Makhalisa. They developed a professional programme of Zimbabwean compositions which featured prominently at the London Africa Centre.

Biddy Patridge's dream is a full Mhepo revival, orchestrating Township Music.

SUMMER BREEZE/ MOSES KABUBI

Moses Bhekilanga Kabubi has seen it all, from township music in the 50's, to "Cha-Cha-Cha-Rhumba", "Simanje Manje", of the 60's, Rock, Afro Pop in the 70's, to Township Music which he still plays. Moses is leader of Summer Breeze, a successful jazz ensemble of veteran musicians. They draw their inspiration from the 50's township music, with varied adaptations.

The group was formed in 1989 in Kariba, with Chris Chabuka at the helm. It is now based in Harare.

Moses Kabubi is a seasoned musician who grew up in a musical family. His aunt Lina Mattaka and mother Judith, were part of the Mattaka Family musicians. He also once played with gifted cousin Eddison Mattaka.

Rute Mbangwa and Summer Breeze

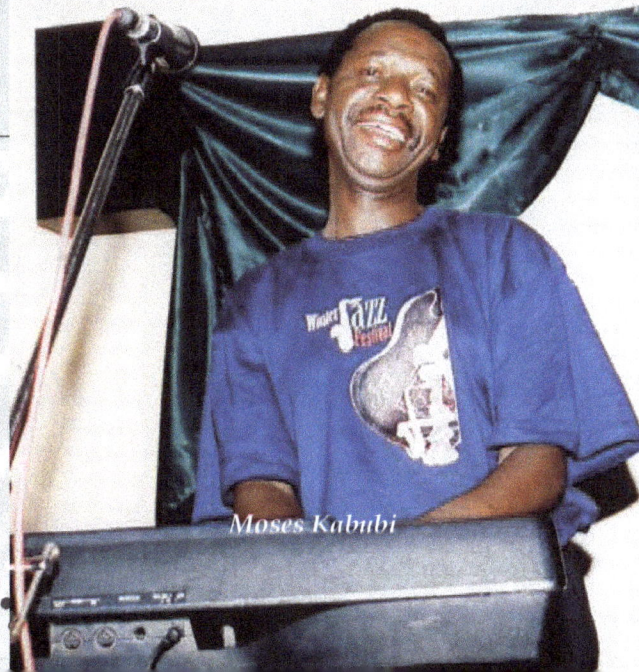

Moses Kabubi

Since 1966 Moses has played with the following groups: Mutanga Band, Springfields led by Thomas Mapfumo, Great Sounds of Eliah Banda and Sound Effects Band. The latter was heavy with rock; the Jimi Hendrix Staff. It consisted of Jethro Shasha, Manu Kambani, Elias Chimwala, Clemency Chinyama and Hilton Mambo. In 1972 Moses grouped with OK Success, then performing at Mushandira Pamwe Hotel. The Pied Pipers replaced the OK's, and incorporated Moses in their midst. Later, he was part of Thomas Mapfumo, at Mushandira Pamwe during 1973-1979.

Moses decided to further his musical expertise at the College of Music for 3 years, where he completed Grade 4 theory. While at the College, he played with the Real Sounds, a Rhumba group from DRC. He had a brief stint with Broadway Quartet, before moving to Lovemore Majaivana, who played a mixture of "Mbanqanga" and Afro-Jazz. The group included Abraham Sithole and Fanyana Dube, who was an articulate Township Musician.

At a time of musical transformations, Moses became more enterprising, teaming up in turn with; Mazana Movement, Summer Breeze, and Real Sounds, once more.

During 1993-2000 he was with Lubumbashi Band, where he helped with their recordings, arrangements and management. He recycled back to Jabavu Drive, and then to Summer Breeze, where he currently leads the ensemle.

Summer Breeze's lineup is as follows: Moses on keyboards; Safeli Sumaili on guitar (Former Harare Mambos and 2D Sounds), Vincent Kapepa on bass (Harare Mambos), Jeff Kumwamba on tenor sax (ex Real Sounds), Malvern Sarutawa on vocals, (former Sisonke of Jonah Mutumha).

The group intends to record some oldies: Kunembaravazi (City Quads), Waterera Zvemakuhwa (Epworth Theatrical Strutters), Nhoro (City Slickers) and many more.

JETHRO SHASHA

The late Jethro Shasha was a celebrated Township Music drummer in the sub-region. He was influenced into the

Jethro Shasha in the mid 70s

musical arena, mostly by The Manhattan brothers, his late brother and father. Jethro's prowess on drums won him accolades and awards at musical festivals, locally and abroad. He loved the drums, as he conceived them to be the basis for musical backing, including dance.

With a musical career dating from the 60's, Jethro's music was influenced by Rhumba, Rock, and Township Jazz; with the latter reigning more on his styles. His tune "*Alois na Jane*", is a reflection of the early influences, a Rhumba - Jazz fusion. Shasha performed with several greats; the likes of Dorothy Masuka, Letta Mbulu, Ray Phiri, Hugh Masekela, and a host of others. He participated in several local and international festivals, drumming his way along, whilst playing his favourite Township Music.

Jethro's musical career began in 1962, with a school band at Mutambara Primary School, near Mutare, where he both sang and played drums. In Masvingo during the school holidays, he met musicians, Maybin Philie, Fred Zindi and Fungai Malianga, who later became the group's business manager. They played at parties, and later in night clubs and hotels, around Harare, Bulawayo, Chiredzi and Triangle. At a contest in Bulawayo (1968), Jethro's group The Four Sounds, came third, with him crowned as the best drummer. Thereafter, they got a contract at the Bulawayo Valley Hotel for a year. In 1969 he played at a Rusape Motel, and later in Harare with The Great Sounds

In 1971 Jethro and friends

Mudzimu: L to R: Ann Ashburn (manager), Brian Paul (Bass), Rick Van Hedeen (saxes), Jonah Marumahoko (guitar), Jethro Shasha (drums & Percussion), Steve Dyer (flute), Louis Mhlanga (guitar).

formed Sound Effects Band, which played Rock Music, having been sponsored by The Machipisa Brothers. They comprised Moses Kabubi, Elisha Chimwala and Manu Kambani. The group played at several venues and recorded such tunes as "Chicago Plane". Manu composed "True my love", and "Nyama Yekugocha", which were recorded by the Shamrock Company.

In 1974 The Sound Effects gave way to the Baked Beans, which had Jethro, Louis Mhlanga and Cookie Tutani. Their popularity took them to Botswana and Mozambique. They recorded "Introduction" and "Poverty". Jethro Shasha soon became a member of the New Tutenkamen, renowned in the seventies, which included Elisha Josamu, Checks Tawengwa, Amanda, Amos Chatyoka and Paul Sekerani. They played jazz and traditional lyrics, and recorded "Tutenkamen Theme", "Sunday Morning", "Togetherness", "True love", "Ane Nungo", "Big brother Malcolm", "Me and Dolly" and the famous "Joburg Bound", among other hits.

Back with Louis Mhlanga, Jethro helped to form Unity, which also included Elton Edwards, Tanga wekwa Sando, Clancy Mbirimi, Barney de Souza and Chris Chabuka.

zimbabwe township music

Jethro Shasha and Derik Huggins

The group recorded "Reminance" in 1977. In 1979 Jethro formed the Movement – which recorded "Chimurenga Funky Movement". They toured Zambia and later settled at Chapels in Bulawayo, during 1980 - 81. Again on the move, he was with Summer Breeze in 1984, and later with Jazz Survivors, whose members were mostly drawn from the Broadway Quartet. They, backed Dorothy Masuka in the recording of "Ningirikiri", during 1986, when they were based at Oasis Hotel in Harare.

Jethro's popularity had spread in the region, as Letta Mbuli invited him on a musical tour BUWA, which toured Paris, Libya, Ethiopia, Ghana, Nigeria, Senegal, Kenya, Zimbabwe and Sweden.

An able musician and administrator, Shasha chaired the Harare chapter of the Zimbabwe Union of Musicians, and was also on the board of the Zimbabwe Music Rights Association. Being an anxious musical scholar, Jethro enrolled at the Zimbabwe College of Music, to study and research on Zimbabwe's indigenous music and its complex inter-linkages.

In the late 90's he moved to South Africa and performed with Musik Ye Africa, with Louis Mhlanga, James Indi and Cookie Tutani; and also featuring alongside Ray Phiri.

Jethro died in South Africa in 2000. He was an gifted composer-drummer, with a passion and zeal for team-work, and the sharing of his love for drums with regional counterparts.

HILTON MAMBO

Hilton Mambo, affectionately known as "Dr. Bobo", has been on the jazz highway for 30 years. He has immensely contributed to the country's

Fungai Malianga, Hilton Mambo and Phillip Svosve

music industry in a variety of ways; as performer, disc jockey, and recording artist/producer.

Hilton was involved in diverse radio programs as a way to promote jazz. Through his shows, Township Music reached a wide audience, often at times when jazz music was constrained for survival. It was sheer pleasure to listen to his selection of music on Radio 3, now 3FM. The programme reflected maturity and grasp of a wide spectrum of jazz; be it local or international, on the part of the presenter.

During Hilton's hectic period, there were also other popular DJ producers; Wellington Mbofana on Radio One, and Ishmael Kadungure promoting jazz on Radio Three.

Hilton Mambo has recorded several artists over the years, since the 70's, with most singles citing him as the producer/engineer.

Mambo joined friends Clancy Mbirimi, David Ndoro and Tony Charles, to form Groovy Union. He later became a session musician with Benny Millers's band, a "white" group which he brought to Mbare to perform, despite segregation laws during of 70's. Later he joined the Soul and Blues Union (SABU), which included, Henry Peters and Mike Lanas. When the band disbanded, he was with BIRTH, an ensemble of 13 artists, which focused on hard rock of the 70's. At the time he was into advertising, working with James Makamba. In 1998 he recorded a single; With You In My Life, which was a hot favourite.

In 2002 Hilton was involved with the National Hunger Jazz Concert, as organiser and performer.

At 52 years of age, the multi-talented jazz-artist is now based in the UK, where he still performs Township Music, with his characteristic husky voice.

FUNGAI MALIANGA

Fungai Malianga

Fungai Malianga's life and love for music cannot be separated. He survived all eras; Kwela, Amarabi, Soul, Rock, Funky and Township Music. His early music was influnced by Lemmy Special, Spokes Mashiyane, City Quads, Louis Armstrong and Jimmy Hendricks. He had a taste of Amarabi, Afro Jazz, Rock and Soul, with a pronounced fusion of Township Music. Malianga's family provided a lot of stimulus; his brothers John and Quinton were well-known musicians, and his father was a reverend and hymnologist of the Methodist Church. Fungai's mother bought the family musical instruments. At the age of 4 Fungai was thus exposed to a variety of instruments; piano, guitars and pennywhistle. Fungai was relatively young when Township Music was at its peak in the 50's. He has, however carried on with the tradition, by recording tunes which were popular in the 50's, in the CD Kwa Mutare Yo!. The CD has hit songs; "KwaMutare" (of Sonny Sondo - De Black Evening Follies) and "Kure Kwatinobva {Makwiro Shamwari}" (of Marshall Brothers). The lyrics have a strong Township jazz flavour, and so is; "Chinzvenga Mutsvairio", which warns, especially men, of the Aids pandemic. Fungai dedicated

Fungai Malianga in 70s

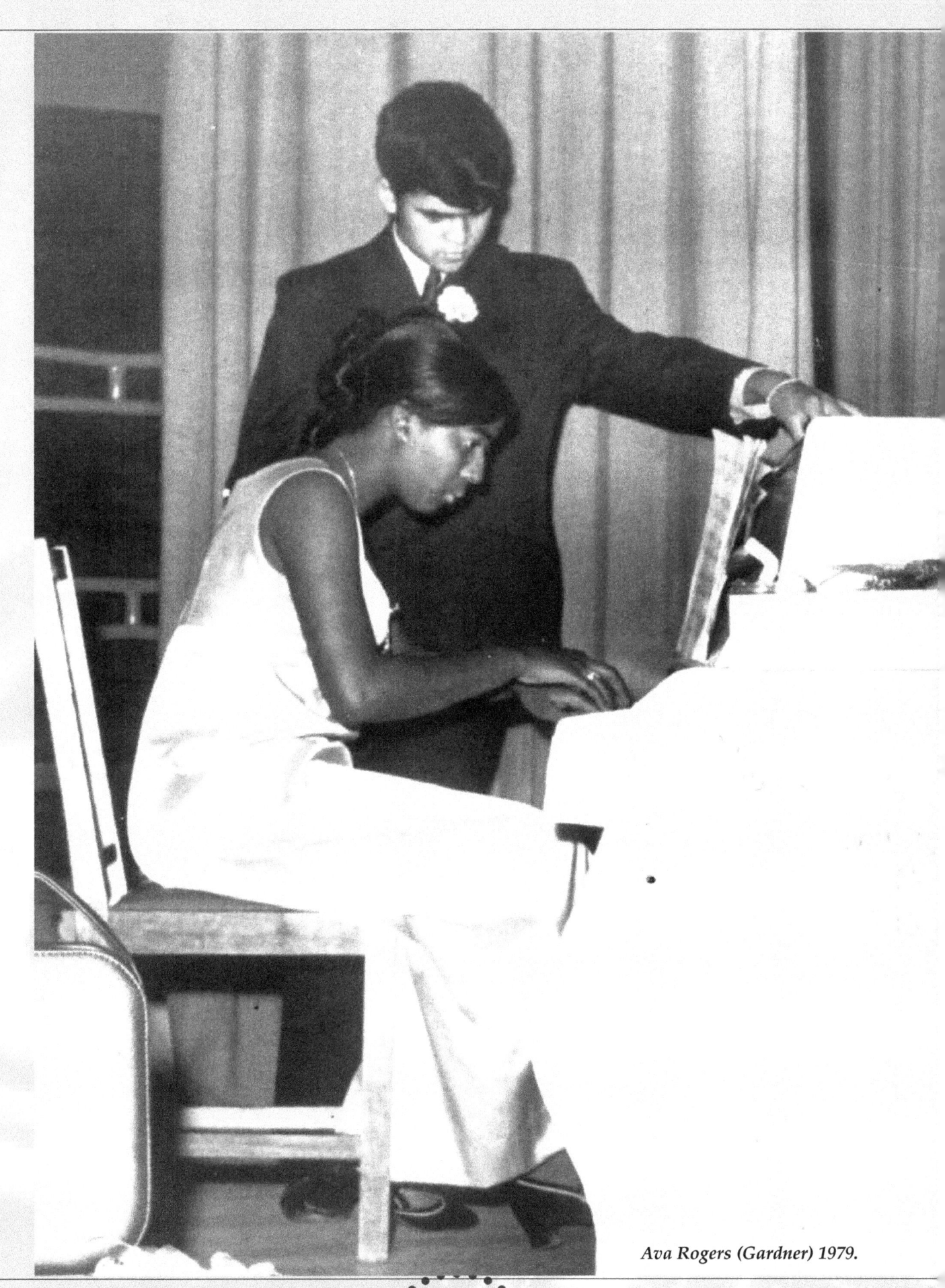

Ava Rogers (Gardner) 1979.

songs to children, highlighting their current plight; as in the 1989 album; 10 Years on Children Survive, whose proceeds he donated to the Child Survival Foundation. Other albums are: "Street Kids" "Jesus Saved My Soul", and "Still Burns Bright", which are exemplary jazz fusion.

At an early age Fungai played with the 2D Sounds, then with Prophets, alongside the late Jethro Shasha..

While teaching Maths at a North London School in the 70's, he and Fred Zindi established the Stars of Liberty, which did stints at Peacock, Ronnie Scotts, 100 Oxford Club and other local night spots.

He also performed with Hot Chocolate's Errol Brown, Eddie Grant and Phil Fearon of Galaxy.

Fungai later joined the Funkies and Abbraka. Finally he returned to Zimbabwe in the 1980's, banding up with some Afro and assorted jazz groups.

In 2002 Fungai was involved in the National Hunger Jazz Concert, as performer and organiser.

He established the Jethro Shasha Drums Scholarship Scheme, for young student drummers at the Zimbabwe College of Music, where the maestro once taught drums.

Fungai is back in London, where he is teaching Maths. Together with Hilton Mambo they are performing jazz in local clubs; and furthering the cause of Township Music.

AVA ROGERS

When she does her repertoire of "Hama neva Bereki", one is immediately reminded of vocalist Faith Dauti's era. Faith sang about township life and its experiences. Ava Rodgers was however brought up in a middle – class suburb Arcadia, reserved for people of mixed race. She nevertheless, appreciated the wonderful tunes which emanated from the townships and which her father also played. Township Music is part of her cultural identity, which bestows upon her, a sense of belonging. She has featured prominently at the Zimbabwe Jazz festivals. At the 2002 National Hunger Concert, Ava sang the old tune "Kure Kwatinobva Makwiro Shamwari", jointly with the original composers, The Marshall Brothers. The audience was left craving for more. Ava's style is that of the 50's township women musicians, as she also finds time to train young ladies refined stage etiquette.

Ava performed with a variety of local musicians, including Chris Chabuka, from whom she learnt a lot."If you did not

Ava Rogers

know your staff well, Chris was always way ahead, as he would use piano chords that only he knew. It was exciting working with Chris," remarked Ava.

On other occasions she performed with Andrew Chakanyuka, Jethro Shasha, Simanga Tutani and Basil Kumpeu. Her current wish is to jazz it along with The Cool Crooners.

Born in 1952, she was named after the famous Hollywood film actor Ava Gardner. A multi-talented artist, Ava made her first stage appearance at the age of three, and played piano at the age of eleven. She attended the Bulawayo Hillside College, where she trained as a teacher, specialising in music.

She got involved with the Reps Theatre soon after college, and produced a musical – Motown, which was quite unique, and another hit, Soul Train. During 1978-79 she featured in a high-flying production; "Svikiro" in 1978-79, by Arthur Chipunza. During the same period, she starred in a musical drama: Rock and Revolution, by Margarita Bouzanis, which aroused a stir in parliament. In 1989 Ava became the first black conductor of the junior combined schools choirs.

Always a first, she was a pioneer black woman musical director at Reps Theatre. Ava intends to record the good-time tunes of the old Township Music era.

Bob "The Headmaster" Nyabinde

BOB NYABINDE

Bob Nyabinde, "The Headmaster," as he is affectionately known, is a unique guitarist/composer who is making ripples on the Zimbabwe music scene. He has brought in a new wave of Township Music; a mixture of Amarabi, Tsababatsaba, Kwela and Jazz. Bob Nyabinde's first album, "Pane Nyaya", abounds in musical comedy with tunes such as Kutsvinya Kunoita Hope (illusion of dreams). The dream is about owning a Mercedes Benz, only to discover it's a far-fetched wish. Bob's music, "Pane Nyaya", has won him the 2003 Zimbabwe Music Awards (ZIMA) accolade.

Although Nyabinde's first album has made him a

zimbabwe township music

household name, he has nurtured his musical career, for the past 30 years. Born in Mutare in 1955, Bob and three friends started on a box guitar, each one playing a portion of the instrument, be it lead, rhythm or bass section. The drummer would play the box part of the guitar. In 1973 his friend Chris Mabika, bought a guitar, and Bob Nyabinde's sister bought yet another guitar, against their mother's will. Bob's launch on the musical bandwagon was more or less complete; his dream had come true.

Two uncles, Dickson and Kingston Nyabinde, were Bob's early influences, alongside musicians such as Quinton Malianga, then a well-known township jazz performer in Mutare's Sakubva Township.

Nyabinde graduated as a teacher in 1975, with Harare as his first port of call, before transferring on promotion to Zhombe, Kwekwe, where he met township musicians Esau Konke and Moses Ngwenya. These added to Bob's grasp of township music. Eventually he moved to Kwekwe as a primary school headmaster, which was to be the launching pad of his musical career. Initially he played his box guitar at a hotel, which was on the brink of closing down, for lack of entertainment. Suddenly life returned to the spot as Bob graduated from being a solo musician, to a band leader. In 1996 he did a demo tape of most of the songs on "Pane Nyaya", which he recorded with the help of Clancy Mbirimi, who produced the album in 2001. Today Bob prides himself as a popular Afro-jazz musician, potently contributing to the tradition of Township Music.

JABAVU DRIVE

Jabavu Drive, a group currently riding high on the Township Jazz circuit, has become more popular than the street from which the name derives. Jabavu Drive actually serves as a highway into Highfields, an early township of Harare.

Jabavu's recent CD is reminiscent of the early

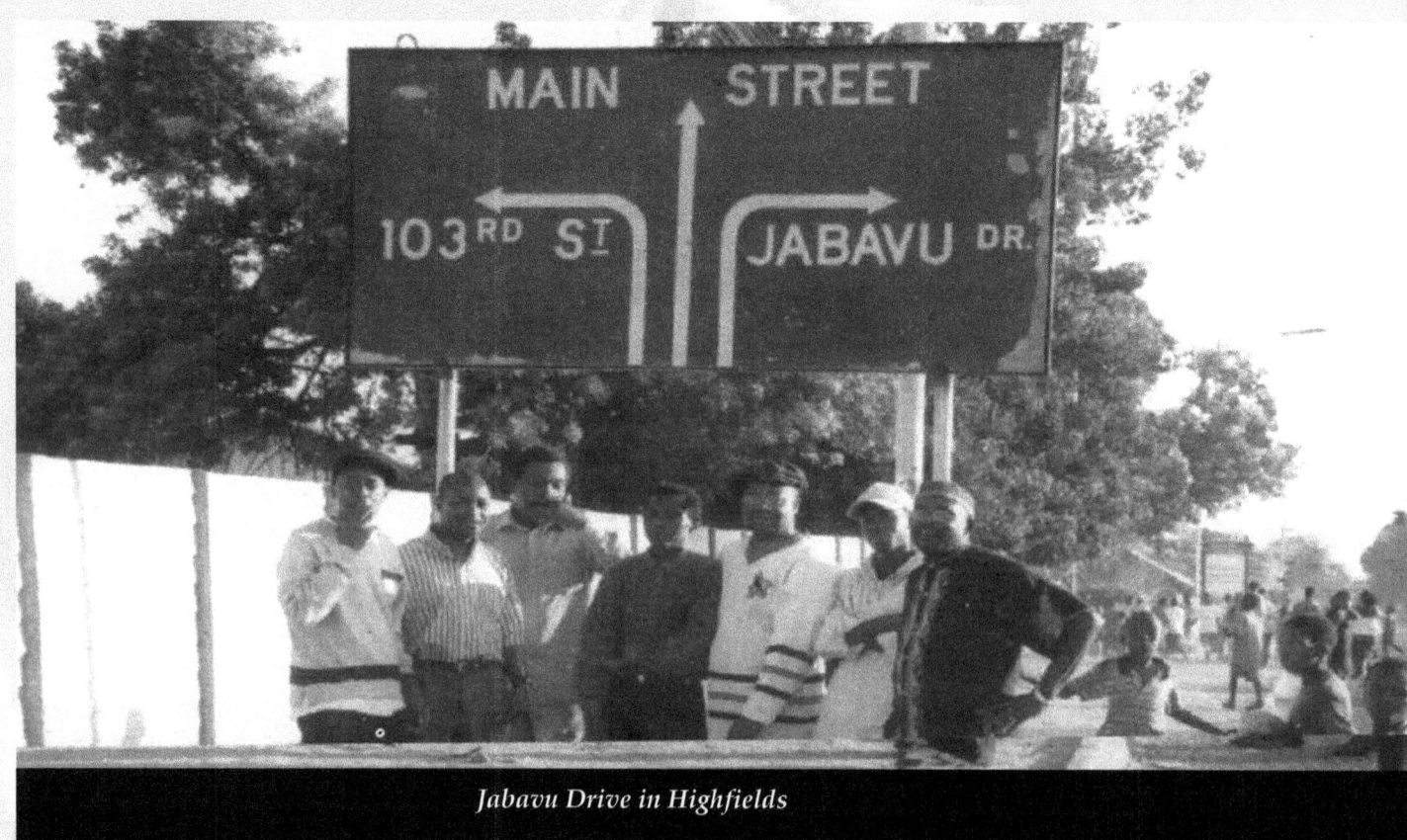

Jabavu Drive in Highfields

township music; a mixture of Jazz, Marabi, Tsabatsaba and Shona traditional music, fused with story telling. The musical themes focus on love, typified by "Isabella", "Moto Moto" and "Jabavu Drive". The album embraces sheer listening pleasure for the jazz lover.

Jabavu Drive was formed in 1998, and consists of seasoned jazz artists, who have persevered and survived as disciples of Township Music. Coming together as a band enabled them to consolidate their varied talents and skills, which they displayed in the 80's-90's.

The group comprises of veteran guitarist Timmy Makaya, formerly of St Paul's Musami band, Phillip Svosve, a prolific lyricist, composer and saxophonist, and Roger Hukuimwe "The Doc", a medical doctor, who doubles as saxophonist and vocalist. Other members are Dave Dimingo on vocals/guitar, Nicholas Mugona on vocals/bass, and Kudzie Makaya, following father's footsteps, on percussion/drums. The late Charles Mangena played vocals and keyboards.

Jabavu Drive is destined for greater heights, having made its mark as a top Afro-Jazz group in the revival of Township Music.

PHILLIP SVOSVE

Phillip Svosve has been on the music scene for the past 35 years, a noteworthy and prolific music composer.

Phillip has written most of the songs on the just released Jabavu Drive CD. A self-taught instrumentalist, Svosve's first instrument was a home-made guitar, but currently the saxophone is his passion.

Once caught up in the Beatles and Rolling Stones craze, Svosve nonetheless stuck to Township Music, which he had grown up listening to. His adolescent years were spent in Epworth, where the Epworth Theatrical Strutters greatly inspired him. It was then that he also learnt piano playing.

As a young man, he witnessed several popular groups and musicians; Capital City Dixies, Golden Rhythm Crooners, Sonny Sondo, Safirio Madzikatire, (whom he later performed with), Willie Dzara, Sam Matambo, and the late Simangaliso Tutani.

Phillip's musical history goes back to 1968 when he joined the Harare Mambos, in which he played for four years, after which he formed Delight. In 1977 he was with Safirio Madzikatire's group, before he created the Four Aces, which recorded "Shava Yawomesa".

In 1983 Svosve regrouped with Madzikatire, in The Ocean City Band, to be later joined by James Chimombe as Chimombe and The Ocean City Band. At one time, the popular and late Biggie Tembo was with the band while Svosve was still a member. Together they recorded two albums; "Out of Africa" and "Jinga, Jinga".
After 13 years with Ocean City Svosve joined Two -Plus –Two in 1996, which he later abandoned two years later, for Jabavu Drive.

With Jabavu his ingenuity for recording came to fruition, as he also continues to play what he loves most; Township Music/Jazz.

ROGER (DOC) HUKUIMWE

Born some 54 years ago in Harare's Highfields, Roger's first musical instrument was a tuning fork, which was to

Philip Svosve

zimbabwe township music

Roger "Doc" Hukuimwe

trigger him off into the exciting world of Township Jazz. During his spare time, "Doc" has certainly taken Township Music to greater heights.

His father, a music teacher, was instrumental to Rogers's love for music, by placing a tuning fork on his ear, which then released vibrating harmonic echoes. Roger played the guitar during primary school, at the age of seven. An uncle based in South Africa used to give him toy saxophones, banjos and ukelele; which all contributed to his inspiration. At St Augustine Mission he met musicians, John and Quinton Malianga; at Goromonzi Secondary School, he met Hilton Mambo, who was a roving musician.

During his medical student days, Hukuimwe was part of the University band, with Lumuel Tsikirayi and Friday Mbirimi. As discrimination was the order of the day, their band could perform for the black section of the University. This did not affect his love of music, as he would often team up with a white band at the university, led by rock guitarist and sound engineer Benny Miller.

Whilst working at Chikwanha in Seke, Roger performed with the Chikwanha Brothers, which included Charles Makokowe.

"Doc" has become a renowned local saxophonist, after acquiring a sound musical background, over the years. Despite playing guitar and keyboards, from a tender age, his favourite instrument is the saxophone. "I had a passion for it, it sounds more mature you know", he casually remarks.

In between his medical duties, Hukuimwe finds time to play jazz. The late Chris Chabuka, once played duet with him at the Red Fox Hotel. He went on to play with Two-Plus-Two, Checks Tavengwa, Sam Banana, Timmy Makaya and Phillip Svosve. When Two-Plus-Two split up, some of the members formed Jabavu Drive, of which Roger is part.

Roger, jazz saxophonist and medical practitioner: has helped other musicians perfect their talent. In Mutare he helped Fanyana Dube to acquire a PA system, which he used until his death. Later, he came up with a project. The Other Four, which witnessed young musicians such as Patience Musa and the late Lenox Chibanda, co-opted into jazz.

Currently Jabavu Drive is recording their own version of Skokiaan (Ndipe Chikokiana), first recorded by August Musarurwa in 1950. Fifty years past, the tune has been caught up in the Township Jazz Craze/revival, which confirms Roger Hukuimwe's assertion; "Township Music has come full circle."

TIMMY MAKAYA

A guitarist of note, **Timmy Makaya** contributed plenty to jazz music in Zimbabwe. His musical profile dates back to the 60's, with The Harare Mambos. Timmy also played with the St. Pauls Musami Band, and helped put it on map, with his unique guitar style. Before teaming up with Jabavu Drive, Timmy had played in the Springfields, Body and Soul, and Two-Plus-Two. Now a talented lead guitarist, he was influenced by, Wes Montgomery and Kenny Burrell. He is also a composer/arranger, as he did Jabavu Drive, an instrumental which graces the recently released Jabavu CD.

TANGA WEKWA SANDO

Tanga Kambadzo WekwaSando was born in Harare's Highfields Township, 50 years ago. He plays a mixture of township music of the 50's, 60's and 70's; Amarabi, Tsabatsaba, Afro -

Jazz, Rock, Soul and Funky. He was influenced by musical cinema shows and tea parties, ability to add feeling to harmony, to convey sadness, joy and finally triumph. It's across the social fabric, laden with messages for everyone.

Tunes about love and happier times, easily appeal to people; "Wake", "Mira Neni," "Paida Moyo," " Nyenyedzi Yomugovera," and "Ndeweku Mbare".

Sando began his musical career with the Society of The Destitutes and Aged, which performed mostly at Christmas parties.

His first professional group was the Harare Mambos, led by Greenford Jangano, which also groomed several young musicians. Greenford was known for instituting and instilling strict discipline into musicians, of which Sando is grateful.

When he left the Mambos, he founded Unity, which

Tanga WekwaSando and his group

which also made him into a good dancer. The Salvation Army Church was a catalyst, as this is where he learnt how to play the saxophone. Sando got additional inspiration from Earth Wind and Fire, Brass Construction, Teddy Pendargrass and Marvin Gaye.

History is retold in Sando's music, which encompasses the spectrum of Zimbabwe society; be it past, present or future. "I want to make a contribution, it's all about contribution, that is shaped by history."

His compositions are inclined to emotional love situations; witty and subtly entertaining. What makes Tanga wekwa Sando's music unique is his not easy to pin Sando's music to one particular genre, although he uses Township Music, as his predominant vehicle for fusion.

A critic had this to say about Sando: "Tanga's style exudes such power and beauty that invokes in Zimbabweans a sense of pride, and of a belonging." Apparently he is aware of the audience's appreciation, and hence he cares. Tanga is an example of an all-rounder. The musical theme cuts

Tanga wekwaSando

zimbabwe township music

comprised of; Elton Edwards, Bunny DeSouza, and Johnny Papas. Louis Mhlanga, Bradshaw Mandishona and Henry Peters joined the band later, and so did Clancy Mbirimi.

They played Funky, Soul, Blues and Jazz, with Louis imitating guitar styles of Santana and George Benson.

The group regularly played to mixed audiences, of blacks and coloureds. Their venues included Mushandira Pamwe, Cannabis, Queens Hotel and the Bulawayo Trade Fair, where they fetched prizes on two consecutive years. Sando thereafter played for Movement, Baked Means, and finally Octave, whose members were; Bothwell Nyamhondera, Jethro Shasha, Louis Mhlanga, Chris Chabuka and Henry Peters.

In 1977 Sando went to the United States to further his studies at the University of Indiana, and majored in International Economics and Finance.

On his way to the USA, he had a stint in Botswana, briefly playing trombone for The Gaborone Town Orchestra.

At Indiana University, he started writing music seriously, and ended up living in a car trailer in the park, to have more time to himself. He recorded music in Bloomington, where he played in a band of white guys.

Being ambitious and adventurous, Sando moved to New York, to try his luck for a music job. He was hired at Tower Records-Departmental Store, in the Intelligence Section. There, he met international artists, such as Janet Jackson, who would sign autobiographies upon release of their records. After three years, he left for the Frankstock Fund which had funded his studies in the States.

When Sando returned to Zimbabwe, he immediately embarked on a musical project with "Giraffe", and recorded such hits as "Mahobho" and "Vakomana Vekwedu", among others. During this time he was a also township councillor of Highfields.

When Giraffe disbanded, he went solo as Tanga wekwa Sando, producing spectaculars like "Wake", "Nyenyedzi Yomugovera" and "Bharanzi". He has produced a fine label "Shungu", which includes "WekuMbare", "KuFio (Highfield)", and "Wangu Wangu". The song "WekuMbare" (of Mbare) is dedicated to township jazz artists; pianist Chris Chabuka, drummer Johnny Papas, guitarist Sam Banana and saxophonist/bassist Simangaliso Tutani, among others. "WekuMbare" had been popularised before by the late Sam Banana.

During, 2004 Sando won the best selling musical artist prize at The National Arts Merit Awards, an overdue accreditation for the man who has fact-tracked Township Music to dizzy heights. Sando is certainly destined for even greater challenges.

Louis Mhlanga

LOUIS MHLANGA

Louis Mhlanga is a gifted guitarist, who has created a unique "Louis beat" which especially identifies with him. He loves his guitar, just the way he strums it. "A guitar is a special thing, it's not just wood and strings," he casually remarks. Louis' music is a mixture of Rock, Township jazz (Afro Jazz) and Rhumba. His musical fusions represent the predominant hectic themes of a once bright era. Township jazz was popular in the 50's-60's, Rumba made its mark in the 60's, Rock was aflame during the 70's. Louis was in the midst of all the craze. It is remarkable how he has integrated these musical blends into one whole. As a guitarist/musician, he is recognised regionally and internationationally, having also made popular performances locally and far-afield.

Louis grew up in a musical family, which included aunt Sarah Mabhokela, who was a township jazz singer of the 50's. Boyhood township Mbare, also played a significant role in moulding his musical career. Mhlanga is currently based in South Africa and plays for Muzik ye Africa (Axemen), which included James Indi and the late Jethro Shasha. They are famed for popular musical recordings, of a highly professional calibre. Louis, is in addition, a gifted director for theatre productions, and has assisted most of the country's premier artists, including Thomas Mapfumo.

In South Africa Louis has performed alongside Ray Phiri, Vusi Mahlasela, Sipho 'Hotstix' Mabuse, Hugh Masekela, Caiphus Semenya and Letta Mbulu. Memorable shows were; The Zimbabwe Jazz Festival, Arts Alive Festival, Grahamstown Festival and The South African Masque Freedom Show, held at France-Montreux Jazz Festival. He represented Zimbabwe at a festival of improvised music in Vevey, Switzerland. Other shows he remembers are Angouleme, the New Morning Jazz Club (Paris) and the Lisbon Cultural City Festival (1994). He was a supporting act for Nigerian / British poet Patience Agbabi at the 1994 Windybrow Arts Festival. Louis also performed in Mozambique, Botswana and Germany. In 1995, he and Vusi Mahlasela, supported the Joan Armatrading show in Johannesburg. Two years later, the pair performed in Harare as a guitarist/vocalist duo, which became the talk of the town.

Louis was special guest/artist at both the National Hunger Jazz Concert (2001), and the National Arts Merit Awards (2002).

Mhlanga started off in the 70's, with such groups as the Baked Beans, Octave, and Unity. The 70's were a hectic era of diverse music forms. Louis fused a variety of scores to produce an African pop brand or the Township Groove. The 70's also posed a difficult time for young musicians due to the turbulent political situation, which forced Louis to leave the country for the UK. There he joined the ranks of Fred Zindi and Joy Welsh in the Stars of Liberty. In London, he also worked with Paul Weller, and some African and Caribbean bands, which included Dennis Brown and Julian Bahula. With fame building up, Nigerian juju superstar 'King' Sunny Ade invited Louis to Lagos to work in the latter's studio. He assisted a number of modern and traditional Nigerian artists, whilst studying the West African guitar tradition. The London and Nigerian experiences helped broaden and enrich Louis' artistic horizons.

He returned to Zimbabwe in 1984, and worked as sound engineer and performer. In 1987, he was with the Baptist Communications Center, producing music for artists from Malawi, Mozambique, South Africa and Zimbabwe. He also produced albums for Thomas Mapfumo, Dorothy Masuka and Ephat Mujuru, among other musicians. During the 80s, he performed with Talking Drum, Ilanga, Mudzimu and Southern Freeway, with late brother Willie (drums) and Steve Dyer, a gifted and articulate musician.

In later years, Louis was sound engineer at Gramma Records (1988), and then administrative manager at the Zimbabwe Ethnomusicology Centre (1992). He settled in South Africa in 1993, where his music is in high demand. South Africa, with its ripened performers and audiences, is destined to catapult him to greater heights. He has just recorded, yet another album with Oliver Mtukudzi,

zimbabwe township music

Chiwoniso Maraire and Busi Mhlongo. His memorable recordings (albums) are: "Mukai", "Song for Nomsa", "Shamwari" and "Tinganekwane". Some of the tunes on the five albums are: "Batho", "Song for Elisha" (in memory of Elisha Josamu, a great composer), "Ndiwe", "Song For Nomsa", "Mari Hakuna", "Gombo Muchochocho", "Gwenyambira","Kugarisana Nevemwe Zvakanaka", "Honaka" and "Distant Lovers". "Distant Lovers", is featured as a sigtune on a popular talk show; "Amai Chisamba Show".

Louis was born in Harare on 10th November 1956, of a South African mother and Zimbabwean father. Indeed, a truly Township Music guitarist/producer

JAZZ INVITATION

Jazz Invitation was born out of The Jazz Moving Café, of Sam Mataure. The group consists of Kelly Rusike (bass) who is leader, Prudence Katomeni-Mbofana (vocals), Filbert Marowa (keyboards), Ritchie Lopez (saxophone), and Victor Duarte (drums).

Kelly Rusike started in the 70's with a family band, which was then based in Kitwe, Zambia, where his father worked as a journalist. The Rusike Brothers consisted of Tawanda, Phillip, Abius and Colleen. Kelly left the group as he is more inclined to Afro-Jazz and wishes to explore features of African Rhythms.

He is a musician/bassist of note, who has contributed immensely to Township Music, having done backing vocals for many jazz tunes, which he helped to produce. Filbert Marova teaches guitar and piano at the College of Music where he also trained. He has played for a number of groups from a young age, becoming currently a seasoned jazz pianist. He grew up listerning to Township Music, as his father once played the Omasiganda (One man –guitar band). Filbert's first group was the Scanners International. At the Zimbabwe College of Music, he met Simanga Tutani, who was an inspiration; and guitarist Jonah Marumahoko. It was then that he got a real feel of how it was to play serious jazz. He later joined Detema Jazz Band, then Straight Marchers, which changed its name to Zebras, later to Savana Cruise. Soon he was with Riders, alongside Clancy Mbirimi and Ray Mashava. Filbert plays for Jazz Invitation, for which he has written songs such as "BP Yangu Yakwira", "Mai Chiuyayi" and "Sondela"; in a recently produced CD; "Rehearsal Room".

Prudence Katomeni Mbofana

Prudence was born long after female giants, Lina Mattaka, Evelyn Juba, Dorothy Masuka and Faith Dauti. Nevertheless, she has created a musical niche for herself as a seasoned Township Musician. "I just go into a natural high, and I am just transferred into a different world," she narrates. The experience is what is termed "improvisation", defined as a nebulous act outside the control of the singer, who is propelled beyond the conscious mastery of what she is producing.

Prudence started off by

Jazz Invitation

Prudence Katomeni Mbofana

an Afro-Jazz album: Rehearsal Room, containg a 50's hit; "Ndafunafuna", a composition of Sonny Sondo. Her voice is enriching throughout the album.

Prudence teams up with top musicians such as The Cool Crooners, who have requested her to feature on their recording tracks. She has also often staged alongside Oliver Mtukudzi and Tanga wekwa Sando.

The vocal artist will scale greater heights, as she regards Township Music as her major springboard.

imitating Makeba and Masuka, before composing and rearranging her own songs. Today she is a celebrated jazz artist in her own right.

Born in Harare in 1977, to a family of musicians; Prudence admired her aunts who sang in the church choir. At school she joined drama and experienced Dub Poets by Albert Nyathi. She later worked with Thando Maclaren, who was involved in theatre and drama productions.

Prudence joined the group called Vice, where she had the first experience as jazz singer. She was the youngest in the group, with most members over the age of thirty. After three years with Vice, she went solo and performed in functions such as Miss Zimbabwe, Miss Universe as well as corporate receptions. During the shows she did copyright versions of Dorothy Masuka and Miriam Makeba.

When Sam Mataure conceived the idea a "Moving Jazz Café", Prudence banded together with Jazz Invitation, comprising of Kelly Rusike, Ritchie Lopez and Filbert Marova. The group produced

Dumisani Ngulube

Dumisani Ngulube is a young Jazz Musician who has gained abrupt popularity. "My whole life is surrounded by music

Dumisani Ngulube

zimbabwe township music 173

from the people", says Dumi as he is affectionately known. Music, like culture, is dynamic, in that and young musicians expeiment with their own unique styles. Dumi adopts the basic elements that he grew up listening to; Amarabi, Kwela, Tsabatsaba and Afro - Jazz. He was born 34years ago in Bulawayo, with his parent's home opposite the Manwele Beerhall, which was a hive of musical activity. Several township musicians played at this prestigious beer-garden, which greatly impacted on Dumi. He was inspired by Don Gumbo, Louis Mhlanga and Jethro Shasha. Simangaliso Tutani taught him how to play keyboards, whilst Chris Chabuka gave him lessons on piano and drums.

On realising his musical talent Dumi joined The Mzilikazi Youth Center in 1977, while still at school. In 1986 after school he was with Amakhosi Theatre Productions,when he sang for drama plays.

His submission to serious music led him to the Zimbabwe College of Music – Ethnomusicology Programme. He learnt both the theoretical and practical aspects of music, and obtained a formal diploma. He subsequently became a lecturer at the same college from 1991 to 2002, and also taught at schools and church organisations.

Whilst lecturing at the College of Music, Dumi performed with local groups; Rusike Brothers, Shaline Robertson, Elias Musakwa, among others.

Once he played "Pansula", Gospel and Reggae before focusing on "Afro Jazz". He performed serious jazz with Uya Moya, alongside Chirikure Chirikure and Ray Mawerera. Subsequently he resigned from lecturing, and formed his own 10-member group. The band's focus is a fusion of African traditional music and Afro-jazz. Ngulube has been playing commercially since 1999.

Amagents comprise of Tonny Tswane/ Drums, John Mambira/Percussions, James Darcy/Lead, Aaron Yafele/ Trombone (now with Jabavu Drive), Faith Ganyau on vocals, and Dumi (keyboards and vocals).

The group has since recorded 3 albums, the first being, "Tshona Langa" in 2000. In 2002 it recorded two CD's; "African Emotion" and "Zvinhu Zvangu". Dumi is a young musician who is versatile, while keeping Township Music persistently alive.

DUDUZILE Tracy Manhenga

"Dudu" was born in Bulawayo in 1981, where she grew up listening to such songs as Yakhal' Inkomo", by Thembi Mtshali, a South African musician. Her mother played keyboards, whilst the grandfather played saxophone. She often listened to the music of Dorothy Masuka and Ava Rogers, who have made inroads for her early initiation into Township Music. At age 16 she sang with her teacher on Prize-giving days. At 17 she joined the Gospel Arch, after which she

left for Siyeza, which featured Henza Mabhiza, of the 90's Southern Freeway fame. In Siyeza she was a lead singer,

Duduzile Tracey Manhenga

often performing versions of Thembi Mtshali or Miriam Makeba.

Eager to advance her musical career, she enrolled at the Zimbabwe College of Music for a National Certificate. In Harare, she was to team up with Dumi and Amagents, led by Dumisani Ngulube, then a lecturer at the College. She used to split her time between performing music and college work.

Manhenga later left Amagents to form a youthful group, Color Blu, which has already recorded a nine-song album, in which she assisted as recording/producer. With a solid theoretical background, Dudu has re-arranged old tunes: "Igqiha Lendlela Ngu Qoqotshwane" and the late Chipunza's "Mvura Ngainaye Makomo KwaMutare".

At the 2001 International and Regional Jazz Festival, held in Harare, Dudu shared the stage with Dorothy Masuka. She has also sung alongside Oliver Mtukudzi, Tanga wekwa Sando and Erica Badhu.

Through youngsters like Dudu, Township Music is evolving as a synthetic version of popular rhythms, blended with contemporary creativity. It will no doubt grow from strength to strength.

Maita Jazz Women's band

An all-female group, the **Maita Jazz Women's** band is a novel outfit which has in a short space of time, spelt out its own niche in the jazz circles. The group is rearing to go; all members of the band playing instruments.

Victoria Zimuwandeyi and Dadirayi Manase

The group artists qualified from the College of Music, in a special programme funded by the Swedish Development Agency. Ultimately, the group fine-tuned their expertise during spare time at their own cost. The saxophonists still continue with their studies as individual students at the college of music. Dedication and sacrifice ultimately pays off; Maita is a smart group to reckon with. It's like listerning to masters of several years' experience.

The band consists of: Susan Ndawi Drums/rythm, Shamiso Chitsinde Bass, Stella Mkundu (Mamvura) Lead, Sophia Madzivanyika (J.B) Bass/voice, Anna Matondo (Sharai/Saru) Rhythm, Marita Tafirenyika (Seby) Keyboard/voice, Victoria Zimuwandeyi (Nakai) Saxophone/voice, who is the youngest and Dadirayi Manase (Choks) Saxophone/percussion who is also the leader of the band.

Currently, the group performs at Thamies Sports Diner on Thursdays and Saturdays; Taste of Africa on Fridays and Sundays. Often they play at private functions and clubs,

Sophia Madzivanyika

Shamiso Chitsinde

Anna Matondo

Stella Mkundu-Mavhura

Marita Tafirenyika

zimbabwe township music 176

such as the Reserve Bank Sports Club. Maita have recorded their first album. They aspire to play alongside jazz greats; of the likes of Abdul Ibrahim, George Benson, Earl Klugh or Hugh Masekele.

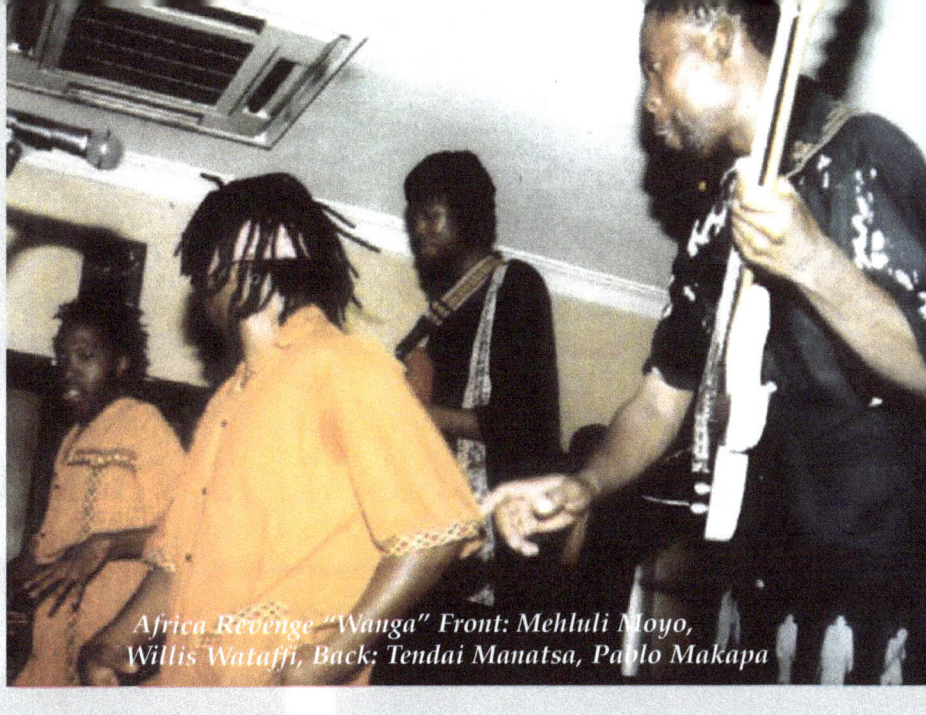

Africa Revenge "Wanga" Front: Mehluli Moyo, Willis Wataffi, Back: Tendai Manatsa, Pablo Makapa

AFRICA REVENGE

Afrika Revenge or "Wanga Boys", is a relatively young musical outfit, which is contributing new dimensions to Township Music. Their offering combines Afro-Jazz and "Mbaqanga", which in turn influence their dancing styles. The main performers are Mehluli Moyo and Willis Wataffi, who both hail from Bulawayo, which has a bearing on their performance styles. Imitating the old Cool Crooners, the group had audiences taken aback by their choreography. Mehluli (24) and Willis (28), are destined for a brighter and hectic future, as they put their solid dedication to the musical cause. The backing group consists of Tendai Manatsa , Victor and Carl Muparutsa. The group sings freely in English, Shona, Xhosa, Zulu and Tswana. It has just released an all-time captivating album, with the smashing hit ; "Wanga", which was voted ZIMA 2004 Song of the Year. They have since scooped two more awards, as Best Male Artist and Best Afro Jazz Artist. Within a short space of time Afrika Revenge have climaxed high on the musical stakes. The sky is the limit!

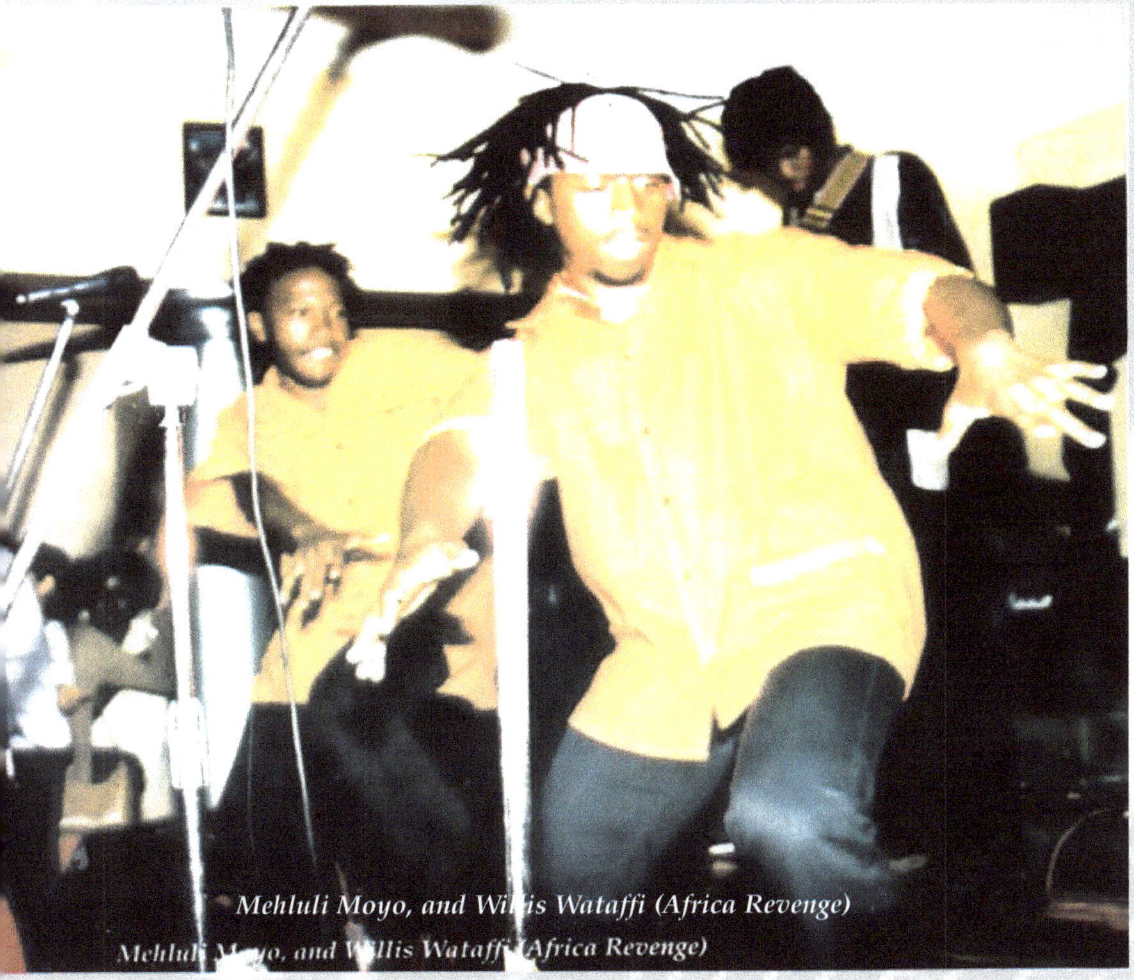

Mehluli Moyo, and Willis Wataffi (Africa Revenge)

Mehluli Moyo, and Willis Wataffi (Africa Revenge)

TODAY'S PROMOTERS

Lenox Chibanda (left), Irene Gwaze (centre) and Gibson Mandishona

From left: Josh Hozheri, Lenox Chibanda and Titus Shangazhike

zimbabwe township music

Paul Brickhill

Lucky Street Blues

zimbabwe township music

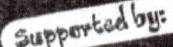
Oliver and Irene Gwaze of Red Fox Motel

zimbabwe township music

CONTEMPORARY PROMOTERS

IRENE GWAZE

Irene Gwaze has groomed several young musicians to artistic fruition. The budding township musicians have often sought the liberal guidance of Irene. The Red Fox Hotel, which her family owns, has become a hub and haven of aspiring and upcoming musicians. She has hosted a number of jazz festivals, including The National Hunger Concert. Some bands she has promoted include The Other Four, Summer Breeze, Cool Crooners, Ernest Tanga wekwa Sando, Africa Revenge, Dumi Ngulube & Amagents, Patricia Matongo and Colour Blu, which she used to manage. She has often offered free accomodation to particular groups, and rehearsing space for upcoming musicians.

Irene's love for Afro-jazz is a result of growing up in Bulawayo's Makokoba Township, where the unique music was flourishing. She is an exceptional female music promoter, who has contributed greatly towards the maturity of young jazz artists. She believes in Township Music, because "it is here to stay, having survived all past odds."

Jackie Cahi

JACKIE CAHI

Jackie Cahi was born in Bulawayo in 1956, but grew up in Harare. She was born at a time when the Golden Rhythm Crooners and the Cool Four were highly popular. Little did she predict that some day she would be the promoter of Cool Crooners. Jackie never grew up in an African township, but as a musician she got familiar with a lot of township music. She became part of a group called Solidarity, just after Independence, which also comprised of Paul Brickhill, Shacky Kangwena and Washington Kavhai. The latter two went on to form the Bhundu Boys. As vocalist, she got exposed to townships, mines, and farms; subsequently the group became a success story of the 80's. Within the musical fraternity, Jackie met the Cool Crooners and eventually became their promoter. She believes the sky is the limit, for the singing quartet.

PENNY YON

Penny Yon has contributed to Township Music as performer and promoter. She joined Mhepo in 1996, after their bass guitarist Sam Zimi fell ill. She stayed with the group for four years as the bassist. She was approached by Chris Chabuka to assist in the organisation of Jazz Festivals, from where Simanga Tutani had left, after his death in 1995. A committee was formed with Penny and Sam Mataure as coordinators of the National Jazz Festival, with Gibson Mandishona as patron. The festivals put many jazz musicians on the map, and helped to market them. Some musicians perfected their skills during the festivals, which also dispelled the myth that jazz was an old people's affair. The Prince Edward Secondary School Jazz Band and The Churchill Jazz outfit emerged in the midst of the festivals. "Young people got to realise that jazz is funky, jazz is wild, jazz is party music," said Penny.

Penny was involved with the festivals during 1996 – 1999. She had to resign, to take up a job in Binga out of Harare.

She did not stop at organising festivals, but also marketed jazz musicians, acting as their agent, since she worked for a tourism company. Her desktop publishing expertise facilitated dissemination and publicity of festival material. She would do posters, newspaper ads, flyers and complementary tickets. At times she used her phone, fax and email for business contacts.

Besides Mhepo, Penny performed with Big Sister, an all-female group, comprising Biddy Patridge, Kundisai Mtero, Ava Rodgers and a Danish Berta Stonebeck, then a teacher at the Zimbabwe College of Music. Big Sister was a hit once upon a time. Penny spends most of her time in Binga, on a project to computerise rural schools. She was pivotal in the revival of Township Music, and in co-ordinating festivals. Thanks to Penny, its now fashionable to be part of the jazz movement.

SAM MATAURE

Drummer par excellence, Sam Mataure has helped to preserve township music by coordinating jazz shows and festivals. He carried on from where the late Simangasliso Tutani left, by way of reviving Township Music and Afro-Jazz. The festivals have also wooed young people into liking Township Music. Sam Mataure says, he has fallen in love with Township Jazz because, "the groove is there, the beat is there, its exciting, it's easy to appeal to the African."

Through assisting Simanga in organising the National Jazz Festival, Sam learnt how to deal with even more challenging tasks, such as coordinating the Regional and International Jazz Festival, which was his brainchild. He, also came up with other themes: Mutare Jazz Festival, The Winter Jazz Festival, Old Timers' Show and The Moving Jazz Café.

Mataure has made a name for himself in South Africa, where he is now based, and where he often performs with top South African musicians

He developed his love for music at a primary school in Sakubva, Mutare, where he learnt how to play drums. In high school he met friends with whom he teamed up to form a band. His passion for drums was influenced by Jethro Shasha and Bothwell Nyamhondera. The Run Family, a popular musical group based in Mutare, was influencial in shaping Sam's musical aspiration.

In 1980, a cousin, Patrick Farai Mahera, establisehd a jazz club in Mutare; Sam formed the group Ekhaya. He would visit Harare to acquaint himself with jazz events, his favourite group being Body and Soul. In 1994 Sam left Mutare to join Thomas Mapfumo in Harare, whom he stayed with for 10 months, before joining Andy Brown. He later decided to return to Mutare where he played for the Zibras Band, with which he organised the first Mutare Jazz Festival. Simanga, of the National Jazz Festival, gave expert guidance.

Sam also assisted in organising such events as Jenaguru, Harare International Festival of the Arts (HIFA) and the SADC Dance Festival. HIFA encouraged Sam to organise the International and Regional Jazz Festival, which drew musicians from different countries, and enabled local musicians to mingle with their international counterparts.

A cross-section of musicians featured at the International Jazz festivals, included Bruce Cassidy (Canada), Ray Phiri (South Africa), Oliver Mtukudzi, Steve Dyer (South Africa), Tanga wekwa Sando, Jazz Ambassadors (USA), Jazz Invitation, Mandebvu and Detema Band.

As Sam organised jazz festivals, he also played drums for Oliver Mtukudzi, who took him to several countries. He has since settled in South Africa, where the prospects are more challenging. He often features alongside Judith Sepuma, Musa Manzini, Louis Mhlanga and Steve Dyer. At age 36, Sam has made significant strides into the Township Music world, where he is poised to scale even greater heights.

Gibson MANDISHONA

Gibson Mandishona grew up in Mbare (then Harare) Township during the fifties, when several musical groups were excelling in showbiz, mostly in the major centres of Harare, Bulawayo and Mutare. He witnessed the unfolding of political scenarios and the temporary fading out of the popular concerts, which gave way to shadowy musical scenes, such as Mahobho, Teen-time and Chachacha. As Mandishona grew up in the vibrant township, he got exposed to the various social scenes at the time, mostly centred at the Boys' Club at Mai Musodzi Hall. They would partake in recreational activities, including cinema

From right to left: Gibson Mandishona, Cephas Mangwana and Bob Marley

shows, supplementary feeding ("stew") and vocational pursuits. His painting: "Double Decker Bus", won him first prize of five pounds in a competition. He used the proceeds to purchase a 4-string "Ukelele" mini-guitar, which was his first inspiration to music. His second inspiration was from his elder sister Grace Mandishona, who sang with the melodious nurses' Gay Gaeties group.

Gibson Mandishona with the Cool Crooners

Whilst in primary school, Gibson played guitar jointly with the late Andrew Chakanyuka, for The Star Gazers group, which comprised Willie Dzara, Bill Saidi, Reuben Dauti and Chesterton Mhango. The singers later formed The Milton Brothers with Faith Dauti, as Gibson also left Harare to attend Tekwani High School in Plumtree. Thereafter, Mandishona taught himself jazz piano and played music at the universities he attended. During his work stint with the United Nations in Addis Ababa (Ethiopia), he was band-leader of a jazz outfit which also included Herbert Murerwa and Cephas Mangwana. He also performed with the Reggae guru Bob Marley in 1978.

During 1980 at Independence, Mandishona was excited to witness a gradual revival of Township Jazz Music, with veteran artists returning home, and banding up with a few who had stayed behind during the turbulent political period. He was also an ardent promoter of jazz, in that he facilitated both Simangaliso Tutani and Chris Chabuka to further their musical expertise with the Boston-based Berklee College of Jazz.

Mandishona also once served on the board of the Zimbabwe College of Music. After Simanga's death, Mandishona was patron of the Zimbabwe National Jazz Festival for three years, which was prelude to the current hectic revival of local jazz. More recently in November 2002, he jointly organised The National Hunger Concert, with Joyce Jenje-Makwenda; at which local jazz artists raised funds for children's charities and hunger-stricken homes. Mandishona is also the editor of the latter's "Zimbabwe Township Music". For him, it is like a journey back to the day he played his "Ukelele" guitar at the Mai Musodzi Boys' Club. Mandishona's

Gibson teaching Joyce how to wind the grammophone

salient message is that today's youth should build Zimbabwe's jazz to even greater heights, blending past experiences with innovative contemporary styles.

SOCIALITES

Mr J.M.N Nkomo president of the the newly-formed S. Rhodesia Congress, (centre) flanked by Dr. S. T. Parirenyantwa and Mr J.G.S. Chingate (L), watches a Salisbury dance troupe as a form of relaxation after two busy days of consultations, interviews, and meetings (1957).

Dr. David Parirenyatwa and son of Dr. Samuel Parirenyatwa follows the tradition 46 years later relaxing at Jazz 105 next to him is Chiza Ngwira (Parade).

Joyce Jenje-Makwenda (right) and sister Josephine Jenje-Mudimbu

The 50s Audiance (Mai Musodzi Hall)   Todays Audiance (2003) Winter Jazz Festival Jazz 105

INDEX

Bibliography and References:
- The African Daily Newspaper
- The African Weekly
- The African Parade
- The Bantu Mirror
- Drum Magazine
- The Radio Post
- Rhodesia Herald
- The Herald/Chronicle
- The Sunday Mail
- Sunday News
- The Daily Newspaper
- Horizon
- Zonk

JOURNALS
- (IAWM) International Alliance for Women in Music.
- Where did we go and What did we learn (NORAD)

VIDEOS
- Zimbabwe Township Music 1930's-1960's – Joyce Jenje Makwenda (1992)
- Christmas With Early Urban Settlers – Joyce Jenje Makwenda (1993)
- Omasiganda – Joyce Jenje Makwenda (1994)
- The Mattaka Family Joyce Jenje Makwenda (1995)
- Epworth Theatrical Strutters – Joyce Jenje Makwenda (1997)
- Have You Seen Drum Recently – Jurgen & Claudia Schadeberg
- The Seven Ages Of Music – The Shadeberg Movie Company
  SHANDA –(Oliver Mtukudzi) – Media For Development Trust

GLOSSARY

Bemba: As Bantu language and name of large group of people living in Zambia and the Democratic Republic of Congo.

Bioscope: (South African) Cinema.

Birthday Parties: Euphemism for singing, dancing, illicit drinking and eventually underground political gatherings in the townships.

Bottle Method: Also known as Hawaiian Method. Guitar playing style using a bottle on the fingerboard to produce required notes.

Chewa: Bantu language spoken by a people of the same name living in Southern Malawi and areas of Western Mozambique.

Colour Bar: Racial segregation based on the notion of white supremacy in colonial Zimbabwe.

Dhepa: Vernacular for Dispensary.

Gule/Gure: Malawian and Zambian religious and secular dance also associated with 'chinamwali', a women's invitation ceremony dance.

Hawaiian: Same as bottle method.

Imbube: A Ndebele secular unaccompanied choral or group singing.

Ingquzu: A lively Ndebele secular vocal style with clapping and measured steps.

Isitshikitsha A secular Ndebele song and dance with clapping and measured steps.

Jerusalema: A Shona secular song and dance correctly called Mbende, characterised by a distinct drumming pattern and clapping.

Jiti: Shona secular song and dance formerly known as Jikinya, perfomed in the manner of a jive.

Loud Speakers: Large loud hailer-shaped devices tied on long poles strategically placed in the townships to amplify radio broadcasts, police messages, and so on.

Mabhavhade: Vernacular equivalent of birthday parties.

Mahobo Parties: Initially inspired by the music of Zax Nkosi, these get-togethers were organized on the same principles as birthday parties.

Marabi: Urban black music developed in the 1920's in South Africa, Blending Western chord polyphonic systems and harmonization with African rhythms.

Mbaqanga: Originally the 1950s popular commercial African jazz, in South Africa, jusing African Melody, marabi and American Jazz. Later it combined new urban traditional sounds and marabi using modern Western musical instruments.

Mbira: Also commonly referred to as the (hand piano), it is the main instrument in the performance of the Shona Spirit and secular music and dance of the same name. It can be played alone or accompanied by drums and rattles.

Mchongoyo: Secular Tshangana traditional song and dance popular in the Eastern districts of Zimbabwe and closely resembling the Zulu war dance.

Ndebele: A people and Bantu language of Zimbabwe and parts of South Africa.

Nyau: Masked dancer chinyau or dancers zvinyau in the performance of Gule\Gure.

Pungwe: Onomatopoeic expression denoting dawn. The name given to an all-night singing party held by guerillas and villagers during the liberation war.

Shangara: Term covering several types of traditional Shona circular song and dance performed with two or more drums, or with clapping and singing only.

Shona: A Bantu language and name of the largest group of people living in Zimbabwe.

MUSICICIANS/PERSONALITIES

Achulu, Duncan 109
Ade, Sunny King 171
Africa, Patience 107
Aghabi, Patience 171
Alpert, Herb 21,101
Allen, Sanchez 145
Allingham, Rob 31,72
Amanda 159
Amatayi, Alan 134
Armstrong, Louis 12,21,56,68,76, 77,78,79,100,101,103, 110,112,153,154,161
Ankar, Paul 21
Armatrading, Joan 171
Ayema Kashimbo, Frank 57
Ayema, Francis Joseph 57
Ayema, Lucy 57
Ayema, Musodzi 57
Badhu, Erica 175
Bahula, Julian 171
Bajila, Patrick 126
Bakasa, Danny 154
Banana, Sam 33,156,168,170
Banda, Eliah 12,30,118,133,158
Banda, Martha 24
Banda, Molly 109
Bandawe, Matilda 107
Bassie, Count 21,69
Benson, George 170,175
Bezuidenhout, Laura 38,
Bhengu, Nicholas 119
Bhika, E 53-

Bhika, Mohammed 52,62
Biko, Steve 110
Bingwa, Mabel 12,22,25,27,51, 70,95,136,137
Bonkwe, Alice 92
Bouzanis, Margarita 165
Brickhill, Roger 78
Brickhill, Paul 9,62,145,180,182
Brown, Andy 184
Brown, Dennis 171
Brown, Errol 164
Burnell, Kenny 168
Buzuzi, Jimmy 145

Cahi, Jackie 13,149,182,183
Cameron, Sheila 62,72
Captain&Mrs Tapfumaneyi 53
Carr, Joe 21,101
Carsten, Nico 21,101
Cassidy, Bruce 66,184

Chabata, Jonathan 27
Chabuka, Chris 12,44,57,128,131, 132,133,143,145,149,153,154,157, 159,164,165,168,170,174,183,185
Chabuka, Leonard 57
Chakachadza, Weston 93,94
Chakanyuka, Andrew 6,12,44,45,76,109,113,128,129,131,132, 144,152,156,185
Chakanyuka, Francis 155
Chamba, Ephraim 61,88,90
Chamunorwa, Isaac 104,105
Charles, Tony 161
Charwe 57
Chataika, Edna 32
Chataika, Jordan 32,61,83
Chatyoka, Amos 159
Chatula, Domingo 119
Chavanga, Jimmy 115
Chaza, Albert 52,110
Chaza, Joseph 120
Chenjerai, Jane 35,42,126
Chenjerai, Petronella 126
Chenjerai, Susan 12,25,31,32,35,82, 83,94,119,123,124,126
Chibanda, Lenox 168
Chibhaga, Musodzi 57
Chibhodhoro, John 133
Chiduza, Nicholas 40,94,122
Chidzanga, Dorothy 119
Chief, Tshekedi 92
Chieza, Jonathan 95,139
Chigoma, Brothers 121
Chigoma, William 149,154
Chigonamubhawa 98
Chikerema, J.R.D 53
Chikoja, Charles 89
Chikukwa, Fanuel 155
Chikupo, Tineyi 83
Chikwanha, Peter 147
Chimbarange, Gilbert 104
Chimbwido, Pat 124
Chimombe, James 167
Chimwala, Elias 158,159
Chinamano, J.M 53
Chinamhora, Chief 57
Chinembiri, Jackson 39
Chingoma, T.C.G 26
Chingate, Schotting 62,53,115
Chingate, Victoria 12,23,24,27,52,62, 110,114,115,117,128,136,137,138,139
Chinhoyi, Matthew 118,155
Chinyama, Clemency 158
Chinyawo, Clement 156
Chipeni, Newman 149
Chipere, Benjamin 61,114

Chipere, Una 122
Chipunza, Authur 155,165
Chiremba, Isaac 104
Chirikure, Chirikure 174
Chitambo, Ebba 42
Chitiyo, McDonald 94
Chitsinde, Shamiso 11,175,176
Chiwareware, Buns 121
Chiweshe, Solomon 38,40
Clarke, Keith 131
Coplan, David 70

Darcy, James 174
Dauti, Faith 6,7,12,13,22,24,25,51,70,109,110, 113,114,117,125,128,132,136,139, 140,164,172
Dauti, Reuben 113,114,115,185
Delgado, Robert 21,101
De Souza, Bunney 159,169
Dhliwayo, Abigail 125
Dick, Flora 12,60,120,138,141
Dimingo, Dave 167
Dludlu, Jimmy 145
Duarte, Victor 172
Dube, Christine 13,22,27,95,139
Dube, Emma 92
Dube, Fanyana 13,151,152,158,168
Duli 121
Dyer, Steve 45,66,144,171,184
Dzara, Willie 113,114,115,185
Dzvowa, Marceline 95

Eastwood, Clint 132
Edwards, Elton 159,169
Ellington, Duke 21,68,69

Fearon, Phil 164
Ferlito, Valencia 66
Fernando, Charles 128,131,132
Fitzgerald, Ella 68,69
Fitzpatrick 92
French Vaughan 156
Fry, Dorcas 116,117

Gadluma, Steven 60
Gallo, Eric 92
Gandari, James 134
Gano, Sylvester 155
Gardner, Ava 165
Ganyau, Faith 174
Garland, Judy 93
Gatsi, Clement 154
Gaye, Marvin 169
Gotora, Freddie 107,121
Gotora, Samuel 88,93,94
Govenda, Valerie 70,110,111
Grant, Eddie 164
Gumbo, Ben 44,47,145,147,148
Gumbo, Don 174
Gutu, Dorothy 119
Gwanzura (Banana Sam)33,156,168,170
Gwaze, Ernest 88
Gwaze, Harry 24,33
Gwaze, Irene 13,62,181,182
Gwaze, Oliver 27,181
Gwaze, Zacharia 96,129,131

Haddon, Eileen 23,28,60,78
Haddon, Mike 78
Hadebe, Josiah 6,8,11,19,20,54, 55,76,81,94,97,151,152
Hamadziripi, Francis 147
Hannan, Grant 157
Hartley, Colonel 57
Hawadi, Oliver 142

Heally, Keith
Heally, Peggy 95
Heath, Ted 112
Hem, Thore 4
Hendrix, Jimmy 158,161
Hlabangana, Cephas 87
Hukuimwe, Roger 9,13,167,168
Huggins, Derik 160

Ibrahim, Abdullah 157,175
Ilunga, Jeff 40
Indi, James 45,142,144,145,160,171

Jackson, Janet 170
Jackson, Mahalia 69
Jaffey, Cy 112
James, Grace 13,140
Jangano, Greenford 46,132,145,149,151,155,156,169
Jangano-Sillah, Virginia 7,13,35,42,109,145,149
Jenje Canaan 4
Jenje, David 4
Jenje-Makwenda, Joyce 6,8,45,120,129,185
Jenje-Mudimbu, Josephine 196
Jera, Nelson 30
Jera, Ruth 116
Jiri, Jairos 56
Jonah 47
Johnson, Frank 112
Jolobe, Churchill 131
Josamu, Elisha 35,44,46,144,145, 149,150,156,159,172
Juba, Eric 44,46,47,144,145, 147,148,153
Juba, Evelyn 6,7,13,18,23,46,91, 92,136,140,144,150,153,172
Juba, Simon 6,18,44,46,91,92,153
Judith 119
Justin, Molly 110
Kabubi Bhekilanga, Moses 133,145
Kabubi, Moses 13,157,158,159
Kabwato, Rex 142
Kachisi, Edwin 118
Kachingwe, Ernest 133
Kadungure, Ishmael 145,161
Kainga, Jeremiah 12,20,24,38,49,89,118,119,120
Kalanga, Daramu 151
Kali, Sam 104,105
Kambani, Manu 132,158,159
Kambarami, Agrippa 156
Kangwena, Shacky 182
Kanyowa, Andrew 21,104
Kanyowa, Nesbitt 21,104
Kanyowa, Peter 21,103
Kanyowa, Tabeth 116
Kapesi, Helen 107
Kapuya, Tabeth 13,24,138
Kashola, Joseph 30
Kassim, Elisha 88,94
Katatu, Daniel 30
Kashiri, William 132,149,150,153,154
Kaunda, Matthew 127
Kavhai, Washington 182
Kazipe, Petros 133
Kessel, Barney 92
Kgasi, Joe 156
Khanda, Edward 151
Khumalo, Bheki 125
Khumalo, Sithembiso 157
King, Dusty 107
Klair, Sam 101
Klugh, Earl 175
Kombe, Tomix 60
Konde, Luke 104

zimbabwe township music

Konke, Esau 166
Kanyere, Winston 104
Kapepa, Vincent 158
Kruger, Klaus 108
Kruger, Rob 30
Kumwamba, Jeff 158
Kumpeu.Basil 13,44,45,143,144, 145,151,155,156,165
Kuretu, Peter 60,104
Kuruneri, Chris 145,147
Kwela, Alan 157
Kyle, Billy 78

Lanas, Mike 161
Last, James 21,101
Lewanika, Chief 57
Lopez, Ritchie 156,172,173
Lunga, Jeff 40
Lunga, Paul 6,9,13,21,27,44,45, 46,62,78,101,102,107,145,152, 153,156,157

Mabhena, Martha 116,117
Mabhiza, Henza 174
Mabhiza, Handsome 42
Mabhokela, Sarah 24, 45,121,144
Mabika, Chris 165
Mabuse, HotStix Sipho 171
Machingura Chada, Solomon 120
Machingura, Jean 119
Madzikatire, Elijah 124,126,133
Madzikatire, Safirio 12,31,32,82,83, 89,94,119,123,124,125,126,131,167
Madzima, John 119
Madzimbamuto, Daniel 28,51,60,63,106
Madzivanyika, Sophia 175
Mafusire-Mpahlo, Moses 6,12,21,27, 88,89,93,94,95,96,122,141
Magaisa 120,121
Mahera, Farai Patrick 184
Mahlasela, Vusi 171
Maishe, Marcello 156
Majaivana, Lovemore 152
Makamba, James 161
Makaya, Kudzi 167
Makaya Timmy 13,155,167,168
Makeba, Miriam 8,44,70,26,106, 107,131,137,144,148,172,173
Makhalisa, Tich 157
Maklema 92
Makokowe, Charles 168
Makore, Pius 126
Makore, Richard 156
Makore, William 60
Makwavarara, Tendai 32
Makwavarara, Tony 152
Makwenda-Jenje, Joyce 6,8,45,120,129,185
Malianga, Fungai 13,38,39,156,159,160,161,162
Malianga John 168
Malianga Quinton 166,168,
Mambira, John 174
Mambo, George 51
Mambo, Hilton 13,145,156,158, 160,161,164,168
Maminimini, Tendayi 35
Manaka, Matsemela 157
Manase, Dadirayi 175
Manatsa, Tendai 177
Manatsa, Zexie 34,42,83
Mandishona, Bradshaw 169
Mandishona, Grace 116,117,158
Mandishona, Gibson 10,13,62,113, 129,145,147,183,184
Mandizha, Dominic 61,133

Mandizha, Themba 94,113,135
Mangena, James 167
Mangwana, Cephas 185
Manhenga, Duduzile 13,145, 174,175
Manyengere, Dan 119
Manzini, Musa 184
Mapango, Nelson 156
Mapemba, Austin 89
Mapemba, Lawrence 89
Mapfumo, Susan 34,35,38,41,133
Mapfumo, Thomas 37,83,89,122,126,133,156,158,171,184
Mapundu, Ngwaru 39
Mapurisana, Terence 145,147
Maraire, Chiwoniso 171
Maravanyika, Jack 32
Marley, Bob 184
Moromo, Curtis 104
Marong-rong, Kid 31,72
Marowa, Philbert 47,145,172,173
Marova, Douglas 104,105
Marozva, Kenny 156
Marsden, Monica 27,51,52,110
Marshall, Ken 52, 110,112
Marumahoko, David 40
Marumahoko, Jonah 6,44,118,129,130, 132,133,143,145,153,155,172,
Marvie, John 104
Masauso, Jerry 128
Masekela, Hugh 21,45,101,102,144,155, 157,159,171,175
Mashava, Ray 172
Mashiyane, Spokes 8,31,72,102,134,161
Masuka, Dorothy 6,7,8,12,18,22,24,28, 44,55,58,60,63,64,66,70,76,106, 107.114,117,127,136,137, 141,143,150,154,159,160, 171,172,173,174,175
Matambo, Sam 27,52,54,61,68,78,84,96, 108,109,110,118,167
Matanhire, Christopher 155
Mataure, Sam 13,62,145,147,172,173,183, 184
Mataya, Clifford 153
Matema, Crispen 39,40
Mathe, Sabelo 8,20,54,76,81,97,151,152
Matondo, Anna 175,176
Matongo, Patricia 182
Mattaka, Eddison 12,61,88,89,90,157,
Mattaka, Lina 7,12,23,24,25,61,88,89,119, 125,136,150,157,172
Mattaka, Kenneth 6,12,18,46,56,61,69,87, 88,89,90,93,94,118, 124,125,131,145,150,153
Matereke, David 121
Matiza, Reginald 122
Matshazi, Mauta 89
Matsika, Getrude 35
Matsvetu, J.B 26
Mawerera, Ray 147,174
Mazabane, Gladys 91
Mazabane, Remington 6,18,91,92,
Mazowe, Shelton 51
Mazowe, Shelly 76,113
Mbangwa, Ruth 157,158
Mbirimi, Bright 33
Mbirimi, Clancy 122,145,149,150,151, 159,161,166,169,
Mbirimi, Friday 13,132,145,153,155,168
Mbirimi, Lovejoy 153,154
Mbirimi, Jonah 94,154,
Mbofana, Comfort 145
Mbofana-Katomeni, Prudence 7,13,35,

109,145,172,173
Mbofana Wellington 161
Mbulu, Letta 44,45,107,144,157,159, 160,171
MbuyaNehanda 57
McEwen 155
McLaren, Thando 173
Meck, John 87
Melusi, Eva 31
Metsi, Gladys 30
Meunier, Patrick 149
Mgcina, Sophie 157
Mhango, Chesterton 113,114,115, 155
Mhlanga, Busi 171
Mhlanga, Louis 11,13,38,39,44,45, 66,142,144,156,159,160,169,170,171, 174,184
Mhlanga, Samuel 118
Mhlanga, Willie 45,171
Mhungu, Jacob 11,20,28,44,54,56,76, 97,98,107,151
Middleton, Velma 78
Miller, Benny 161,168
Miller, Glenn 69
Misheck 154
Mkundu, Stella 175,176
Mkuze, Never 42
Mlenga, Rashid 88
Mobape, Mrs 124
Modikwane, Florence 13,139,
Moeketsi, Kippie 106
Mokone, Mike 156
Montgomery, Wes 168
Moore, Timothy 156
Moore, Ricky 156
Moore, Robert 156
Moyo,Chiundura,Aaron 72,73
Moyo, Dave 156
Moyo, Emma 91,93
Moyo, Mehluli 177
Moyo, Mehluli 125
Mpisaunga, Ruth 12,24,52,119, 110,120 145
Mpofu, Isaiah 61
Mqadi, Flyn 60
Msengezi, Patrick 94
Msonda, Joseph 33
Msora-Mattaka, Bertha 12,32,61,88, 89,90,
Mtenda, Junior 125
Mtero, Kundisai 183
Mtshali, Thembi 174
Mtukudzi, Oliver 34,37,40,66,83, 171,173,175,184
Mtunyani, Steve 27,52,84,108, 109,112,145
Muchawaya, Peter 119
Muchirahondo, Bradshaw 156
Mudukuti, Minos 147
Mujuru, Ephat 102,171,
Mugabe, Robert 96,113
Mugona, Nicholas 167
Mukonorwi, Daniel 20,99
Mukarati, Tinashe 9,146
Mukosanjera, Titus 108
Munangatire, Herbet 63
Munangatire, Wilson 60,120
Munemo, Davis 153
Muparutsa, Blessing 145
Muparutsa, Carl 177
Muparutsa, Victor 177
Mupungu, Ivy 101
Murambiwa, Raphael 51
Murerwa, Herbet Dr 6,185
Murombedzi, James Dr 4
Musa, Patience 145,168

Musabaika, Joseph 35
Musakwa, Elias 174
Musarurwa, August 9,12,21,54,55,75, 76,78,82,100,101,103,106,152,155,168
Musarurwa, Tandiwe 103
Mushayabasa, Mrs 35
Musoni, Ben 61
Mutare, Square 121
Mutariyana, Lenos 133
Mutendevure, Richard 153
Mutumba, Jonah 145
Muzambiwa, Chiremba 104
Mwale, Alan 124
Mzingeli, Mrs 53
Nakapa, Pablo 145
Nathenson, Albert 111
Ncube, Jacob 46,145
Ndaba, Timothy 72
Ndawi, Susan 175
Ndebele, Martha 92
Ndinda, Albert 12,27,27,28,60,62,120, 121
Ndlovu, Emlot 73
Ndlovu Nevada, Never 153

Ndlovu, Temba 20
Ndoro, David 161
Ndoro, Joyce 13,24,70,95,136,139
Ndoro, Sylvia 24
Nelson, Sandy 21
Neganje, Gideon 38
Ngoyi, Andrew 30,123
Ngulube, Dumi 13,129,173,174,175
Ngwenya, Moses 166
Nindi, Rowland 147
Nkala-Makhalisa, Barbara 8
Nkata, Alick 12,20,21,61,117, 118,133,128,131
Nkomo, Joshua 92
Nkonde, Rufus 31,73
Nkosi, West 34, 40,149
Nkrumah, Kwame 78
Nsabila, Joseph 30
Nyabinde, Bob 13,145,150,165,166
Nyabinde, Dickson 166
Nyabinde, Kingston 166
Nyamhondera, Bothwel 170,184
Nyamundanda-Jones, Rennie 13,90,95, 136,140
Nyandoro, Christine 30,125
Nyaruka, Mura 155
Nyathi, Albert 173
Nyathi, John 132,133
Nyikadzino, Matthew 127
Nzimande, Hamilton 34,40

Onayadis ,Nikki 32
Operman, Edith 154

Papas, Johnny 130,132,145,169,170
Partridge, Biddy 13,45,47,145,156,157, 182
Paul, Bryen 157
Paul, Les 94
Paver, Betram 59
Paver, Cedric 59
Pazarangu, Margaret 13,24,27,95,136, 141
Pedzi, Joshua 127
Pendagrass, Teddy 169
Peters, Henry 130,156,161,169,170
Petersen, Oscar 132
Philie, Maybin 159
Phiri, Charlotte 90
Phiri, George 42
Phiri, Isen 153

Phiri, Ray 45,66,144,159,160,171,184
Phuzutshukela 76
Piccard, Nikki 40
Piliso, Nteni 101
Pindurai, Mabel 26,154
Presley, Elvis 32
Pswarai, Edward.Dr 62

Rachabane, Barney 157
Ratebe, Dolly 44,106,144,148
Rezant, Peter 101
Richard, Cliff 32
Rhodes John, Cecil 132
Robertson, Shaline 174
Rogers, Ava 13,127,161,164,174,183
Rosin, Muriel 109
Rululimi, Albert 31,77
Rusike, A, B.C 60,121
Rusike, Abius 172
Rusike, Colleen 172
Rusike, Phillip 174
Rusike, Tawanda 172
Rusike, Kelly 156

Sabeta, Francis 156
Sadza, Jack 39,40
Saidi, Bill 94,113,114,115,185
Samantha 47
Samkange, Stanlake 78,94
Samuels, Nigel 156
Sarutawa, Malven 158
Satchmo 78
Savanhu, J.Z 53
Samkange, Rose. Mrs 117
Sango, Peter 133
Selani, Timothy 148
Sekerani, Paul 159
Semenya, Caiphus 171
Sepuma, Judith 184
Shamu, Webster 40,83,85,126
Shamhuyarira, Nathan 121
Shandavu, Fazo 89
Shandavu, Willy 89
Shonhiwa, Sam 154
Shasha, Jethro 23,33,40,43,44,45,132, 133,143,144,156,158,159,160, 164,165,170,171,174,184
Shonhiwa, Samuel 132
Sheba, Thandi 90
Shimulambo, Edward 133
Sibanda, George 20,54,76,81, 97,98,151,152
Sibanda, Pasika 60
Sikhova, Timothy 129,131,132
Sikhuza, Solomon 152
Sikibuya, Godfrey 30
Silla, David 150
Silla, Paul 145,149,151
Simemeza, Herbet 103,104,105
Sisimayi, George 12,30,134
Sithole, Abel 145,147
Sithole, Abraham 158
Sithole, Ephrage 134
Sithole, Ernest 91
Sithole, Ndabaningi 52
Sithole, Jonah 37
Sithole, Sinwametsi 47
Sithole, Susan 119
Smath, Jimmy 132
Soka, Albert 127
Soka, Ernest 127
Solani, Tethiwe 116,117
Sondai, Willy 113,125
Sondo, Sonny 6,21,22,27,28,52,76, 84,95.96,108,109,110,111,117,122, 124,132,161,167,172

Sondo, Sylvia 12,22,125,138
Sparks, Mr 100,122
Special, Lemmy 8,72,73,161
Stanley, Adrian 52,110,120
Stonebeck, Berta 183
Sumaili, Safeli 158
Svosve, Phillip 13,160,167,168
Sylvester, Victor 69

Tabva, Kenny 51
Taderera, Elizabeth 32,124
Takadiyi, Boniface 145
Takaingofa, Marko 20
Tafirenyika, Marita 175,176
Tamburayi, Peter 155
Tavengwa, Charles 41
Tavengwa, Checks 44,46,144,145,159,168
Tembo, Biggie 167
Tembo, Kaisano 40
Thodlana, Lucky 47,145,147,148,153
Tickey 27
Tikili, Jerry 42
Thodlana, Henry 44,62,153
Tracey, Andrew 81
Tracey, Hugh 15,61,81
Tredgold, Barbara 27,51
Travers, Pat 12,22,23,49,52, 78,110,111,112
Tsikirai, Lemuel 168
Tswane, Tony 174
Tutani, Cookie 44,143,145,159,160
Tutani, Simangaliso 6,9,12,25,26,28, 43,44,62,76,107,109,112,117,118,128, 129,130,131,132,133,147,153,154,155, 165,167,170,172,174,183,184,185

Vambe, Lawrence 59
Vaughan, Sarah 68
Vera, Jerry 41,156
Vera, Tsitsi 156

Wataffi, Willis 177
Watson, Jack 112
Waungana, Webster 40
WekwaSando, Tanga 13,44,145,149, 159,168,169,170,173,175,182,184
Wella, Paul 171
Welsh, Joy 171
West, Dotty 107
White, John 8,11,20,55,56,98,99,
Williams, Stanley 111,112
Williamson, Eric 154

Xahe, Arthur 109

Yafele, Aaron 174
Yafele, Miriam 13,24,136,141
Yon, Penny 13,47,147,156,183
Young, Tommy 78

Zengeni, Agnes 12,91,93
Zimi, Stan 156,183
Zimuwandeyi, Victoria 175
Zindi, Fred 38,39,45,144,159, 164,171

GROUPS/BANDS

Aaron Thurston Trio 66
Abbraka 164
4 Aces Wild Flower 37,38
African Kid Brothers 51
Africa Revenge 13,44,145,177,182
African Boogie Four 59
African Melodians 24, 59,141

African Writers 155
Afrocubans 149
All Stars Group 118 133
Ambassadors 111, 184
Arcadia Rhythm Lads 23,27,50,70, 109,111,112,115
Axemen 45,144

Baked Beans 37, 159 170
Bantu Actors 6,12,18,21,59,86,87,88, 89,90,93,94,118,123,124,128,136
Bantu Glee Singers 89
Beatles 30,107,167
Bhundu Boys 182
Big Sixteen 183
Big Three 128
Birth 161
Blind Eye 37
Body and Soul 44,168,184
Brass Construction 169
Breeze 37
Broadway Quartet 27,28,45,83,107, 129,130,131,132,149,155,158,160
British South Africa Police Band 70
Bulawayo Choral society 92
Bush Babies 125

Cantos Quatet 151
Capital City Dixies 51,132,154,167
Champ 152
Chikwanha Brothers 168
Churchill School Jazz Band 145,146,183
City Crakers 26
City Quads 6,12,22,23,24,35,50,51,54,56, 57,58,60,61,68,70,81,92,96,106,108,109, 110,111,112,114,115,117,122,128,131,132, 133,137,151,154,158,161
City Slickers 12,22,27,51,70,90,121,122, 158
Cold Storage Band 21,100,101
Colour Blu 44,125,145,182
Combination 151
Cool Crooners 1,13,44,47,80,115,144, 145,147,148,149,153,164,165,173,177, 182,183
Cool Four 6,22,50,54,62,64,70,104,106, 151,153,182
Crazy five 134
Crazy Kids 58,128,132,154
Crooners 47
Cyclones 32

2D Sounds 158,164
De Black Evening Follies 6,12,21,22, 23,24,25,27,49,51,56,58,59,60,61,69,70, 88,92,93,95,96,104,106,108,113,114,115, 122,124,128,133,139,141,150,154,161
Detema Jazz band 150,172,184
Dhama 37,38
Double Shuffle 37
Dr Footswitch 37,38,42
Dumi Ngulube& Amagents 145 174,175,182

Earth, Wind& Fire 169
Ekhaya 184
Elbow 151
Epworth Theatrical Stratas 6,12,21,51, 61,70,103,105,128,158,167
Expensive Bantus 88
Eye-Q 37
Eye of Liberty 33,37,38,40,83
Follow me Boys 108
Four Aces 167
Four Sounds 159
FrontLine Kids 39
Funkies 164

Gaberon Town Ochestra 170
Galaxy 164
Gay Gaeties 12,23,24,27,51,52,59,62, 106,110,114,115,116,117,128,136,137, 138,139,145
Golden Rhythm Crooners 6,54,55,62, 106,114,115,148,167,182 47
Golden Gate quartet 69
Gospel Ark 174
Gipsy Caravan 33,37,38
Giraffe 170
Great Sounds 30,133,158,159
Green Arrows 34
Groovy Union Band 150,161

Hallelujah Chicken Run 37
Happening 156
Happily 156
Harare Drive 44,145
Harare Mambos 13,38,45,83,109,132, 145,148,149,150,151,155,156,158,167, 168,169
Harlem Swingstars 106
Hot Chocolate 164
Hot Shots 122

Ilanga 171
Ink Spots 94
, 11,148
Intombi Zesi Manje Manje 30
Izintombi zikaMthwakazi 31

Jabavu Drive 13,44,102, 145,155,158,166,167,168,174
Jacaranda 153
Jairos Jiri Band 31,37
Jazz&Pop Band 153
Jazz Impacto 44,46,107,145,153,156
Jazz Invitation 13
Jazz Merchants 153
Jazz Moving Café 122,173
Jazz Revellers 122,133
Jazz Survivors 160
Jerry de Vorse Band 62
Jobs Combination 152
Joelson Brothers 154

Kachingwe Ernest 123
Kalanga Boys 60
Kay Jays Combo 112

Limpopo Jazz Band 30,37,38
Lubumbashi Stars 58
Lucky Street Blues 44,180

Mahotela Queens 20, 24,30,119
Maita women's Ensembles 13
Maita Women's Jazz Band 175
Mandebvu 184
Manhattan Brothers 70 94,125,137, 148,158

Marshall Brothers 12,127,161,164
Mary Andrews& Swingstars 104
Mashonaland Melodies 59 120, 121
Mutanga Queens31
Mattaka Family 61,87
Mazana Movement 158
Mbare Trio 44,145,150,153,154
Menton&Sisters 118,120
Mephis Band 37
Merry Makers 6,12,18,54,55,59,91, 92,93,140
Mhepo 13,145,156,157,182
Militia Army Band 156
Milton Brothers & Faith Dauti 12,24,51,
70,113,114,115,139,140,185
Mills Brothers 68,70,94,108,111,114,148
Morden African Stars 51,123
Moving Jazz Café 47
Movement 37,40,45,133,144,159,170
Mubvumbi Brothers 24,141
Music yeAfrika 45,144,160,171
Mutanga Band 157
Mysterious three 93
Mverechena Band 37

New Tutenkhamen 35,80,159

Ocean City Band 167
Octave 170,171
OK Success 30,38,123,151,158

Players Gold leaf 149
Prestley Kids 154
Philharmonic Stars 59
Pied Pipers 37,38,83,126,127,158
Pine Tops 44,78,128
Pirate of the High Seas 153
Prince Edward Jazz Band 145,183
Prophets 164

Real Sounds 158
Rhodesia Police Band 122,124
Rich Maize 123,124
Riders 172
Rolling Stones 30,107,167
Run Family 184
Rusike Brothers 172,173

Safe Brothers 123,131
Safirio Madzikatire&Sea Cottage Sisters 123
Santana 170
Savanna Cruise 172
Savutha 74
Scanners International 122
Sea Cottage Sisters 125
Season 37
Shaka 37,38
Shelton Brothers 128,154
Showdown Quakers 140
Sisonke 158
Siyeza 174
Six Hits Mood 29
Soul& Blues Union 37,38,42, 156,161
Sound effects 33,158,159
Southern Freeway 45,144,171,174
Springfields 118,132,133,157,168
St Pauls Blues Band 155,156
St Pauls Musami. Band 167,168
Star Gazers 94,113,185
Stars of Liberty 37,38,164,171
Straight Marchers 172
Stratas 104
Submarine 151
Summer Breeze 13,44,145,151,157,158,160,182
Sunrise Kwela Kings 151
Sweet Rhythm Band 21,100
Swing Jazz Brothers 113

Talent Band 46,88,145,153
Talking Drum 171
Tanhatu Marimba 101,102
The Other Four 182
Theodora sisters 90
Three Brothers 59
Too Open 145
Trio State Boys 131
Tumbuka Ensemble 126
Tutenkhamen Band 35,37,45,46,144,145
Twelve Bar Blues 22,122

Two Plus Two 44,46,145,167,168

Unity 159,169,171

Vice 172
Volcanoes122

Wells Fango 37,38,42,46,83
Woody woodpeckers 148
Woogie Boogie Swingsters 60

Yellow Blues 25, 138

Zebras 172
Zebrons 30,132
Zibras Band 184

TUNES/SONGS

Abazali bami 84
African Emotion 174
Aloius na Jane 45,144,159
Amainini handeyi kumusha 151
Ana Amai vane rugare 126
Anenungo 159
Anopenga Anewaya 30,13

B.P yangu yakwira 172
Baba ivai nomoyo muchena 119
Baba VaBhoyi maita Seiko 34
Baba va Ngirande 15
Baby Tsware 70
Baleka Mfana 1148
Bata Mahuhu 156
Batho 171
Bibi uya kuno 134
Bharanzi 170
Bhurugwa rako rine chigamba 99
Bhutsu Mutandarika 37
Blue Sky 148,149
Bromley 119
Brother Malcolm 159
Buhera 150

Calling Your Name 38,40,83
Catch up 156
Chaminuka 96
Chechule Ana vala Bottom 34
Chelete 129
Chembere dzomira-mira 37
Chemutengure 156
Chengeta vabereki 98
Chicago plane 159
Chimurenga funky movement 160
Chimwemwe Chamulungu 104
Chinzvenga mutsvairo 161
Chiperoni 117
Chipo Chiroorwa 34
Chipo mwanawaBaba 84,109
Connie 133
Corner Boys 156

Dai ndiri muumbi 94,96
Dai tiri Kwa Hunyani 31,123
Dunah 17
Dhalala Kece 84,108
Dhali Iwe 126
Distant lovers 172
Edge City 156
Elokitshini 91
Ekhaya baya Ngibiza 141
Ewe Dubu 96

Farai mose 114

Follow me boys 108
Fungai Mudiwa 126

GoliGoli 95
Gomo guru re mbire 104
Gumbo muchochocho 172
Gona ra Machingura 155
Gwabi Gwabi Kuzwa Ngilentombi yami 8, 95

Hakunamumwe84
Hama nevabereki 114,164
Hamba Notsokolo 8,106
Handidi kuenda kuTanganyika 141
Have I told You Lately 117
Honaka 172
Hondo ye Chindunduma 125
Hwahwa Ndichazourega 70,104

Iam a Country Boy 38
Imali yamiphelel Eshabini 8,32
Imbote 117
Ibhulugwe lami 148
Igqiha Lendlela Ngu Qoqotshwane 175
Imi munosara nani Ndaena 20,24,38,49119,120
Inyama ye Mbongolo 152
Introduction 159
Isaac Hauchandida here 125
Isabella 116
Isono Sami 106
Ishe komborera Africa 112
Isimanga 152
Iwe neni Tinebasa 150
I wish I Could fly 104
I Wish You were mine 36,37,80
Iwe Maggie 83
Iyo Ipathapatha 8,82

Jesus save my soul 156,164
Jingajinga 167
Joburg Bound 35,159
Josephine 150
Julieta uko Wapi 134

Kugarisana newe zvakanaka 172
KanaUsingandide 122
Kanonkope 117
Kudendere 150
Kudzidza Kwakanaka 21,70,104
KuFio 170
Kumadokero 69
Kunembaravazi 84,158
Kune muti unonzi muonde 119
Kuraura 156
Kure kwatinobva 127,161
Kushaya Amai 98
Kutapira kunoita Manhanga 38
KwaHunyani 126
KwaMutare 161
KwaMutare yo! 166
Kwenya Mhedzi dzako wega Moloyi 35

Lamulela 84, 109
Lindi 109
Lindi mwana akanakisisa 8
Lizofika nini Ilanga 8,22,61,82,84,118,109,110

Made in Zimbabwe 156
Maggie 117
Mahobo 170
Mai Chiuyayi 172
Makokoba 117
Makomo e Kwa Mutare 56,95,96
Mapapiro 156

Maybe Tommorow 38,83
Mbuya Nehanda 150,151
Me and Dolly 159
Mhere yarira 104
Mira neni 169
Motomoto 166
Muchenjeri 35
Mukai 171
Mupfuhwira 133
Music in An African Township 22,61,84,108
Mvura ngainaye 155,175
Mwari hakuna 171
Mwedzi muchena 126

Ndafuna funa 8,35,94,109,150,151,173
Ndakanga Ndakaroorwa Kwa Murewa 34
Ndakanga ndichifamba 119
Ndapera Nechachacha Amai 30,134
Ndatemwa negogo 31,123,125
Ndatenga moto 124
Ndati Bhutsu Yangu Tapera Hiri 30
Ndewe ku Mbare 169,170
Ndipe chiKokiaan 101,168
Ndine Musikana wangu 124
Ndinoda Mangwiro Mukwasha 104
Ndiwe 72
Ndoenda 45,144
Nekweba 117
Ngatimbofunga nguva yeucheche 127
Ngidhingi Imali 152
Nherera 133
Nhingirikiri 160
Nhoro 70,122,158
Nyama yekugocha 159
Nyatheluqihile 84, 109
Nyenyedzi ye Mugovera 169,170

Out of Afrika 167

Paida moyo 169
Pane nyaya 165,166
Pendeka 97
Poverty 159
Put another chair at the table 114
Rehearsal room 172,173
Reminance 159
Romours are flying 69,88
Rosvikazuva 114
Rova Ngoma Mutavara 34
Rudzi Rwevatema 104
Rufaro mu Zimbabwe 150
Ruvimbo mwanawe 127

Sabona Fish 8
Sarura wako kadeyadeya 149
See it fade 38
Siya waitanda 150
Shava yaomesa 167
Shamwari 171
Shumaira 38
Shungu 170
Skokiaan 21,76,82,100,101,102,103, 144,152,155,168
Sondela 172
Song for Elisha 171
Song for Nomsa 171,172
Sono Sami 96
Still burns bright 164
Street Kids 164
Sunday morning 159

Tamba Suzana 150
Tambai mose 104
Tarasikirwaa nevabereki 114
Tave munyika itsva 104
Ten years on Children survive 161
Tiki yangu 127

Tingachate here 126
Tingane kwane 171
Togetherness 159
Torai Mapadza muchirima 35
True Love 159
True my Love 159
TshonaLanga 174
Tutenkhamen Theme 159

UmaDlamini 148
Umbolidwa Tidzaimba 87
Unolishwa 106
Unondiroora rini 126
Uri Denga rangu mwanawe 104
Usandimirire paghidhi 35,126
Uya Moya 174
Uzangenzani Malayisha? 8

Vakomana Vekwedu 170

Wacitumuzi 84
Wake 169,170
Wanga 177
Wangu Wangu 172
Waterera zvemakuhwa 158
Watchout Big Storm Is Comin 38
With you in life 161
Wonder baker 120

Yakhali Inkomo 174

Zai Regondo 126
Zimbabwe Jive 153
Ziwerewere 34
Zonki insuku 84
Zvanhasi ndezveduwo 83,150
Zvino uno voruzhinji 127
Zvinhu zvangu 174

PLACE NAMES

Addis Ababa 185
Africa 79
Arcadia 49,112,164
Austria 131
Avondale 147

Blantyre 78,136
Bloomington 170
Binga 183
Boston 129,133,185
Botswana 60,92,107.159,170,171
Britain 106
Bulawayo 1,6,8,18,27,31,34,37,38,41,44, 46,48,50,51,54,56,60,62,70,72,78,89,91,97, 100,101,103,104,106,109,118,120,121,127, 137,144,145,150,152,156,157,159,160, 174,177,182
Bulawayo Hillside College 165

Canada 152
Cape Town 106
Central Africa 27,61,88,89,117
Central/Southern Africa 110
Charter Road 53
Chegutu 127
Chikwanha 168
Chinhoyi 100
Chiredzi 159
Chiredzi School 90
Chishawasha 57
Chitsere School 114,140
Chizhanje 57

Congo 136
Copperbelt 136

Dar esSalaam 131
Democratic Republic of Congo 30,32,38,83,118,128,158
Dete 152
Domboshava 41
Domboshava School 87,88
Djibouti 131
Epworth Mission 104
England 134
Ethiopia 45,76,131,145,160
Europe 27,131

Fort Victoria 15,81
France 131
Francis Joseph Street 57
Francis town 92

Gaborone 92
Germany 20,22,108,121,131,171
Ghana 78,160
Golden city 139
Golden Valley Mine 87
Goromonzi District 34,41
Goromonzi Sec School 154,155,168
Gweru 8,20,56,98,113,120,121,149,151

Harare Airport 77,78,79
Harare 6,18,21,31,32,34,35,38,39, 41,44,46,49,50,54,62,70,72,78,88, 90,92,93,95,97,100,101,16,108,113, 114,118,120,121,122,131,132,139,140, 141,150,154,155,156,157,159,160,166, 168,171,172,182,183,184,185
Harare hospital 92,114
Highfields 31,35,40,52,134,140,167, 168,170
Hungary 109

Iminyela Beerhall 8
Italy 131

Johannesburg 19,53,107,139,171
Juru Growth point 34
Kariba 98,152
Kariba Dam 52,109
Kenya 76,78,131,160
Kitwe 78,120,172
Kwekwe 100,166

Lake Chivero 31
Lagos 78,171
Libya 160
London 45,107,112,144,156,171
Lusaka 21,61,79,117,120,131
Luxembourg 131

Magaba 49
Makwiro 100,127
Malawi 14,59,76,78,87,107,118, 120,132,138,156,171
Makokoba 6,48,54,103,152,185
Matopo 137
Marirangwe 128
Marondera 35,113
Marshall Hartley School 100
Mashonaland 53
Mashonaland East 34
Masvingo 15,81,108,120,128,159
Mazowe 57
Mazowe Secondary School 155
Mbare 6,50,52,54,57,108,110,123,124
Mbare musika 94
MbareTownship 40,49,94,109,114,

119,128,133
Methodist Mission 104
Moleli 100
Mozambique 14,20,113,121,151,159, 171
Murewa 87
Musami Church School 8
Mutare 40,41,44,56,62,95,106,120, 121,131,152,159,165,168,184
Musarurwa Kraal 100
Musarurwa Village 103
Mutambara Primary School 159
Mwenezi 98
Mzilikazi Township 37,41,54,91,103, 107
Mzingwane School 153
Nairobi 78
National lines 50,51,57
New Orleans 79
New Lines 50,119
New Location 50
New York 170
Nigeria 28,160
Northern Rhodesia 14,136
Nottingham University 134
Ntabazinduna 97
Nyasaland 14,107,118,138
Nyatsime College 94,110
Nyon 148

Old Bricks 49,50,11,113
Old Mutare Mission 122

Paris 112,160,171
Pelandaba/T/Ship 103
Poland 131
Portugal 156
Portuguese East Africa 14,118
Plumtree 120,185

Regina Mundi School 113
Rhodes University 81
Rhodesia 32,63,103,115,118,138,151
Rusape 123

Sakubva 106,184
Salisbury 21,34,39,50,53,54,61,64,79, 90,101,136,139,140
Salisbury African School West 140
Sarahuru 98
Selukwe 63
Seke 168
Senegal 160
Serowe 94
Simonstown 89
Sinoia 100
Sophia town 104
South Africa 8,30,31,34,40,44,45,59, 63,70,73,76,81,89,90,94,95,98,104, 106,115,119,125,143,144,160,168, 171,184
Sourthen Africa 20,45,89,117,140
Southern Rhodesia 72,78,108,117, 118,136
St Augustine Mission 168
St Pauls Mission 155
Stockholm 112
Switzerland 56,121,131,145,148,156

Tekwane High School 185
Triangle 151,159
Tunisia 131

U.K 106,117,157,161,171
Uganda 45,76,131
University of Indiana 170
University of Zimbabwe 154,155

USA 68,70,95,103 125,129,170,170
Vervey 171
Victoria Falls 46,121,151,156
Waddilove School 93

Zambia 14,28,32,44,45,57,59,76,77,79,
107,110,115,117,118,120,129,130,133,
144,149,172
Zhombe 166
Zimbabwe 6,8,28 30,32,57,59,69,70,72,
76,81,82,85,87,100,107,110,115,121,129,
132,136,143,160,164,168,170
Zvimba Reserve 100,103,113
Zvishavane 51

VENUES

Alabama 147
Anglican Cathedral 27
Arcadia Community Hall 53,128
Ardbenie 150
Art Gallery 155
Athenium Hall 110

Bantu Sports Club 19
Beatrice Cottages 150
Beit Hall 32,56
Basement 147
Bhika Brothers Restaurant 52
Blue Lagoon 53
Bonanza 41
Book Café 62
Bulawayo Sun hotel 147
Bulawayo Trade Fair 170
Bulawayo Valley Hotel 159

Cannabis 170
Castle Hotel 150
City Hall 56,92
Club Flamingo 155
Club Tommorow 150
Crown Plaza Monomutapa Hotel 47,150

Cyril Jennings Hall 52

Dartmouth Hall 53

Elizabeth Hotel 41,150,156

Federal Hotel 41,52,131,150,152,155

George Hotel 44,147
Glamis Stadium 78,154
Goodwill Centre 128
Gwanzura Stadium 41

Happy valley Hotel 156
Harare City Centre 41
Harare Showgrounds 60
Hari Margolis Hall 32

Ikon 147
Ikwezi BeerHall 56,78

Jamaica inn 41
Jazz 105 62,147
Jewish Theatre 92
Job's Night Spot 41,157

Kambuzuma Hall 41
Karimapondo Restaurant 52,53,62
Kaufman 49
Kudzanai Hotel 52

KwaBhora 41

LasVegas 150
LeCoq D'or 53
London African Centre 157

Machipisa Beer Garden 159
Machipisa Night Club 155
Mai Musodzi Hall 18,25,32,49,
50,54,56,57,70,96,108,110,111,113,
115,119,125,128,131,184
Manhattan 147
Mannenburg 62,147
Manuele beer Garden 56,174
Marisha 41,156
Mazowe hotel 155
Mbare Market 15,49
Mbare Vito Tavern 155
McDonald Hall 41,50,51,54,153
Moffat Hall 56
Mushandirapamwe Hotel 35,41,158,170
Mutanga Night Club 30,41
Mverechena 41

New way Hotel 34
Nyamanhindi Farm 40

Oasis Hotel 44,160,147
100 Oxford Street Club 38,164

Palace theatre 109
Peacock 164
Pelandaba Hall 41
Pelandaba Township 56
Presbyterian Church 125

Queens Hotel 41,170
Rainbow Theatre 154
Recreation Hall 49,57
Red Fox Hotel 27,62,147,168,181,182
Reps Theatre 52,110,112,165
Reserve Bank Sports Club
Roma Catholic Church Hall 91
Ronniescots 164
Rufaro Stadium 57
Runyararo Hall 51,96,117

Sakubva Beit Hall 106
SkyLine Motel 133,142,156
Simba Night Spot 41
Smokeys 147
Southerton Night Club 152
Stanley Hall 18,54,56,89,91,92,93,
103,118,140,153
Stanley Square 37, 41,48 100
Stodart Hall 32,40,50,51,63,122,154
Stones Bar 150
Sun City! 44

Taste of Africa 175
Thamies Sports Diner 175
Tsimba Hotel 41

Valley Hotel 159
Vashee Hall 54
Victoria Falls Elephant Hotel 150

Wembly Stadium 107
West End Clubs 106
Woodpecker Inn 131
White City Stadium 41

EVENTS/ PUBLICATIONS / INSTITUTIONS

African Banking Corporation 62,147
African Daily News 25,53,58,59,88,89,114,115,121,136
African Distillers 147
African Methodist Episcopal Church 139
African National Congress of Bulawayo 121
African News 64
African Parade 59,60,63,106
African Service radio 114,138
African weekly 59,119
Agricultural Show 122
Alliance Francais 147
Amakhosi Theatre Productions 174
American Embassy 101
Angouleme 171
Arts Alive Festival 171

BAT 147, 149
Bantu Mirror 59
Baptist Communication Centre 171
BBC 106,118
Berkley College of Jazz 185
Berkley College of Music 129,133
Bhika Brothers 53
Boys Clubs 6,25,27,132,153,184
Broadcasting Corporation & Cultural Services 110
British South Africa Police 57, 78,106,118
Bretheren in Christ Church 8
BUWA 45,160

Castle Brewery 53
Centinary 137
Central African Broadcasting Cooperation 21,61,117,118
Child Survival foundation 164
Christmas Parties 96
City Council 25
Cliff Richards Shadows Concert 155
Coca-Cola company 128
Coronation 121
Criminal Investigation Department 100
Cultural Syndicate 60,63,106

Daily News 115
Drum 59

Eistedford Competitions 32
Ethnomusicology Programme 129,174

3Fm 161
Federation 22,23,63,68,128,137
Federal Broadcasting cooperation 21,61,81,90,
98,109,118,127,129
Federal Parliament 23,109
Federation of Rhodesia and Nyasaland 21,52,82
Federated Union Of Black Artists 157
Fereday & Sons 89
Ford Foundation 4
France–Monreux Jazz Festival
FrankStone Fund 170
Freedom Struggle 38
FUBA 157
Gallo 20,30,31,34,35,40,72,81,
82,83,84,100,103,107,117
GAMMA Sigma Clubs 23, 62
General Election Campaign 107
General Service Radio 114

Gonakudzingwa Prison 60
Grahamstown Festival 171
Gramma 147,171

Harare Beatrice Cottages Cemetery 110
Harare Hospital 23,115,117
His Summer Holiday 32
House of Hunger 126

I will wait 91
ILAM 81
IGI Insurance 147
Independence 85,107,110,129,131, 156,185
Independent Television 106
Interfin 62,147
International & Regional Jazz Festival 175,184
Inter racial Association 23,60
International Library of African Music 81

Jairos Jiri center 54,109,151
Jairos Jiri Fetes 8
Jazz Appreciation Club 78,110
Jenaguru 184
Jethro Shasha Drums Scholarship Scheme 164

King Kong 63
King Solomon's Mine 132
Kwanongoma 8
Lets Go Show 112
Liberation Struggle 83,148,151
Lisbon Cultural City Festival 171

Macbeth 120
Machipisa Brothers 159
Mai Musodzi Boys Club 6,154
Mahobo Parties 28
Malawi Congress Party 107
Manchester Garden 117
Manica Post 129
Marx Brothers 63
Mashona Uprising 57
Mattaka's money 90
Mattaka buys a Bicycle 90,91
Mattaka& Son 90
Mattaka Family 12,90,123
Mbare Boys Club 128
Meet The Mattaka Family 88
Methodist Church 49,88,161
Metro Studios 150
Mhuri yava Mukadota 123,124,126
Ministry of Education and Culture 62
Ministry of Information 27,60,61,82,90, 118,132
Miss Harare 139
Miss Rhodesia 95
Miss Universe 172
Miss Zimbabwe 173
Mobile Cinema 82
MoonRise 147
Mukadota 123
Mukadota Family 125
Music ye Zimbabwe 39
My Story 76
Mzilikazi Youth Centre

NAMA 85,117,171
National archives of Zimbabwe 82
National Hunger Jazz Concert 127,161,164,171,182
Neria 110
New Morning Jazz Club 171
Norad 4
Nyasha 91
Nyatsime College 28

Omasiganda 45

Perfoming rights Society 103
Poised in the Sun 110,112
Pop Music Group 39

Queen's Command Perfomance 109

Ready Steady go Show 106
Red Army 121
Reflections 110
Reformed Industrial Union 121
Rhodesia Broadcasting Corporation 61,125,133,134
Rhodes Centenary Exhibition 22,106
Rhodes& Founders Holiday 51
Rhodesia College of Music 32
Rhodesia Herald 59,88,103,112
Rhodesia Iron&Steel Company 100
Rhodesia Television 112
Radio 1 161
Radio 3 161
Rokhana Mines 28
Roman Catholic Church 57,78
Roots Rocking in Zimbabwe 39
Rothmans 78
RTP 147
Rufaro Mumba 61,90
Runyararo Drama Group 27,28,51,52,110

Salvation Army Church 169
Second World War 57
Shamrock Company 159
Shanty Town Review 63
Shebeen 63
Smith Government 37, 152
Social welfare Department 109
Society of the Destitute & aged 159
South Africa Masque Freedom Show 171
Southern Rhodesia African National Congress 121
Southern Rhodesia Youth League 121
Sparks Distributors 147
SR National Congress 63
Sun City Afro Jazz orchestra Band Show 45
Sun Valley 26
Sunday Mail 145
Swedish Development Agency 175

Talent Contest 27
Teal Record company 83
Thabiso Boys Club 153
The British Council 147
The Sister Barbara 109
Tower Records Department Store 170
Township Troubadours 45
Troubadour 82,83,85,106
Trutone 82,83
Trust Bank 62

UNIP 115,131,133
Unilateral Declaration of Independence 28,39,59,152
United Methodist 149
United National Independence Party 115,129
Universal 1 Jazz Label 147
United States Information Service 78
University of California 91
University of Zimbabwe 32,91

Victoria Bakery 26
Voice of America 68

Windybrow Arts Festival

Wizard of Oz 93
Women's Volunteer Service 109
Wonder Bakery 120

Yellow peril 121
ZAPU 118,154
ZBC/TV 45,82
ZIMA 85,165,177
Zimbabwe College of Music 39,44,46,132,133,145,154,156,160,164,172,174,183,185
Zimbabwe Ethnomusicology Centre 174
Zimbabwe Jazz Festival 175
Zimbabwe Music Rights Association 160
Zimbabwe Music Corporation 147
Zimbabwe Publishing House 91
Zimbabwe Union of Musicians 150,155,160
Zion Christian Church 8
Zonk Magazine 19,59
Zonk Recording Company 134

PICTURE CREDITS

1. National Archives- Radio Post, African Daily News, African Parade, Herald, Sunday Mail, (p7)-Dorothy Masuka, (p7) Faith Dauti,(p7) Virginia Silla (p7) Dorothy Masuka, p14 (Mbare in 1958), (p18)The Bantu actors, (p20) Alick Nkata, (p21) August Musarurwa, (p21) Sonny Sondo, (p22) -De Black Evening Follies, (p23) Victoria Chingate, (p24) Dorothy Masuku & Sarah Mabhokela,(p25) Harry Gwaze, (p26) Simangaliso Tutani & The City Crackers with Mabel Pindurayi, (p27) Albert Ndinda, (p28) Runyararo Drama Group& Dorothy Masuka, p30 - OK Success & The Mahotella Queens, (p31) Safirio Madzikatire, (p34) Oliver Mtukudzi, (p37) Thomas Mapfumo, (p40)-Webster Shamu, (p42) Soul and Blues Union, Dr. Footswitch, Virginia Sillah, Zexie Manatsa, Jonah Mutumha, (p44) Dorothy Masuka - (p46) The Harare Mambo, (p51) - Monica Marsden & the Runyararo Group, (p51)- George Mambo and Showdow Quakers, (p53) - Mahommed Bhika, Sonny Sondo & Samangaliso Tutani, (p55) The Merry Makers, The Golden Crooners, Dorothy Masuka, (p57) Mai Musodzi standing, (p58) - Grand show by the City Quads, De Black Evening Follies & Dorothy Masuka, (p59) - Lawrence Vambe, (60) The Kalanga Boys, Daniel Madzimbamuto, (p61) Ephraim Chamba, Dominic Mandizha & Jordan Chataika, (p63) - An article on Music Festival (p64)An article on Music Festival & The Cool Four, An article on Dorothy Masuka, (p68)-Louis Armstrong, (p70) Miriam Makeba, (p75) - August Musarurwa, (p76) - Dorothy Masuka and August Musarurwa, (p79) Louis Armstrong, (p82) Do0rothy Masuka, (p83) old Radio, (p86)-The Bantu Actors, (p88)- The Bantu Actors, (p91) The Merry Makers Group, (p91) Dr Joshua Nkomo, (p93) Moses Mpahlo Mafusire, (p95) The De Black Evening Follies With Joyce Ndoro, (p96)Moses Mpahlo-Mafusire and Robert & Sally Mugabe's Wedding entertained by the De Black Evening Follies, (p102) - Peter Rezant, Louis Armstrong and August Musarurwa & The Cold Storage Band, (p106) Dorothy Masuka+ Dorothy Masuka introducing - "Miss Wonderful", (p109) - City Quads & Faith Dauti, (p110) - Sonny Sondo, (p112) - The Arcadia Rhythm Lads, (p114) - Faith Dauti & Milton Brothers, (p115) Victoria Chin gate, (p116) The Gay Gacties performing, ((p117) Alick Nkata, (p121) - Albert Ndinda eating bread, (p122) The City Slickers, (p123) - Madzikatire & Children, (p124) Safirio Madzikatire, Pat (Chimbwido) Chenjerayi, Susan Chenjerayi and Elijah Madzikatire, (p125) The Sea Cottage Sisters, (p128)- Simangaliso Tutani and Crazy Kids, (p131) Andrew Chakanyuka, ((p132)- Simangaliso Tutani, Sonny Sondo, Faith Dauti and Chris Chabuka, (p136) Lina Mattaka, (p137) Mabel Bingwa, (p138)-Sylvia Sondo & Flora Dick, (p148) Christine Dube & Joyce Ndoro, (p140) Evelyn Juba, (p141) Dorothy Masuka & Margaret Pazarangu, Miriam Yafele, (p150) (2nd photo) Virginia Sillah Jangano, (p160) Fungai Malianga,

Hilton Mambo & Phillip Svosve, p198 - Photo of Socialites in the 50's & Schotting Chingate, Joshua Mqabuko Nkomo and Dr. Samuel Parirenyatwa

2. David Kofi
(p9) Simangaliso Tutani, (p11)Jacob Mhungu, (p11) Jacob Mhungu, (p44) Simangaliso Tutani, (p98) Jacob Mhungu, (p111) Pat Travers, (p113) Bill Saidi, (p120) Albert Ndinda & Joyce Jenje Makwenda, (p129) Simangaliso Tutani and Joyce, (p137)-Victoria Chingate, (p138) Tabeth Kapuya,

3. Lee Maidza
(p 7) Prudence Katomeni.-Mbofana , (p163) Fanyana Dube and Summer Breeze, (p153) Mbare Trio; Friday, Lovejoy Mbirimi and William Kashiri, (p154) Friday Mbirimi, (p169) Summer Breeze and Rute Mbangwa, (p177) Bob Nyabinde, (p181) Tanga wekwa Sando, (p172) Prudence Katomeni -Mbofana and Jazz Invitation (p173) Prudence Katomeni-Mbofana, (p173) - Dumisani Ngulube (p174) Duduzile Manhenga, (p177) Africa Revenge, (p181) Africa Revenge, Dumisani Ngulube & Duduzile Manhenga, Africa Revenge -Willis Wataffi and Mehluli Moyo, (p186) Dr David Parirenyatwa & Chiza Ngwira, Josephine Jenje Mudimbu & Joyce Jenje Makwenda, Photo of Today's Socialites in 2003,

4. Josephine Jenje Mudimbu
(page 9) -Paul Brick hill, p14 (Grammaphone), p23,Gramophone, p192 - 1. Mannenberg (Paul Brickhill), p193 - Oliver and Irene Gwaze, p194 - Jackie Cahi, p197-Gibson Mandishona & Joyce Jenje-Makwenda.

5. Sam Mhirizhonga
(p4) Dadirayi Manase, (p11) Shamiso Chitsinde, (p41) Mushandira Pamwe, (p49) Mai Musodzi, (p50) Stodard Hall, (p73) Aaron Chiundura Moyo, (p94) McCloud Chitiyo, (p135) Dadirayi Manase, (p164) Ava Rogers, (p175) - Victoria Zimuwandeyi & Dadirayi Manase, & Sophia Madzivanyika, (p176) - Anna Mat ambo,, Shamiso Chitsinde, Stella Mkundu - Mavhura, & Marita Tafirenyika, (p199) -The author - Joyce Jenje-Makwenda

6. Gibson Mandishona (Source)
(p166) The Gay Gaeties posing, (p184) Gibson Mandishona, Cephas Mangwana & Bob Marley Gibson Mandishona, (p185) - Gibson Mandishona with the Cool Crooners, (p68) The Mills Brothers (The Anthology -1931-1968) (DECCA MCA © 1995 MCA Records Inc. MCAD2-11279)

7. Jazz 105(Source)
(p9) -Roger Hukuimwe, (p9)Tinashe Mukarati, (p146) Prince Edward Jazz Band, Tinashe Mukarati & Churchill Jazz Band, (p147) Oliver Hawadi, (p179) - Josh Hozheri, Lenox Chibanda & Titus Shangazhike -Adverts: Patience Musa, Victor Kunonga, Jazz Invitation and Sanchez

8. Roger Hukuimwe
(p102) Jabavu Drive Band (p166)Jabavu Drive Band, (p167) - Phillip Svosve (p168), Roger Hukuimwe

9. Tanga wekwa Sando (Source)
(p169) Tanga wekwa Sando.

10. Ava Rogers Source
(p163) Ava Rogers.

11. Terrence Mapurisana.(Source)
(p9) Paul Lunga, (p45) Paul lunga, (p47) Moving Jazz Café, (p71) Emmloty Ndlovu (p74) Emmloty Ndlovu & Robbie Kruger, (p102) Hugh Masekela, Paul Lunga, (p152) Paul Lunga, (p156) Mhepo.

12. Jethro Shasha (Source)
(p33) Varouis Artists of the 70's -(Jose and company), (p43) Jethro Shasha, (p73) Jethro Shasha, (p132) Chris Chabuka, (p143) Jazz Survivors, (p158) Jethro Shasha, (p159) Jethro Shasha and Mudzimu, (p160) Jethro Shasha and Derek Huggins.

13. Jackie Cahi (Source)
(p5)- Cool Crooners, (p47) Cool Crooners, (p80) Cool Crooners, (p147)- Cool Crooners, (p148) Cool Crooners, (p182) Jackie Cahi.

14. Fred Zindi (Source)
(p9) Simangaliso Tutani (p38)-Fred Zindi , (p44) Jack Sadza, (p45) Chris Matema, (p124) Safiriyo Madzikatire, (p130) The Broadway Quartet, (p144) Elisha Josamu, (p149) Green Jangano & The Harare Mambos, (161 - Green Jangano and The Harare Mambos.

15. Louis Mhlanga
(page 11) -Louis Mhlanga, (p142) Louis Mhlanga, Jethro Shasha,James Indi & Cookie Tutani.

16. Goerge Sisimayi (Source)
(P31) George Sisimayi, (p134) George Sisimayi.

17. Susan Chenjerayi .(Source)
(p29) Susan Chenjerayi and friend, (p31) Susan Chengerayi, (p82) Susan Changerayi, Safiriyo Madzikatire & unidentified actor (p125) Susan Chenjerayi with The Sea Cottage Sisters & Safiriyo Madzikatire.

18. Zimbabwe Women in Culture in Southern Africa
(p7) Evelyn Juba (Margaret Waller-ZWICT), (p18) Evelyn Juba (Margaret Waller), (p23) Eileen Haddon.(Margaret Waller), p162 - Virginia Sillah Jangano (Tessa Colvin).

19. Jeremiah Kainga
(p118) Jeremiah Kainga

20. Herbert Simemeza (Source)
(p104) Nesbit Kanyowa.

21. Peter Musarurwa
(p9) -August Musarurwa, (p100) August Musarurwa.

22. Rob Allingham
(p11) Josaya Hadebe, (p19)-Josaya Hadebe singing under a bridge, (p97) Josaya Hadebe, (Zonk Magazine).

23. Bailey African History Archives (BAHA)
(p67) The Manhattan Brothers, (p70) The Manhattan Brothers.(The Very Best of Manhattan Brothers-Gallo), ((p72) Spokes Mashiyane, (p102) Spokes Mashayane.

24. Priscilla Sithole (Source)
(p48) Stanely Square, (p50) Macdonald Hall, (p54) Stanley Hall.

25. Ministry of Information
(p17) Joyce Ndoro, Cool Four, (p103) The Dpworth Theatrical Strutters (p104) Andrew Kanyowa (p105) The Epworth Theatrical Stutters.

26. Jean Paver (Source)
(p59)-Cedric Paver

27. Janup Deans (Source)
(p78) Louis Armstrong and the Pine Tops.

28. Zimbabwe Township Music Video (Joyce Jenje Makwenda)
(p7) ,Lina Mattaka, (p11)- John White, (p24) Lina Mataka, (p87)- Kenneth Mattaka, (p88) **Lina Mattaka**, (p92)- Evelyn & Simon Juba, (p99) John White, (p105) The Epworth Theatrical Strutters (p127)- The Marshall Brothers (Photographer-Joyce Jenje-Makwenda), (p178) Lenox Chibanda, Irene Gwaze and Gibson Mandishona.

29. Mike Mwale (Source)
(p32) Jordan Chataika, (p41/81) Webster Shamu label, (p81 Shungu Label) (p81) Afro Soul Label, Rugare Label & Tuku Music, (p102) Louis Armstrong -Brunswick Records, (p69) Ella Fitzigerald.(Phill Stern- Album; Produced by Norman Granz MGV-4003).

30. Jack Maravanyika (Source)
(p32) Jack Maravanyika.

31. Sister Helen Maminimini (Source)
(p35) - The two singing Nuns

32. SFM (Source)
(p36) - The New Tutenkhamen LP, (p80) - Cover I wish you were mine -Tutennkhamen LP

32. Gilbert Neganje.(Source)
(p37) Gyps Caravan.

33. Solo Chiweshe (Source)
(p40)-Movement.

34. Rhoda Isaacs - Sheer Sounds.(Source)
(p45), Louis Mhlanga, (p170) - Louis Mhlanga.

35. Basil Kumpeu (source)
(p46)-Basil Kumpeu, (p107) Dorothy Masuka, (p143) Basil Kumpeu, (p155) Basil Kumpeu,

36. Ismail Bhika (Source)
(p52) Mahommed Bhika.

37. Sam Mataure (Source)
(p62) Sam Mataure, (p183) Sam Mataure

38. Penny Yon
(p65) The Zimbabwe Festival of Regional & International Poster, (p66) Festival Flyer with photo and programme.

39. Sheilla Cameron
(p74) Isavhuta (Phaphama Promotions)

40. Andrew Cinema (Source)
(p77) Louis Armstrong and his wife.

41. Andrew Tracy (Source)
(p81) Hugh Tracey.

42. Steven Mutunyane- (Source).
(p22) City Quads, (p84) City Quads LP Music In The African Township, (p108) City Quads.

43. Bertha Msora- Source
(p89) **Bertha & Edison Mattaka**, (p90) Bertha Mattaka Msora .

44. Ephat Mujuru (Source)
(p102) Ephat Mujuru .

45. Rumbidzai Chipendo (Source)
(p102) Tanhatu Marimba

46. Ruth Mpisaunga (Source)
(p119) - Ruth Mupisaunga (1), Ruth Mupisaunga (2).

47. Pat Travers (Source)
(p22) Pat Travers, (p111) Pat Travers and the Ambassadors.

48.Jane Changerayi (Source)
(p126) Jane Chenjarayi instead.

49. Simon Kofi (Source)
(p133)- Eliah Banda, (p121)-David Matereke.

50. Fungai Malianga (Source)
(p161) Fungai Malianga, (p162) Fungai Malianga.

51.Macloud Chitiyo (Source)
(p80) Troubadour Label,(p84) Gallotone Label.

PHOTO RESEARCH AND COMMISSIONING OF PHOTOGRAPHERS -JOYCE JENJE MAKWENDA
© Copyright reserved.

ACKNOWLEDGEMENTS

A big thank you to all musicians whose contribution made this project possible, particularly the late big brother Simangaliso Tutani, who was pivotal during the painstaking initial stages. At times he would introduce me personally to the old musicians.

A close colleague, Gibson Mandishona, himself a jazz pianist/guitarist; spent hours, editing and managing this project, despite other pressing commitments. Thank you Samanyanga –Unendoro!

Takesure Handiseni had the onerous task of providing expert advice on text production and design. Complementary contribution from Patrick and Tendai Nyamhunga involved index compilation and information on the history of music-recording. Saki Mafundikwa for designing the cover and advice on publishing.

Special Mention also goes to Rob Allingham for allowing me access to his library and availability to assist (the history of recording 1930's -1960's); Mike Mwale for using his music library, Fred Zindi for providing some photos and sharing experience on book production; Tsitsi Dangarembga for advice on project fundraising; Chris Timbe for facilitating the project at the Zimbabwe College of Music; Dr Herbert Murerwa for his invaluable comments; unfailing support and persistent motivation from friends and associates too numerous to mention, but typified by: Barbara Nkala (sis Babs), Alexander Kanengoni, Hope Chigudu, Margaret Dongo, Rhoda Mandaza (my ek se), Masepeke Sekhukhuni, Gunilla Selerud, Virginia Phiri and Claude Maredza.

The book could not have been realised, without the inspiration, moral and financial support of my parents, David (Murehwa) and Canaan (MaDube); (*NDINOTENDA, NGIYABONGA* (THANK YOU); and my children, who had to bear with me, whilst working on the book: Tandiwe, Simbarashe, Naomi, Edward and grand-daughter Nontando Mya. Caleb Dube, mentor and guardian, was a source of unflinching support.
Thanks to my dear sisters; Juliet, Joseline, Josephine-Spiwe, for always "being there", whilst the product was unfolding. My brother Emanuel, a special friend, who realised my talent as we grew up, has ever supported my efforts.

Time and space do not permit the mention of several contributors, for their liberal assistance in the fulfilment of my aspired project book.

THANK YOU ALL!

Joyce Jenje Makwenda, September 2004

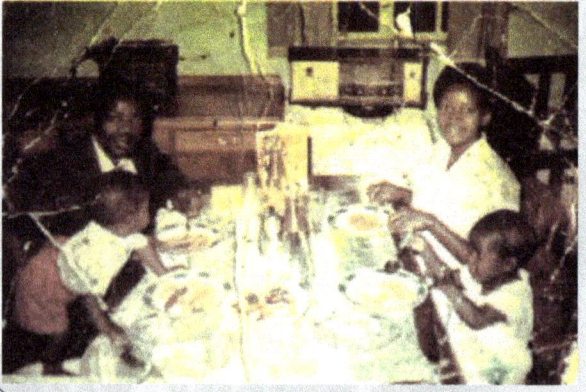

Joyce Jenje (right) with parents, far right Canaan (Madube) mother, Left David (Murehwa) father, and brother Emmanuel left in 1961 at the Jo'burg lines (Majubheki) Mbare (Harare).

The Author

JOYCE JENJE-MAKWENDA

Joyce Jenje- Makwenda was born on 24th March, 1958 in Mbare Township, then called Harare, being a third generation of the early urban settlers. Her paternal grandparents were amongst the original inhabitants of Mbare, where the father David Jenje had grown up. David used to narrate stimulating and evocative tales, about the lives and experiences of black Zimbabweans during the early period of urbanization. These included music of the 50s, which has had a lasting impact on Joyce's appreciation of Township Jazz. Himself, an avid jazz enthusiast, as a young man, David often sold concert tickets at community halls to gain free admission at the shows. In this way he became fully abreast with the music and musicians of the time. These contacts were soon to become an invaluable asset and launching pad for Joyce's quest to research on township music.

Joyce's mother, Canaan Jenje, was a woman pioneer journalist of the late 50's, who played the singular role of nurturing, guiding and monitoring the aspiring researcher's findings from a variety of print media. Earlier, the parents had encouraged Joyce to take up music seriously, having noticed her youthful leanings. Ultimately she opted for the arduous research and documentation of Zimbabwe Township Music.

The research task on the history of Township Music began in earnest during 1984. Initially it consisted of a mere collection of interviews from musicians who were popular during 1930-1960. The objective was to better understand the entertainment culture of the earlier generation in urban Zimbabwe. Having amassed adequate information on the country's musical history, Joyce's passionate ambition has been to document it in the form of a film.

She boasts of five prestigious accolades to her credit:

- **Zimbabwe Township Music Documentary-1993**
  (Southern African Film Festival-Special Mention)

- **Best TV Producer of the Year-1993**
  (Reuters- National Media Awards)

- **Second Best TV Producer of the Year –1994**
  (Reuters –National Media Awards)

- **Freelance Woman Journalist of the Year- 1999**
  (UNIFEM- Federation of African Media Women of Zimbabwe (FAMWZ)

- **Population Development and Gender Writer of the Year-2002 (UNFPA**—Zimbabwe Union of Journalists.

A mother of four; two girls (Tandiwe, Naomi) and two boys (Simbarashe, Edward), Joyce also graces up a grand-daughter, Nontando Mya. She has lived to the challenge of archiving deeper into the roots of Zimbabwe Township Music, a challenge she will bequeath to both contemporary and tomorrow's youth.

Joyce's offering on township music has been her childhood dream, come true. Indeed, it is a timeless and rich source on the evolution and development of music that has uniquely characterized Zimbabwe.

Gibson Mandishona, July 2004.

EPILOGUE

Township people dancing to a song from the loud speaker

www.ingramcontent.com/pod-product-compliance
Lightning Source LLC
Chambersburg PA
CBHW061128010526
44116CB00023B/3000